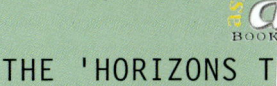
THE 'HORIZONS T...

Director & author of the series
Roland Neveu

Design, production, prepress
Extra image Co., Ltd.

Author of the Phuket guide
Hamish Keith

Main photography
Hamish Keith, Roland Neveu, Dede Lurde

Maps, drawings
Denis Loisel, Extra image

Pictures editor
Roland Neveu

Text editing
Graeme Loveridge

Publicity, distribution
Extra image Co., Ltd, Ko Pinpibal

Published by
Asia Horizons Books Co., Ltd.

www.asiahorizons.com

MILLENNIUM EDITION

Blazing new paths in travel

Trails of Myanmar

Bagan

A visit to Myanmar is an exciting combination of tradition, culture and nature.
Discover the magnificent plain of pagodas and temples at BAGAN.

Explore the former royal capital MANDALAY with her golden pagodas on the banks of the legendary Ayeyarwaddy River. Stroll through dazzling, colourful markets and

Mandalay

Yangon

trek to minority villages around INLE LAKE. Whether you leave the beaten track or follow the trodden path, whether you prefer individual a la carte tours or travelling on scheduled programs, with ASIAN TRAILS you are always on the right track.

15th Floor, Mercury Tower, 540 Ploenchit Road, Bangkok 10330 Thailand
Tel: (66 2) 658-6080-89 Fax:(66 2) 658 6099 E-mail: res@asiantrails.org

471 Pyay Road, Kamayut Township, Yangon, Union of Myanmar
Tel: (951) 524 978   –   Fax: (951) 524 978

Prices are quoted in baht (**B**) and US dollars ($)

	PAGE Nº
ABOUT THIS GUIDE 5	

SOUTHERN THAILAND BASICS
- OVERVIEW 17
- TRAVELING TO THE SOUTH 20
- PHUKET ISLAND AND THE ANDAMAN COAST 23

PHUKET ISLAND
- PHUKET BASICS 33
- DIVING IN PHUKET 45
- PHUKET TOWN 57

PUKHET BEACHES
- PATONG BEACH 63
- KARON BEACH 77
- KATA BEACH 84
- PHUKET SOUTH BEACHES 88
- BEACHES NORTH OF PATONG 95

KOH PHI PHI
- THE MAIN ISLAND 103
- PHI PHI LEH AND MAYA BAY 111

PHANG NGA BAY
- PHANG NGA BASICS & ATTRACTIONS 113

KRABI AND AREA
- KRABI BASICS 115
- AO NANG BEACH 121
- RAILEY BEACHES 128
- KOH LANTA 135
- TRANG & TARUTAO 143

ANDAMAN COAST
- KHAO LAK 145
- SURIN AND SIMILAN ISLANDS 150
- RANONG 151
- KHAO SOK FOREST 152

BACK OF THE BOOK – CONTENTS 157

INDEX 166

MAPS (BIG MAPS -SOUTHERN THAILAND & PHUKET- END OF THE BOOK)
- THAILAND ENTRY POINTS 16
- AO NANG & RAILEY 173
- PHUKET BEACHES: PATONG, KARON, KATA 174, 175
- PHUKET TOWN 176-7
- KOH PHI PHI 178
- PHANG NGA BAY 179
- KOH LANTA 180

Our favorite places...
We award this cup to places getting our highest recommendation. Please send us your comments on these selections: comments@asiahorizons.com

AN "AsiaHorizons Guidebook" PUBLISHED BY:
Asia Horizons Books Co., Ltd. — a company registered in Bangkok, Thailand.
HORIZONS Travel Guides are produced by Extra Image Co., Ltd. and
asiaHORIZONS is pending registration.
www.asiahorizons.com is the property of Roland Neveu.

Every effort has been made to ensure the information in this book is correct at the time of printing. However, the publisher cannot be held liable for its accuracy, as situations can change rapidly in the region.

All rights reserved. No part of this book may be reproduced, stored in a retrieval system or transmitted in any form or by any means (electronic, mechanical, photocopying or any other, including the Internet) without the prior written consent of Asia Horizons Books Co., Ltd. and its representatives worldwide.

Information regarding this publication, advertising in future (yearly) issues or distribution can be obtained from:
(☎) 662-933 8214 or (📠) 662-933 6328 in Bangkok, Thailand.
or by e-mail: info@asiahorizons.com

© **June 2000**   **ISBN 974-85984-8-9**

AUTHORS

Hamish Keith

Hamish Keith first went to Samui ten years ago and immediately fell in love with the island. Since then he has owned and operated a boutique shop and restaurant on Samui and an adventure travel company in Bangkok. He now resides in Bangkok, but escapes to paradise whenever possible, and as well as penning this guide book has contributed stories and articles to several publications. If he is not at home he can usually be found leading mountain bike tours somewhere in South East Asia.

He can be contacted at: hamishk@loxinfo.co.th

Main photography

French-born **Roland Neveu** has been living and traveling in Asia for more than 20 years. He is an internationally-recognized freelance photojournalist and was one of the few Westerners to witness the fall of Phnom Penh to the Khmer Rouge in 1975. His pictures have appeared in hundreds of publications around the world. He spent three years covering the civil war in Lebanon for *Time* magazine and photographed the wars in El Salvador and Afghanistan. He documented the devastating effects of Aids in central Africa. He worked as official stills photographer on the production of many Hollywood movies. Among his credits are Platoon, Casualties of War, Born on the 4th of July and Thelma and Louise. In the early 90s, Roland launched a publishing company. This series of guidebooks is one of his main interests and is a way to convey his knowledge of the region to the world at large.

Full PHOTO credits on page 159.

This book was written with information available as of :
April 2000

The ASIAHORIZONS guidebooks series comprises the following titles:
  Cambodia – ISBN – 974 89446-9-7
  Vietnam – ISBN – 974-89447-1-9
  Thailand – ISBN – 974-86535-2-8
  Laos (1999) – ISBN – 974-87034-4-4
  Koh Samui – ISBN – 974-87161-1-2
  Phuket & Andaman Coast – ISBN – 974-85984-8-9
The first 2 titles are also available in French.
Titles in preparation (to be published in 2000):
  Angkor – ISBN – 974-86535-9-5
  Cambodia (new edition) – ISBN – 974-85984-9-7
  Yunnan
  Bangkok
  Lanna – Northern Thailand

About this Guide

Introduction

Phuket is Thailand's largest island and its most popular tourist destination. Well over two million visitors a year flock to its beaches, which have gained a well-deserved reputation as being among the best in the world. Separated from the rest of Thailand by a short causeway, Phuket has grown up separately from the rest of the country. Historically influenced by an incongruous collection of foreign forces as well as surviving domestic tussles Phuket has a flavor and appearance that is quite unique. It is located midway along Thailand's Andaman coast, a rugged and beautiful stretch of tropical shoreline studded with islands and beaches that were once infested with pirates. The entire coast has become a powerful magnet attracting tourists from all over the world. The diversity and strength of its allure is universal and very few visitors are anything less than overwhelmed by the range of attractions this coastline has to offer. Phuket is the upmarket part, Krabi is the trendy scene, Koh Lanta is where the backpackers go and Khao Lak is unspoilt. Hidden amongst all these touristic gems are huge savannas of untouched southern Thailand, all raw and wild and very interesting.

Phuket is a fully-fledged international tourist resort with some of the most luxurious hotels in the world and its fair share of mawkish tourist attractions. However the island is large enough to accommodate its visitors and still have plenty of space left over. It is 550 square kilometers in size, twice as large as Penang and six times bigger than Hong Kong. It is almost the same size as Singapore and it is sometimes said to be half as efficient, but twice as much fun. Phuket has room for the outrageousness of Patong, the opulence of Bang Tao and the peacefulness of Nai Yang. It has rainforests, mangrove forests, rubber plantations and a busy commercial capital that pays little attention to the hoards of foreigners frolicking on its beaches. Its innumerable attractions and mesmeric pace of life have drawn a steady trickle of settlers from all over the world to join an already disparate community of Thais,

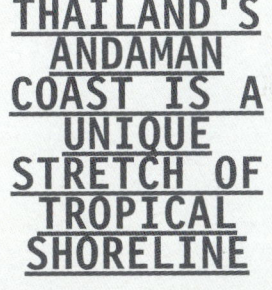

THAILAND'S ANDAMAN COAST IS A UNIQUE STRETCH OF TROPICAL SHORELINE

Phuket's Liveaboard and Adventure Tour Specialists

PADI Instructor Courses
with Course Director Bent Posejpal

Located directly across the street from the Dino Park in Kata Beach, Phuket, we offer a full range of diving and sailing services.

Siam Dive n' Sail, Co. Ltd.
Tel: 66-76/330-967/ Fax: 66-76/330-990
Email: info@siamdivers.com
www.siamdivers.com & www.idc-thailand.com

ABOUT THIS GUIDE

Chinese and Malays into a cultural melting pot that has prospered steadily throughout history. Strategically located in the Andaman Sea protecting the rugged treasure of Phang Nga Bay, rich with tin and rubber and now tourism Phuket has been blessed in almost every way. Unique in that it has been able to market its attractions with extraordinary success without detracting –too heavily – from them. It has marketed itself successfully – some would say mercilessly – as an island paradise.

For those who feel that Phuket is overly packaged, then it is only a short boat road to a host of destinations all along the coast. Beyond the cinematic scenery of Phang Nga Bay lies Krabi, where powder white beaches curl up between the toes of towering limestone pinnacles. Even the most fevered Hollywood imagination would struggle to conjure up a location this dramatic. The beaches of Krabi are where the adventure junkies hang out: rock climbing, scuba diving, sea kayaking and game fishing are just some of the dishes on the menus of Railey, Ao Nang and Phi Phi. The twin towers of Phi Phi Don overlook two of the most photogenic bays this side of Hollywood. Home to an eccentric combination of upmarket resorts and a vibrant travelers scene which has been fuelled by the release of the controversial movie "The Beach".

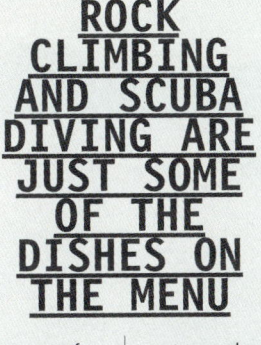

ROCK CLIMBING AND SCUBA DIVING ARE JUST SOME OF THE DISHES ON THE MENU

Further south are a myriad of tropical islands that have hardly been touched by the double-edged blade of tourism. Koh Lanta is the largest and most accessible and has become a favorite resting place for weary travelers. With seemingly endless beaches it is a rising star on the Thai tourist production line. But if peace and quiet is still not enough then the islands of Trang and Tarutao can provide as close to a desert island experience as is possible without being marooned.

North of Phuket is another endless horizon of tranquil coastline. With the islands and reefs of the Similans and Surin providing some of the best diving in the world and the unchartered waters

ABOUT THIS GUIDE

of Burma just over another horizon there is enough here to keep the most restless explorer occupied for a lifetime.

Using this guide

This guide brings you all the necessary information you will need to reap the maximum enjoyment from your time in Phuket and along the Andaman Coast. It has been designed to help travellers and tourists decide where to stay, what to do, where to eat, what to expect from their stay and much more. It will help you strike out to places that you may otherwise never know of. To break free from the packaged programmes that many tourists follow and discover the real Thailand. The beaches of Patong, Karon and Kata are still the main draws for most of Phuket's visitors and we hope that this book will not only help you discover what lies beyond the convenience of these resorts, but also treasures that can be discovered within them. It should be essential reading for anyone considering a trip to the region and an indispensable source of information for those who decide to visit this beautiful part of the world. As well as tips for travelers and inside information on the people who live in the area, there is a guide to each beach destination. These beach guides should tell you everything you need to know to get the most out of your holiday. Up to date information on where to stay and where to eat as well as practical information on how to get things done. The map in the corner of each page will show you where you are and our detailed maps will help you navigate your way around. Of course we have not been able to list every resort, restaurant and bar, but we have tried to cover the best each beach has to offer. We are confident this book will help you more fully appreciate the best that these tropical islands has to offer - but in the end it's up to you to enjoy your

ABOUT THIS GUIDE

time in paradise.

Remember Phuket and the other resorts along the coastline are developing at breakneck speed - places open and close every day and we have tried to anticipate this whenever possible. Entrepreneurs will supply you with lots of guides and handouts with free information on where to go and where to stay, but they are little more than advertising sheets pointing you towards their sponsors' resorts and restaurants. We have reported Phuket and the region as we see it, not as we are paid to see it.

ACCOMMODATION AND OTHER PRACTICALITIES

Naturally accommodation is a vital concern for any traveler. Unfortunately it is not possible to list every single resort in all the regions covered by this book. We have, however, listed a broad range of the most appropriate resorts, guest houses and hotels. We have listed all the best places, the "hottest deals" and point out some of the stinkers you should avoid. At the top of the range we list the amenities and facilities that are on offer, but when a number of places have similar services we will say so. We assume that all rooms over Bt1,000 have air-conditioning (if they don't we say so). Likewise at the budget end we assume all rooms over Bt200 have attached bathrooms and anywhere that requires you to share facilities we say so. We list the price range of rooms in each resort and have tried to incorporate seasonal variations - the bottom price should be the cost of the cheapest room in

Using this guidebook...

Asian Adventures

Asia's Premier Adventure Holiday Company

Diving
Trekking
Biking
Sailing
Kayaking

Tel: (076) 341799
Fax: (076) 341798
E-mail: info@asian-adventures.com
Web: www.asian-adventures.com

ABOUT THIS GUIDE

the low season, while the top price is the most expensive room in peak season.

With restaurants we have estimated what a meal for one person should ordinarily cost, and as this can vary on each menu we have given a price range that should help guide your choice.

We also like to have an opinion on everything and our researchers have tested everywhere that we have recommended or panned.

A NOTE ON OUR MAPS

Maps in Thailand can vary significantly from one to another. On the one hand, foreign-edited maps (which often come from the same original source) can contain serious errors in regard to the placement, or even existence, of roads, for example. On the other hand, there are locally produced maps that may contain errors regarding "contours" and the identification of secondary and tertiary highways, not to mention misleading distances of scale. It's rather difficult, therefore, to strike it just right. What we have done to try and resolve this problem is to refer to all available material to double check our maps, but it is still impossible to guarantee that they are significantly more accurate than those produced by "specialists". In short, it's best not to trust any single map and be ready for the unexpected.

OUR GUIDEBOOKS

Our series of guidebooks on Southeast Asia already has six titles on the shelves of bookstores, including this most recent addition. Like this book, the others in the collection have been researched and written only by people, usually journalists, who live in Southeast Asia and who are completely famil-

ABOUT THIS GUIDE

PHUKET COUNTRY CLUB
27-hole Golf Course

tel (076) 321 038 - 41 (4 lines) fax (66 76) 321 721
e-mail: info@phuketcountryclub.com

iar with the people, culture and traditions of the countries we cover.

All the books we publish have a root level of information and once one has been written, we take it on the road for a "test drive" before publication.

The series is going to grow rapidly from 2000 onwards. A complete series on Indochina, plus Burma, should be in place at the end of this year, then we'll cover China, with the first title planned for Yunnan (mid-2000).

Bon voyage!

SIAM SAFARI
SOUTHERN THAILAND

Tel 076 280116, Fax 076 280107
Email: info@siamsafari.com
www.siamsafari.com

International award winning Ecotours
Phuket   Samui   Krabi

JUNGLE SAFARI'S
KHAO SOK & PHANGNGA

Calendar of commemorations

January	1st: New Year's Day		Paddy harvesting	Super sunse...
February	Chiang Mai Flower Festival		Chinese New Year	
March		8th: International Women's Day		
April	6th: Chakri Day			Songk... (Tha... New Ye...
May	International Worker's Day		Beginning of rice-planting cycle	
June		From June: Fruit fairs countr...		
July				
August				
September				
October		Ok Phansa-Thot Kathin (end of Lent) Phuket vegetarian Festival		
November				
December		5th: HM the King's Birthday Phuket King's Cup Regatta 10th: Constitution Day		

FESTIVALS AND EVENTS IN THAILAND

				Rain fall	Average temp. night/day
				no rain	19/30°C
	Full moon Day: Makha Bucha				21/32°C
					22/35°C
				hot and dry	24/35°C
Yasothon Rocket festival		Full moon Day: Visakha Bucha		beginning of the rainy season	24/34°C
	Pi Ta Kon festival Dan Sai-Loei				24/32°C
Full moon Day: Asaratha Bucha		Khao Phansa (start of Lent) Ubon candle festival		hot and humid	24/32°C
12th: HM the Queen's Birthday					24/31°C
				heaviest rain	24/31°C
		23rd: Chulalongkorn day			23/30°C
Full moon Day: Loy Krathong		River Kwai Bridge Festival		end of the rainy season	22/32°C
		31st: New Year's Eve			20/30°C

THAILAND – VIETNAM – FIJI
LAOS – PHILIPPINES

SEE YOUR WORLD

IN A NEW WAY

ASIA'S PREMIER SEA KAYAKING COMPANY

Call Us Today About Your Next Vacation at 212-252
Award Winning International Standard in Five Countries
Day trips To Two-Weeks;
Custom Charters and Management Training our Specialty.

SeaCanoe International, Ltd.
Tel/Fax: (66-76) 212-252 or 212-172,
For information,
email: info@seacanoe.com   Website: www.seacanoe.com

Thailand Basics

TOURIST TIPS

Dos and Don'ts

Thailand is justly celebrated for its tolerance and hospitality, and the average tourist will have no difficulty in adjusting to the local customs. All the same, as when coming into any unfamiliar society, a visitor may find it helpful to be aware of certain dos and don'ts and thus avoid giving accidental offence. Basically, most of these are simply a matter of common sense and good manners - not really all that different from the way one would behave in one's own country - but a few are special enough to be pointed out.

THE MONARCHY

The Thai people have a deep, traditional reverence for their Royal Family, and a visitor should also be careful to show respect for the King, the Queen, and the Royal Children. In a cinema, for example, a portrait of the King is shown during the playing of the Royal anthem, and the audience is expected to stand. When attending some public events at which a member of the Royal Family is present, the best guide as to how to behave is probably to watch the people around you and do what they do.

RELIGION

Thai law has a number of special sections concerning religious offences, and these cover not only Buddhism, the religion of the majority of the people, but also any other faiths represented in the Kingdom. It is, for instance, unlawful to commit any act, by any means whatsoever, to an object or a place of religious worship of any community in a manner likely to insult the religion. Similarly, "whoever causes any disturbance at an assembly lawfully engaged in the performance of religious worship or religious ceremonies" is subject to punishment, as well as "whoever dresses or uses a symbol showing that he is a priest or novice, holy man or clergyman of any religion unlawfully in order to make another person believe he is such person."

In less legal language, here are a few tips on what to do and what not to do on a visit to a religious place:

☞ Dress neatly. Don't go shirtless, or in shorts, pants, or other unsuitable attire. If you look at the Thais around you, you'll see the way they would prefer you to be dressed -- which, in fact, is probably not very different from the way you'd dress in a similar place back home.

The tranquility of Phuket's beaches is legendary.

VISITING THAILAND

☞ It is all right to wear shoes while walking around the compound of a Buddhist temple, but not inside the chapel where the principal Buddha image is kept. Don't worry about dirt when you have to take them off; the floors of such places are usually clean.

☞ In a Muslim mosque, men should wear hats and women should be well covered with slacks or a long skirt, a long-sleeved blouse buttoned to the neck, and a scarf over the hair. You must remove your shoes before entering the mosque and you should not be present during a religious gathering.

☞ Buddhist priests are forbidden to touch or be touched by a woman or to accept anything from the hand of one. If a woman has to give anything to a monk or novice, she first hands it to a man, who then presents it. Or in case of a woman who wants to present it with her hand, the monk or novice will spread out a piece of saffron robe or handkerchief in front of him, and the woman will lay down the material on the robe which is being held at one end by the monk or novice.

☞ All Buddha images, large or small, ruined or not, are regarded as sacred objects. Hence, don't climb up on one to take a photograph or, generally speaking, do anything that might show a lack of respect.

SOCIAL BEHAVIOUR

It is easy to get along with Thai people, especially in Samui where they are used to westerners and their strange ways. However they will appreciate it if you respect their customs - it shows politeness and this is a virtue they value very highly indeed.

☞ Keep smiling and people will like you. A smile has a thousand meanings, but will always be well received. It can be used as an apology, an excuse, for thanks, as a sign of embarrassment and of course as a sign of pleasure. Remember you are in the land of smiles and a smile here never hurts or offends - so, keep smiling.

☞ Bargain with good humor. Not only is it fun but will also help you to get the best prices.

☞ Beckon waiters or anyone you wish to talk to with the hand, palm downward, fingers straight and waving up and down. Don't crook your finger, clap, and snap your fingers or hiss.

☞ Thais do not normally shake

Northern Thailand: the other very popular destination in the Kingdom.

VISITING THAILAND

Tourist tipss...

hands when they greet one another, but instead press the palms together in a prayer-like gesture called a *wai*. Generally, a younger person wais an elder, who returns it. Watch how the Thais do it, and you will soon learn.

☞ It is considered rude to point your foot at a person, so try to avoid doing so when sitting opposite anyone. And in accordance with the belief that the foot is the lowest limb, DO NOT point your foot to show anything to anyone - use your finger instead.

☞ Thais regard the head as the highest part of the body both literally and figuratively. As a result they DO NOT approve of touching anyone on that part of the body - even in a friendly gesture. Especially avoid patting a Thai on the head (even children) or ruffling their hair. Similarly, if you watch Thais at social gatherings, you will notice that young people go to considerable lengths to keep their heads lower than those of the elders to avoid giving the impression of "looking down" on them. This is not always possible, of course, but it is the effort that counts.

☞ Public displays of affection between men and women are frowned upon. You may see some very Westernised young Thai couples holding hands, but that is the extent of the displaying of affection in this polite society.

☞ Losing your temper, especially in public, will more than likely get you nowhere. The Thais think such displays denote poor manners, and you are more apt to get what you want by keeping a cool head and concealing your emotions.

☞ Never publicly humiliate Thai people, it causes them to lose face, which is the worst thing that can happen to them. Not only is it unkind, but their reaction may also be unpredictable.

☞ DO NOT be surprised if you are addressed by your first name; for instance, Mr. Bob or Miss Mary instead of by your surname. This is because Thais refer to one another in this manner, usually with the title "Khun" (Mr., Mrs., or Miss) in front. Follow the customs of the country as far as possible, and you will definitely make people more friendly toward you.

☞ Flatter when appropriate. Thais love it, and remember their nationalistic feelings are usually high.

☞ Do not hesitated to say "thank you" or smile your appreciation. The Thai phrase is "*Kop Khun Krap*" by a man and "*Kop Khun Kha*" by a woman.

Relax, take it easy - at least at the beginning of your stay. You will soon come to appreciate and enjoy the Thais laid-back attitude to time and punctuality. Keep pressure for when you get home!

TIMELY SAFETY TIPS

In recent times there have been several instances of robbery, rape and murder of tourists which have made headlines around the globe. As in any country, Thailand has its problems with unpleasant incidences, although they are not too often direct at tourists. Whenever this happens, it causes great embarrassment among the authorities.

Here, like everywhere, one should be aware of the risks posed to the lone traveler. Exercising the same caution when getting in taxis or going about at night as you would in your own country is probably the best advice. Thailand is quite safe, but just don't take it for granted! With 60 million people, there's bound to be some miscreants.

Traveling South

GETTING TO PHUKET

BY AIR
Thai Airways
The national carrier has over 10 flights a day from Bangkok directly to Phuket International Airport. The cost is B2,300 each way. There are direct flights from Phuket to Trang (B520) and to Haad Yai (B910) every day. There is a daily direct flight from – but not to – Chiang Mai (B3,950).

THAI Airways also flies from Phuket to Singapore every day (B4,000), Penang (B2,230) 3 times a week, Kuala Lumpur (B3,730) once a day – twice on Fridays and Sundays. (Theses are O/W rates).

Thai Airways International Phuket Office: ☎ 212 946
Bangkok: ☎ (02) 280 0060

Angel Airlines
Does not operate anymore. It was a short life private airline.

Bangkok Airways
Flies from Samui to Phuket twice a day for B1,530 each way (plus a hefty B400 airport tax levied by the Samui Airport - which is owned by the airline).
Bangkok Airways Phuket Office: ☎ 225 033-5
Bangkok: ☎ (02) 229 3456

INTERNATIONAL FLIGHTS
Many other airline carriers and charter companies have offices on Phuket and fly to destinations all over the world. Some regional airlines are:

Dragon Air (Hong Kong)
☎ 215 734, 217 300-1
Silk Air (Singapore)
☎ 213 891
Singapore Airlines
☎ 213 891
Malaysian Airlines
☎ 216 675.

BY BUS
There are buses to and from nearly everywhere in Thailand from the Bor Kor Sor Bus Station in Phuket town. For buses to Bangkok we strongly recommend that you take an air-conditioned bus, preferably a 24 seat VIP vehicle where the seats recline almost to horizontal. Buses depart from Phuket every hour from 14.00 until 22.00.

If you are coming from Bangkok, regular air-con buses depart from the Southern bus Terminal every hour from 15.00 until 22.00 and tickets cost B356. VIP buses depart at 17.30, 18.00 and 18.30 and cost B690. Tickets for VIP buses can be bought from any travel agent and will usually include a minibus pick up at your hotel.

Bor Sor Kor Bus Station
☎ 211 480
Southern Bus terminal
(air-con) ☎ 434 5558
(VIP) ☎ 434 7192
For buses and boats to Krabi, Phi Phi, Koh Lanta and other parts of the Andaman Coast please refer to the relevant sections in this book.

DRIVING: THAI LAW

Thai law requires car drivers and front seat passengers to wear seat belts. Motorcyclists are also required to use crash helmets, though you will notice many people on Phuket openly flouting this law. It is advisable that you use both. There are sometimes impromptu road blocks and you can be hit with an on the spot fine for flouting the law. An International Driving Permit, or a license from your home country, is required for all car and big bike rentals. The local police will check from time to time - so be warned.

GETTING TO THE ISLANDS

Many companies also offer minibuses to destinations all over south Thailand and as far as Penang in Malaysia. Although they are sometimes quicker than regular buses they are not nearly as comfortable – unless you are lucky enough to get one that is running empty. A minibus – or *rod tou* in Thai – to Surat Thani will cost **B**250, Krabi **B**200, Haad Yai **B**300, Penang **B**500, and tickets are available from any travel agent.

ARRIVING ON THE ISLAND

The two main gateways to Phuket are the international airport and the bus station. Transport from the airport is restricted to two operators, both of which have large desks outside the arrival hall. Fares are fixed and transport is by shared minibus or private taxi. The fares are clearly marked, but the staff will try to encourage you to take a private taxi rather than a shared bus. A bus to Patong costs **B**120; Kata is **B**180. A taxi to Patong costs from **B**400. Taxis to Krabi cost **B**2,000 and Khao Lak is **B**1,080.

> If you have arranged for a hotel or tour company to pick you up, proceed beyond the taxi desks and you will find a scrum of drivers and hotel staff holding name cards and banners.
>
> From the bus station it is easy to get a tuk tuk to take you to your destination, otherwise make your way to Ranong road where the local *songtaews* wait.

GETTING AROUND

Phuket is a big island and it can take a surprisingly long time to get around it. This is immediately apparent on arrival as transfers from the airport in the north to Patong and the other resorts in the south take over an hour. Due to the sort of petty political pressures that still hinder economic progress in Thailand there is a very inefficient transport system on Phuket. Public transport radiates from Phuket town and is designed to suit the needs of the local people. Tourists are supposed to hire tuk tuks – who have a powerful lobbying voice – to travel around the island.

PUBLIC TRANSPORT

There is a public transport system during the day that covers the entire island. Transport is by *songtaew* – which translates as two rows – large six wheel trucks converted into colourful people carriers. These Phuket buses provide a reasonably efficient and very economical way to explore the island, but can be time consuming, especially during school hours when scores of uniformed children are crammed inside. Mostly they start and end their journeys in Phuket town so their routes are not necessarily convenient for tourists trying to get from beach to beach. Destinations are clearly marked on the front and you can just flag them down. A journey will cost from **B**10 to **B**50 depending on the distance. The *songtaews* start their journey from Ranong road in Phuket town and run from 07.00 to 18.00.

TUK TUKS

Tuk Tuks line the streets of Patong, Karon and Kata and will take you anywhere on the island for a price. They are a fast and reasonably efficient way to get around the island, but their drivers have a bad reputation as hustlers and con men. Many of them try to double up as travel agents and tour guides offering round-the-island trips at tempting prices. These trips are almost certainly a tour of establishments that pay commissions and you will most likely spend the day being bullied and pestered by pushy salesmen. Prices for transport around the island are fixed. Journeys inside Patong cost **B**20, Patong to Phuket town is **B**150; Patong to Karon **B**100; Patong to Phuket Airport is **B**400

GETTING TO THE ISLANDS

ROAD DEATHS ON PHUKET

A telling statistic: last year, 179 people were killed and more than 10,000 injured in motorbike accidents on the island.

MOTORCYCLE TAXIS

Motorcycle taxis are available all over Phuket town and Patong. Short journeys cost **B**10, with prices rising to **B**50. Many motorcycles don't like to go outside their town. Always ask the price for a longer journey before you get on the bike.

CAR AND BIKE HIRE

Renting your own vehicle is the best way of getting around for it allows you to explore the many small roads and tracks that lead off into the interior jungles or down to one of the many deserted beaches. Suzuki jeeps represent 99% of the cars hired while the 100cc Honda Dream motorcycle is by far the most common rented bike. Larger sports bikes and 'choppers' are also readily available if you want a bit more power and style. There are dozens of rental shops all over the island; mostly small businesses, discounts can be negotiated when renting for an extended period. Beware of jeeps without full insurance, there are many that don't have it, and many stories of tourists who have landed in serious trouble following accidents. Reputable rental companies Avis and Budget both have offices on the island and offer a wide range of vehicles and deals, often as good or better than the smaller operators.

DRIVING SAFETY TIPS
Renting the Vehicle.

Most rental companies will hold you responsible for any damage occurring while you are renting the vehicle. Make a note on the contract of any dents, scratches or missing parts before you drive off with the vehicle. If you have never driven a vehicle before, do not hesitate to ask for instruction. Make sure everything on the vehicle is functional. Brake lights and turning signals, low and high beams should all be working properly.

Phuket & Andaman coast

OVERVIEW OF PHUKET AND THE ANDAMAN COAST

History

Phuket was once connected to the mainland by a land bridge and up until as recently as the 18th Century people were able to cross to the island on elephant back. During the first half of the last millennium there was little to distinguish Phuket from the rest of the Andaman Coast. It had a very small population and with its lack of a river estuary was not suitable as a settlement. It is likely that its first inhabitants were Mokken sea gypsies, a pre-Malay race the decedents of whom can still be found today. In 1225 AD a Chinese chronicler noted that "Silan" – as Phuket was then known - was part of the powerful Srivichai Empire from Sumatra and was most likely controlled from the port of Takua-pa.

The first Siamese control over the region came after King Ramkamhaeng ascended the throne in the Sukhothai era and began to unify the Tai tribes from Chiang Mai as far south as Nakhorn Si Thammarat. Phuket became important as it had an abundance of natural resources. Its dense forests sustained tigers, elephants and rhinoceros and its seas were a breeding ground for fish and pearls. The seas off Thailand's west coast were becoming busy shipping lanes and Malay pirates, Arab traders and European adventurers began to exploit the resources under the watchful eyes of the ruling Thai families. But it wasn't until tin was discovered in the 17th century that Phuket assumed any real economic and political importance,

In 1662 Dutch traders were allowed to set up a trading post on

TIN MEN

Tin was an incredibly precious commodity from the 16th century to the early 19th Century. It was used to make nearly all the necessities of war - spear tips, body armour, swords, muskets and bullets. Possession of it, therefore, led to considerable power. From the 16th century through to the 18th century Phuket was exploited by Thais, Burmese and Europeans and crude mines were dug and fought over. When the Chakri Dynasty finally asserted itself over the island trading started in earnest and Phuket became one of the most prolific tin producers in the region. Demand boomed, as the new regime needed coins and roof tiles and the industrialising west cried for tin-cans and electronics. Huge open mines were dug out of the earth and Chinese coolies were brought in to sort through baskets of clay and silt. The mining was overseen by European contractors with little or no regard for the land they worked. A strange waste land, devoid of vegetation scarred the island until the offshore dredgers arrived. At the turn of the century technological advancements meant that it was more efficient to dredge the tin from the ocean floor and huge pumps, excavators and furnaces chugged away just off the shoreline. As the century progressed world demand for tin diminished and many foreign companies towed their equipment away. There are still a few old dredgers left in Phuket bay, but the mines have now melted back into the landscape and have been redeveloped to make way for tourists. The most spectacular example of old mines being ameliorated are the lagoons at Phuket Laguna on Bang Tao beach.

PHUKET & REGION

THE HEROINES MONUMENT

In 1785 the Burmese sent their powerful navy to invade Phuket. With the Chakri Dynasty still in its infancy in Bangkok and instability and uncertainty rife throughout Siam, it seemed an opportune moment to seize the wealthy island. Despite a warning from Sir Francis Light, the people of Phuket seemed ill prepared to defend themselves. The Burmese invasion, consisting of a fleet of warships carrying 3,000 troops, swiftly overran Takua Pa and lay siege to Thalang. Phuket was without a ruler, as the governor had recently passed away, and was at odds with Rama I - the new ruler of Siam – over unpaid taxes and so very vulnerable to an attack. To compound their problems, the Siamese had detained the governor's wife, Chan, a grand daughter of the Sultan of Kedah. As the Burmese swept south from Takua Pa, Chan was able to escape from her captors and with her sister Mook was able to rally the people of Thalang to fight the invaders.

Although hopelessly outnumbered the two sisters had stockades built to defend the town and ordered everyone, including women and children, to fire muskets and other ordinance at the Burmese. Through determination and cunning the women were able to outlast their foes, and eventually the Burmese – frustrated and out of supplies - had to retreat. One of their ruses had been to get the women of Phuket to dress up as soldiers and carry coconut palms, cut and dried to look like weapons, and march down to Bang Tao bay as the Burmese landed. They then retreated to the stockades, making the Burmese think they would have to fight a long protracted war with a large well-armed force.

In reward for their bravery, Rama I conferred the title of Tao Tepkrasatree on Chan and Tao Srisunthorn on Mook. A statue to honour the achievement of the two heroines now stands at a busy crossroads south of Thalang.

the island and it began to gain a great deal of attention from the expanding European colonial powers. A French missionary became governor of Phuket and based his capital in Thalang, and at the same time the British East India Company was looking for a port to control the straits of Malacca. The company's captain, Francis Light, married a Phuket girl and lobbied heavily for Phuket to be taken as a British possession, but Britain ended up occupying Penang Island instead.

In 1767 the Burmese sacked Ayuthaya and the Thai kingdom fell into disarray. Phuket was attacked on a number of occasions and was occupied by the Burmese and Malays at different times, but always managed to beat off the invaders. As the Chakri Dynasty in Bangkok managed to reunite the Thais and the Burmese and Malays capitulated to the British, Phuket once again fell under the auspices of the rulers of Nakhorn Si Thammarat, who enjoyed Bangkok's patronage, and the foreign tin mining companies were able to return. As the island had only a small population, thousands of Chinese coolies were brought up from Penang to work in the mines.

As they did in Penang, the Chinese immigrants soon began to dominate the island. In 1876 two Chinese sects fought bloody battles with each other, before going on a murderous rampage. The local people were able to crush them, but the Chinese soon rose to ascendance using more subtle methods. The Chinese settlement in Phuket town surpassed Thalang as the island's main town and quickly became the hub of its commercial activity. Phraya Ratsada, the first Chinese

PHUKET & REGION

History...

governor of Phuket, came to power in 1890 and during his reign –1890 to 1909 - the island prospered enormously. Grand European-style houses were built and the Standard Chartered Bank set up its first Thailand branch. He was also accredited with introducing rubber trees to Phuket.

Phuket soon became Thailand's wealthiest province and even when a global oversupply of tin caused the price to plummet, it managed to retain its wealth by becoming an important rubber producer until tourism took over. In 1970 *Newsweek* magazine published an article proclaiming Phuket as the most exciting travel destination in Asia and within a few short years Phuket was transformed from an industrial island into a tourism machine. The opening of Club Med was the first great step propeling Phuket into the public eye and all through the early 1970s hotels rushed to claim their small pieces of paradise. The Chinese business acumen and their ability to raise money from the booming Sino financial centres of Singapore and Hong Kong helped Phuket take the tourism industry by storm. The timing was just right for Phuket to emerge as an ideal holiday destination. A massive increase in European demand for beach holidays and their willingness and desire to travel further afield, plus the emergence of efficient tour companies seeking new and exotic destinations, meant there was a huge market for Phuket. As Thailand's infrastructure improved and Phuket gained its international airport in 1976, it soon became almost entirely a tourist island.

Geography

Phuket is 543 sq km and the largest island in Thailand, although as recently as 500 years ago it was connected to the mainland. It is now separated from Phang Nga province by a 600-meter channel, which is spanned by two bridges. The island is 50-kilometers long and 20-kilometers wide at its broadest point. The interior is mountainous with granite peaks reaching as high as 530-meters. The dense jungle that once covered the island is now largely gone. The only protected area is around Khao Phra Thaeo, which has been declared a national park. The west coast has 35-kilometers of almost continuous sandy beaches and this is where the majority of its tourist development has taken place. The east coast is a mixture of mud flats, mangroves and coral beaches. There are 32 smaller islands surrounding Phuket, most of which are uninhabited apart from some resort developments. Tourism

PHUKET & REGION

RUBBER ISLAND

As the tin mining industry began to go into recession the ingenious people of Phuket had to to look for other sources of income. In 1899 Phraya Ratsada, the then governor of Phuket, visited the rubber estates of British Malaya and in 1901 he planted the first rubber tree in Trang. The climate and soil conditions in South Thailand were found to be ideal for the Indian rubber tree and the Thai government distributed seeds throughout the area. Chinese smallholders in Phuket took advantage of the opportunity to go into business on their own as many of them had been laid off by the tin companies. Phuket quickly transformed itself into a rubber-producing island and sent sheets of latex to the markets in Northern Malaya. By 1936 40% of Phuket's surface was covered by rubber plantations and Thailand supplied 4% of the world's rubber. By the mid 1990s Thailand had become the largest exporter of rubber in the world, producing over 2 million tons a year, earning around **B**60 billion annually. Even though it has been surpassed by tourism, It is still an important industry on Phuket, earning around **B**800 million a year. Rubber plantations can be seen all over the island, particularly around Nai Harn, Nai yang and along the road to the airport. If you want to see the 'tappers' in action you will have to get up early, as rubber is collected before dawn.

is the island's primary industry with agriculture and fishing as other considerable economic contributors. The main cash crop is rubber, followed by rice, coconut, pineapple, durian and other fruits.

Phang Nga province is directly north of Phuket and is best known as the home of Phang Nga Bay, the island studded Marine Park that covers 400 square kilometers of the Andaman Sea. The limestone islands – known as karsts – are spectacular geological anomalies formed over millions of years. The northern coastal section of Phang Nga province is a sparsely populated area and is home to several national parks, including Khao Lak, which is adjacent to a beach area undergoing rapid developments. South of Phuket and stretching 200-kilometers along the Andaman coast is Krabi province. With 200 islands and a host of national parks Krabi has an incredibly diverse topography. Geographically its coastal regions are an extension of Phang Nga bay and are punctuated by awesome limestone cliffs. The most famous of these formations are the Phi Phi Islands, which have now become a popular tourist destination. However there are many other islands further south that are only now being discovered by more adventurous travelers.

.People

Phuket has a population of around 215,000, of whom an estimated 60,000 live in Phuket town. 73% of the island's population are Buddhist, 23% Muslim and 3% Christian. Most of Phuket's residents are ethnically Thai, with a large Chinese minority – estimated at 35%. However a considerable number of Chinese immigrants have assimilated into Thai society through marriage and have taken Thai names and are considered to be Thai. The Chinese on the island nearly all hail from the Hokkien Region, which is also where the majority of Chinese in Singapore and Penang originally came from. Phuket has the largest Hokkien community in Thailand – most Chinese in Bangkok come from the Tsiou Tsou region and speak a different language.

As in many other parts of Asia the Chinese dominate the commer-

PHUKET & REGION

cial aspects of the island's economy and are therefore the most influential group on Phuket.

Indonesian and Malay cultures have also left their mark on Phuket and the other southern provinces. About 35% of Phuket's population follows Islam and there are mosques all over the island – indeed there are more mosques than Buddhist temples. Most of Phuket's Muslims live in the north of the island and traditionally are farmers and fishermen. Some of them still speak the ancient Malayan dialect of Yawi. The coastal parts of Krabi are predominantly Muslim and the Phra Nang peninsular and Koh Lanta are almost entirely Muslim. The aboriginal seafaring people known as Chao Leh, or Sea Gypsies are spread throughout the islands off the Andaman coast, although the pressures of modern life are forcing them further into the peripheries of society. They are also predominantly Muslim and speak their own languages, although there are strong elements of animism in their culture.

Tourism

Tourism is Phuket's number one industry. Last year an estimated two-and-a-half million foreigners and around seven hundred thousand Thai tourists visited the island. It earned around **B**50 billion in revenue. Of the foreign tourists, 26% were Asian, 21% German, Swiss and Austrian, 11% British, 10% Scandinavian, 5% from Oceania, 5% Italian, 4% from North America and 3% French. Approximately 405,000 of the island's population derive an income directly from tourism. There are just over 20,00 rooms available in 303 registered establishments and the average occupancy rate is 67.7%, which any hotel manager will tell you is very healthy. However most of the up-market hotels claim to have 90 to 100% occupancy all through the high season.

Krabi has come storming onto the international tourist map in the last few years, and now that it has an international airport arrivals are expected to grow even faster. In 1999 an estimated 1.1 million tourists visited the province, roughly 40% of whom were foreign. Phang Nga, with far fewer facilities and rooms, managed around 200,000 visitors, of whom 35% were foreigners – and of the foreigners over 50% were German.

To say that tourism has shaped Phuket's development over the last two decades would be a gross understatement. A great deal of the money that pours into the island does manage to find its way

PHUKET & REGION

back into the infrastructure and Phuket has much better roads and amenities than anywhere else in Thailand. As soon as you cross the causeway you notice the wide-open roads and large well cared for houses. There is an aura of affluence that could not exist without the foreign tourists. Ever the entrepreneurs, the people of Phuket have been quick to provide them with whatever they want, and due to the massive numbers they are dealing with everything in Phuket is contrived to cater for the mass market. It is a path that Phuket has eagerly followed and most of the people seem happy to deal with the tourists as long as the money keeps rolling in.

Seasons & Weather

Tourism in Phuket and along the Andaman coast is traditionally very seasonal and dependent on the weather. The southwest monsoon comes from the Indian sub-continent and sweeps along the coast from June to September, bringing rough seas and rain. Although the rain is not continuous during this time the sea is usually too rough and dangerous for swimming and the beaches are often covered in debris. The rest of the year can be split into two; the cool season, from November until January; and the hot season from February until May.

From late March until the rains come it can get very hot with temperatures averaging around 35 degrees centigrade and sometimes climbing as far as 40 degrees centigrade. The coolest month is January with temperatures in the high twenties; January, February and December – in that order - experience the least rain and are usually the best months to visit. The wettest months are October, September and June; the rest of the time there is usually enough sunshine to keep everyone happy.

In terms of visitors Phuket has a very distinct high season, which is reflected in the prices charged for most available accommodation. The season begins promptly on November 1. This is when high season room rates are enforced and bargaining becomes difficult. From mid December through to mid January it is peak season and rooms are often difficult to find, if you intend traveling during this period it is best to make reservations in advance, especially if you plan to travel during the Christmas/New Year period. Mid January until the Songkran festival (13th and 14th of April) are back to high season and prices finally come down to earth on June 1st.

Low season can be a great time to visit Phuket, especially if you are interested in the cultural aspects of the island. Room rates are very reasonable and of course there are a refreshing lack of tour buses and package groups. During July and August the weather is often quite good and the beaches are less wind swept.

Krabi is less attractive during the low season as its beaches are its major attraction. The Phra Nang peninsular is often cut off and many places simply shut down. Phi Phi also becomes something of a ghost town and also suffers an erratic ferry service. The same can be said for Koh Lanta as, unlike Phuket, if it does rain for more than a few days there is very little to do.

Gastronomy

A SHORT GUIDE TO EATING ON PHUKET

Phuket has to be one of the world's greatest eating destinations. The range, quality and value for money that can be found in the mind-boggling myriad of eating establishments is nothing short of phenomenal. Every kind of cuisine is represented on this truly cosmopolitan island, including some of the most varied and interesting food in

PHUKET & REGION

A typical outdoor restaurant of the South Thailand.

Thailand. The melting pot of Thai, Chinese and Malays produces a fantastic array of flavors to satisfy Thailand's most popular pastime...eating. All visitors to Phuket should make a pilgrimage to the taste temples of Phuket town and Rawai Beach. Thai cuisine is now firmly established as one of the world's favorites, it is also one of the most distinctive cuisines in the world and a major motivating factor for choosing Thailand as a holiday destination. It is spicy and aromatic and Thai chefs like to use lots of garlic, chillis, lemon grass, coriander and a host of other herbs, spices and flavorings. It has a well deserved reputation for being hot and spicy and the fearsome *prik kee noo*, or mouse shit chilli, is a vital ingredient. You will find that in most tourist areas the food is toned down to suit the western palate, so if you like your food hot make sure you tell the waiter to serve it *pet pet* or spicy. However if you do not like it hot you will need to memorize the phrase *mai pet* or not spicy – it may be the most useful phrase in the Thai language. Southern Thais have a slightly different cuisine to their north and central relatives. They like to use a lot of coconut in their curries, which often have a strong Malay or even Indian influence. They are also known throughout Thailand for having the spiciest cuisine, so be careful. Of course fish and seafood play prominent roles.

The main staple food in the Thai diet is rice, which is eaten with most meals; southerners eat plain rice or *khao blao*, while sticky rice or *khao niaw* is more common in the north and the northeast, or Isaan province. You will find a lot of Isaan food available in Phuket as there are many migrant workers from this region on the island. They bring with them a distinct culture, language and cuisine which is more Lao than Thai.

On the beach

Most hawkers on the beach are from Isaan and one of their favorites is *som tam* or papaya salad, sometimes called "*papaya pok-pok*" a spicy salad mixed in a large pestle and mortar which is carried in rattan baskets balanced on the end of a stick slung across the shoulders and carried up and down the beach. This is often eaten with sticky rice and can be very spicy, so make sure you ask for just one or two chillis. Other snacks you will see carried up and down the beach are *por pia thod* or spring rolls; *gai yang* or grilled chicken; and *moo yang* or grilled pork. You will also see whole chickens roasted over a barbecue rotisserie: these are chopped up into pieces when you order one and are absolutely delicious. Fruits are also

PHUKET & REGION

widely available an you can get a whole pineapple (*sap pa rot*), watermelon (*taeng mo*) or papaya (*ma la gaw*) chopped into bite size pieces for around **B**20. Many of the beaches have large clutches of semi-permanent restaurants serving authentic Thai seafood. Surin, Rawai and even Karon are excellent places to sit and enjoy the tantalizing aromas and ribald pleasures of eating al fresco.

Street food at the market and in the towns

One of the best places to try real Thai food is at the markets where small stalls will sell ready cooked food and snacks. Curries are usually cooked in the morning and poured into large metal pots, which are displayed at the market or in small restaurants all over the island. You just lift the lid and take a look inside and order whichever one takes your fancy. There will usually be a wide selection and may include; *gaeng som pla* - sour fish curry, which will be very spicy; *gaeng kiaw wan gai.*- sweet green coconut curry with chicken; *gaeng ped nuea* - hot coconut curry with beef; *kai parow moo* - hard boiled egg and pork belly in a rich soy sauce to name a few. The curries are served over rice and cost **B**10 to **B**20 each. You will also see a lot of food in glass showcases; the most common offering is *kuay-tiaw nam* or noodle soup. There are many kinds of *kuay-tiaw* and you first choose the type of noodles (*sen*) you want and then the ingredients – the most popular being beef or fish balls or fresh sliced pork or beef. A bowl of soup will cost you **B**20 to **B**30. One of Phuket's trademark dishes is *khanom jiin naam ya* - noodles covered in a yellowfish curry, served with a plate of fresh vegetables. Another is *khao yam*, a delicious fusion of rice, lemongrass, dried shrimp and beansprouts.

Phuket town is the best place to try street food as it seems that every third shop is a restaurant. Krabi town is also very good, otherwise try the food market in Patong or check out Thalang or Rawai.

Food stands

Thai people love to eat at any hour of the day or night and you will see mobile and permanent food stands anywhere there is likely to be a crowd. Standard ready to eat offerings are *sateh, nua, moo gai* or satay sticks of beef, pork or chicken; *sai krok* or Thai sausages which can be round instead of sausage shaped; *hoy tawd* or mussels fried in a pancake batter; *roti* or Indian pastry which is expertly prepared in front of you and served with a choice of fruits or sweet sauces. You may also notice the pungent aroma of *pla muk ping* or grilled dry squid, which is eaten with a chilli sauce and has

Fresh fruit is in abundance througout the year.

PHUKET & REGION

an interesting flavor to say the least. Famous Phuket/Hokkien dishes are; *hokkien mee*, a yellow noodle soup served with shrimps. In the travelers outposts of Krabi and Phi Phi there are always lots of stands selling sandwiches, burgers, hot dogs and other western fare.

For dessert there is *pon la mai* or fresh fruit inside a pushcart: just point at what you want and it will be served with a spicy sugar dip.

Restaurants

You will find literally hundreds of different types of restaurant on Phuket. Opening a restaurant seems to be what anyone deciding to stay on the island does. Italian, French, British, Spanish, German, Austrian, Swiss, Israeli, Swedish, Mexican, Korean, Indian, Chinese, Japanese and more are all represented, as well as Thai, of course.

The Thai restaurants on Phuket either aim at the tourist market or at the local market and there is a great deal of variation between the two. The local restaurants are often small unfussy affairs and may or may not have menus in English. During the day Thai people normally eat one plate meals such as *khao pat* or fried rice; *khao man gai* – sliced Hainan-style chicken served on rice cooked in broth; *khao moo daeng* – marinated pork on rice with a sweet red sauce; *khao naa ped* – duck on rice. Or noodle dishes such as; *pad si yiw* – noodles fried with soy sauce; *pad thai* – Thai fried noodles with ground peanuts and dried shrimp; *raad na* – large flat noodles in a thick gravy; *ba-mee haeng* – wheat noodles with vegetables and meat. For high quality Thai restaurants serving authentic Thai cuisine you will need to go to Phuket town.

In the tourist areas you will find that most Thai menus are fairly similar. Here are a few dishes we recommend that you try; *gaeng mussaman* – muslim curry, usually with beef cooked until it is very tender, peanuts and potatoes; *pad kraprao gai* – chicken fried with holy basil, often very spicy. *Gai pad met mamuang* – chicken fried with cashew nuts; *tawd man pla* – fried fish cakes; *yam nuea* – grilled beef salad (careful: Thai salads are usually very hot and spicy); *gaeng kari* – Indian-influenced curry; *gaeng panaeng nuea* – pan fried beef in a thick curry sauce; *tom kha gai* – coconut soup with chicken, lemon grass and galangal. Vegetarians should ask for *ahaan jay* of which there is usually plenty; *pad pak ruam met* – fried mixed vegetables; *pak pad nam man hoi* – vegetables fried in oyster sauce; *pak bung fai daeng* – morning glory fried with garlic and bean sauce

Eating seafood is one of the best things about visiting the coast,

Tourism facts...

Beach side restaurant - the temptation is everywhere.

PHUKET & REGION

it is always fresh and there is a huge amount of choice. Most restaurants display their selection outside in large trays packed with ice. You simply pick the fish (*plaa*) or crustacean you want and tell them how you want it cooked. This will either be *pao* - barbecued and served with a selection of sauces; *tawd kratiem prik thai* – deep fried with garlic and pepper; *tawd raad prik* – deep fried and covered with hot and sweet chilli sauce; *neung manao* – steamed with lemon and aromatic herbs; *sam rod* – three flavors (sweet, sour and of course spicy). Prawns (*gung*) come in various sizes and variety from giant king prawns to river prawns and can also be served in different dishes, some popular ones are; *tom yam gung* – hot and spicy soup with lots of lemon grass and other herbs; *gung ob gruea* – pot roasted with salt; *gung chup bang tawd* – deep fried in batter; *gung nueng kratiem* – steamed with garlic. Crab (*boo*) is also a favorite and can be served steamed, barbecued or as a curry – *boo bong kari*. Lobster (*gung mangkawn*) is usually the most expensive dish on the menu and can also be steamed (*nueng*) or barbecued (*pao*) or in many of the larger restaurants served with thermidor or hollandaise sauce. You will also find baby clams (*hawy lai*), green mussels (*hawy malaeng phuu*), scallops (*hawy phat*) and oysters (*hawy nang rom*). Seafood restaurants vary in price and quality, and a good rule is to look for busy places as you can usually be sure that they have the freshest offerings.

If you venture away from the tourist centers you will find prices go down and there are some excellent authentic seafood restaurants, the only problem you may find is the language barrier.

When Thai people order food they are very specific and often menus are purposely vague to allow the individual room to describe exactly how the dish should be cooked.

In the more local places you may well just have to leave the details to the chef and maybe even discover a delicious new eating experience.

Dr No island from 007 "The man with a Golden gun".

Phuket Basics

INTRODUCTION

Phuket is unashamedly a package tour destination. Two-and-a-half million tourists visit each year and although the majority of them come to soak up the sun, there are a large number of people who need and expect more from their holiday than just a beach. Phuket has a number of natural attractions to lure you out of your sunbeds, most of which have been well marketed by local entrepreneurs and are easily accessed by the masses. There are also a considerable amount of man made attractions ranging from world-class golf courses to bungy jumping and shows and museums and on and on. Very few people can complain that there is not enough to do on Phuket. Some of the sights listed below are very easy to find and visit on your own, however for some we recommend you take a guide or book a package.

Natural Attractions

Cape Phromthep
Phuket's most visited viewpoint commands a stunning view across Kata, Karon and Patong Bays. It is at the far south of the island and a beautiful place to watch the sun disintegrate into the Andaman Sea at the end of the day. Don't let the busloads of Taiwanese tourists put you off. It's worth a visit if you have a car or motorcycle for the day.

Laem Sing Beach
A beautiful hidden cove between Kamala Bay and Surin Beach. The beach is not visible from the road, but a small carpark marks the entrance, which is the start of a rocky path down to the beach. There is a small restaurant with sunbeds for rent. A perfect beach to spend the day on, but during high season it regularly gets visited by speedboats and coach tours, however they don't stay long. Come early in the morning or late at night to get a feel of what Phuket was like before tourism.

Nai Yang National park
At the far north of the island well away from jetskis and intrusive beach vendors lie Nai Yang and Mai Khao beaches. A 15 kilometer stretch of sand and mangroves that was declared a national park in 1981 and is now administered under the umbrella of Sirinut national park. Nai Yang (translates as "in rubber") is best known as the breeding ground for Olive Ridley turtles and the much rarer giant leatherback. There is a visitor's center on Nai Yang Beach with accommodation and information on the flora and fauna of the area.

Sirinath National Park
Running along the coast up from, and including, Nai Yang Beach is a 12-kilometer mangrove forest. This fascinating and incredibly diverse ecosystem is usually impenetretable, however the innovative park authorities have devised an ingenious way for visitors to get deep into the mangroves.

They have constructed an 800 meter elevated walkway through one square kilometer of mangrove bayou. Taking a walk along the wooden path you have a chance to see a wide range of birds, monitor lizards, tree climbing snakes and longtail macaque monkeys, as well as enjoying the forest. And the best thing is…it's free.

You can take a **songtaew** from Phuket town to Ban Chatchai, which is a ten-minute walk from the park. Or take a bus across the causeway to Phang Nga, jump out on the other side of the bridge and walk back across the old Sarasin Bridge into the park.

PHUKET ISLAND

Khao Phra Taew Forest Reserve

Just a few centuries ago all of Phuket was covered in lush tropical rainforest, which was home to tigers, leopards, elephants and rhinocerus. The 2,333 hectares that make up Khao Phra Taew is all that is left of that wilderness. Protected since 1977 and designated a non-hunting area, this tropical monsoon forest rises to 424 meters above sea level. It is a stunning contrast to the noisy beaches and commercialism of the south west of the island and really worth making the effort to visit. Although there are no elephants or tigers left, there are gibbons, langurs, monitor lizards, monkeys, flying foxes and colorful hornbills, all of which can be seen on treks.

Operators on Phuket organize treks or you can go on your own. The walks to Ton Sai or Bang Pae waterfalls are both marked from the visitor's center and for longer treks you can go with a park guide, payment is by voluntary donation. Siam Safari and Adventure Safari both organize hikes and tours that will typically include a visit to the gibbon rehabilitation center, a 3-4 hour trek and a visit to a local rubber plantation.

To get to the park take a *songtaew* to Thalang and then either walk or take a taxi the 3 kilometers to the visitor's center.

Phuket Nature Tour ☎ 255 522.
Siam Safari ☎ 280 116
Adventure Safari ☎ 341 978

Gibbon Rehabilitation Center

Located near Bang Pae Falls in Khao Phra Taew. This charitable center adopts and rescues gibbons that have been kept in captivity and re-introduces them back into the wild. White handed gibbons used to be common inhabitants of the island's forest, however due to their cuteness and peaceful nature they have been poached to near extinction and are more easily seen in the bars of Patong than in the wild. It is open to the public (10.00 to 16.00) and is financed by donations. This is the place to get photographs of gibbons (Not on the streets of Patong). ☎ 260492.

Kathu Waterfall

These large multi tiered waterfalls just outside Kathu are a great place for a swim. There is a sala for changing in and it is a 100 meter climb up the bank next to the falls to some quiet pools that are perfect for a dip. Best visited in the monsoon and avoided at weekends.

Koh Lone

This large island in Chalong bay is worth a visit. It is very quiet with a couple of small fishing villages and no development. Passenger boats make the 20-minute journey regularly from the pier at Ao Chalong.

Pearl Farms

There are a number of pearl

Rafting in shallow waters in Phang Nga province.

PHUKET ISLAND

farms off the east coast of Phuket producing cultured pearls. Naga Island Pearl and Pegasus Pearl Co. farm invites visitors for daily tours to the island where you are shown around the facilities where they demonstrate the nurturing and finishing process. An interesting day trip that costs **B**1,100 including transfers from your hotel and lunch. Contact any travel agent to book.

Rubber Plantations
There are still numerous rubber plantations on the island. It is interesting to get up early and watch the rubber tappers at work. They work between 02.00 and dawn and will happily tolerate curious bystanders. There are plantations on Highway 4028 between Ao Chalong and Kata Beach and on Highway 4031 in Thalang District.

Sea Gypsy Village
The most commonly visited sea gypsy village is on Koh Sirey an island very close to Phuket town. Although there is some pretty scenery the sea gypsy village is very poor and dirty and overwhelmed by tour buses and visitors who turn this sad spectacle into a human zoo.

Temples & shrines

Chinese temples
There are a number of lavishly decorated Chinese temples in Phuket town and Kathu. Strikingly different from the Buddhist temples, they are worth taking a look at. If you are visiting during the vegetarian festival at the end of October (see page?) then they should not be missed. The most impressive temples are at Kathu and Put Jaw in Phuket town.

Wat Chalong
The island's most important Buddhist temple is located on Highway 4021 between Ao Chalong and Phuket town. It is a large and ornate temple, but has become famous throughout Thailand for its spiritual power rather than architectural merit. It is associated with three revered monks, all great healers, so people come to regain their physical and spiritual powers and buy amulets to protect them from misfortune.

Wat Phra Thong
Another temple worth visiting, located on Highway 402 between Thalang and the airport. The temple was built around a large gold Buddha image that is half buried in the ground.

Man-made Attractions

Thai Village
Two shows a day (11.00 and 17.30) give an insight into tradi-

Natural attractions...

Phuket Chineses's community is very visible during festivals.

PHUKET ISLAND

tional Thai culture. You get to see shadow puppets, Thai boxing, fishing and tin mining - all from the south, plus dancing and wedding celebrations typical of the north. Afterwards there is an elephant show and display of Thai crafts. There is also a beautiful orchid garden. It is unashamedly touristy, but also quite interesting and if you are flying in and out of Phuket without seeing anything else of Thailand then it is well worth visiting. Entrance is **B**230 and tickets including transport can be bought from any travel agent. Located on highway 402. ☎ 214 860, 214 861.

Phuket Shell Museum
A huge building dedicated to seashells - selling them as well as exhibiting. There is some quite interesting stuff on display and more than a few pretty souvenirs for sale, but as an excursion? One for rainy days only. Located on highway 4024. Open 08.00 - 19.00. ☎ 381 266.

Phuket Marine Biological Center
A good place for anyone interested in marine biology and underwater life. The displays are becoming a little run down and there is not enough information, but at **B**20 entrance you can't complain. Open 08.30 to 16.00 and located at the end of Highway 4129 at Cape Panwa.

Phuket Butterfly Garden and Aquarium
North of Phuket town is another aquarium and butterfly garden. The displays here are much more impressive and there is a lot of information in English. A pleasant hour or so of light entertainment for a family. Entrance is **B**150. ☎ 215 616.

Thalang National Museum
Located beside the heroines monument. Provides an interesting introduction to Phuket's history and culture. There is extensive coverage of sea gypsy traditions and a 10-foot tall statue of Vishnu dating back to the 9th century. It is far more practical and informative than anywhere on the island, but not particularly well presented. What is a must visit for culture vultures may be a bit dull for others. Entrance: **B**30.

THINGS TO SEE AND DO

BUNGY JUMPING
Just outside Patong off the road running to Phuket town. This operation consists of huge crane supporting a platform high above a lake for bungy jumpers. The owners boast a 100% safety record and although the operation appears a bit lackadaisical they have an excellent reputation. First jump costs **B**1,400.
Bungy Jump ☎ (076) 321 351.

GO KART
There is a 600 meter figure of eight track on Hy 4029, 2-kilometers from Patong. They have 100cc and 230cc karts and charge **B**800 for 30 minutes.

ELEPHANT TREKKING
There are a number of Elephant camps dotted around the island, mostly on the outskirts of the major beach resorts. They offer short elephant treks into the island's interior, usually to a viewpoint. Rides cost **B**400 to **B**500 and ensure that you don't leave Thailand without the obligatory "I rode an elephant" photo. A good experience and you will be helping to keep elephants legally and gainfully employed, as tourism is one of the few ways elephants can now earn their living.

Kalim Elephant Trekking
North of Patong. ☎ 290 056.
Siam Safari
Ao Chalong ☎ 280 116.
Nai Harn safari
At Nai Harn Bay
Kata Safari
South of Kata Bay
Karon Lagoon Elephant trekking
North of Karon

PHUKET ISLAND

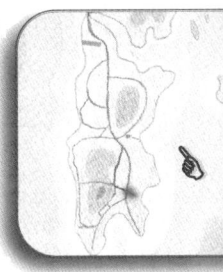

PHUKET FANTASEA

A wildly ambitious $20 million cultural theme park near Kamala Bay which compares itself to a Las Vegas extravaganza showcasing Thai culture. As a spectacle it is certainly amazing with 30 or so elephants, mock battles, pyrotechnics and aerial ballet in an auditorium that seats 2,000 just part of the entertainment. It is certainly not for serious students of Thai culture, but is a beautifully choreographed and delightful piece of theatre. The park opens at 17.30 and a cultural shopping village and fairground set in a mock Ayuthaya or Angkorian city greets the visitors. Everything is on a grand scale and works very professionally, and although it is designed to help you spend your money as quickly as possible one cannot help being impressed by its

THE ELEPHANT HELP PROJECT

A conservation project initiated by Siam Safari Nature Tours and The Dusit Island hotel to get tourism to help elephants in Phuket. The project objectives are to raise funds from tourism and use the money to run elephant welfare and conservation schemes in Phuket and southern Thailand. At present there are very few traditional sources of funds left to help elephants in Thailand and so "Elephant Help" runs fund raising activities and events, sells stickers and T-shirts, collects donations and runs an elephant adoption scheme to help the creatures. A long-term objective is to help establish a sanctuary in Phang Nga province.

Some of the main problems elephants used in tourism suffer from are due to a lack of facilities and research. There are no emergency treatment facilities for elephants and a lack of specialist vetinary equipment. There is also a lack of land space for elephants, especially when they become old and sick and can no longer work. One of the project's aims is to control the amount of elephants brought to work on the island. One hundred years ago wild elephants would have roamed Phuket Island. In 1994 there were only 15 elephants there and these were used at tourist attractions. At the end of 1994 Siam Safari started the first elephant treks on the island and from their success came the elephant trekking operations. At the end of 1998 there were an estimated 150 elephants on the island.

Elephant trekking has now spread to Phang-Nga, Krabi and Surat Thani provinces and has provided a lifeline for the creatures. There is not enough forest left to return them to the wild and taking tourists for rides is far healthier than begging on the streets of Bangkok and other major cities, something that has become a worrying trend since Thailand's economic troubles started. It is estimated that about 35% of Thailand's captive elephants are in full or part time use in the tourism industry. This number is growing rapidly as there are few other alternatives left for captive elephants. It is important to establish better welfare and conservation programs to help protect elephants in Thailand so they can survive into the next century. Elephants are the very symbol of Thailand. Thailand without them would not be Thailand.

This project is also supported by the Tourism Authority of Thailand, Thai Airways International, Phuket Tourist Association, Phuket Provincial Livestock Office, Phuket Provincial Forest Office and Thai Hotel Association - Southern Chapter.

Elephant Foundation of Thailand ☎ **(02) 278 0924 or (076) 280 107,** email: eceath@samart.co.th

PHUKET ISLAND

buffet hall holds 4,000 people and the food is OK but not really worth **B**500. It is probably best to skip the early section and arrive in time for the show, which starts at 21.00 and lasts an hour and 20 minutes. The show costs **B**1,000, show and buffet is **B**1,500 and transfers can be arranged each way - tickets are available from any travel agent ☎ 271 222,
email: *info@phuketfantasea.com*

PAINTBALL ASIA 'TOP GUN'
Organised war games for all the family, as well as a shooting range. A well run facility with decent equipment and showers and lockers. Located near Ao Chalong, it costs **B**500 for 40 shots. ☎ 280 130.

PHUKET LAGUNA RIDING CLUB
A horse-riding club set inside the Laguna complex, but open to non-guests. They have some great trails along scenic beaches and around the lagoons.
☎ 324 099.

PHUKET RIDING CLUB
Horse riding enthusiasts can enjoy a ride along the beach or through the forest on well-kept Australian horses. There are guided and non-guided tours and a dressage-riding ring for beginners or children. An hour's ride costs **B**500, open 07.00 to 18.30. Located on Viset Rd. close to Ao Chalong. ☎ 288 213.

PHUKET WATERSKI CABLEWAYS
There is a cable ski operation near Kathu Waterfall, but the water is murky and uninviting. Fortunately the machine runs so slowly it is difficult to fall off.
☎ 321 767. **B**500 per hour

PHUKET ZOO
A large zoo with 100 kinds of birds and elephants, tigers, giraffe, crocodiles as well as numerous other animals. The animals are quite well looked after, even though some of them live in cramped conditions. The main attraction is the shows where you can see elephants at work, crocodile wrestling and monkeys picking coconuts. There are also tame (or drugged) tigers to pose next to for photographs. Located on Soi Parlai off Highway 4021 between Ao Chalong and Phuket town. Entrance is **B**400.
☎ 381 227.

TOUR OPERATORS
Adventure Safari
70/85 Rat-U-Thit Rd, Patong
☎ 341 988.
Island Safari
Moo 6, ☎ Chalong Bay, Phuket. ☎ 281 281.

The world famous King's Cup Regatta in full sail.

PHUKET ISLAND

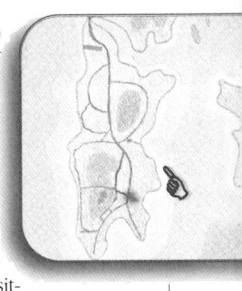

Phuket Nature Tours
62/23 Chao Fa Rd. Phuket
☎ 255 522, 📠 381 655.

Phuket Trekking Club
94/23 Soi Patong resort, Bangla Road, Phuket ☎ 341 453.

Siam Safari
70/1 Moo 10 Chao Fa Rd, Chalong ☎ 280 116, 📠 288 107, email: info@siamsafari, www.siamsafari.com

PHAN NGA BAY TOURS

Phang Nga Bay is one of the most beautiful places in the world. A sheltered bay of blue and green calm, clear water dotted with amazing, misshapen limestone karsts (see page? for more details) extending northwest from Phuket to the mainland. There are a variety of ways tourists can explore the bay, its islands and the mysterious *hongs* (*bong* is the Thai word for room or caves). The Thai government has declared the area a National Park and seemingly restricts the number of visitors and their impact on the environment, however Thai private enterprise is notoriously difficult to control and in high season there are literally thousands of tourists, in a variety of watercraft, in the bay.

CANOE AND KAYAK TOURS

Sea canoeing has burst onto the Thai tourist scene in the last ten years, promoting a clean, eco friendly alternative to boat trips to Phang Nga bay. Pioneered by the innovative Sea Canoe Company, which brought foreign experience and marketing skills, as well as an inexhaustible energy and desire to explore the fantastic sea *hongs*, it has become a phenomenally popular way to view the bay. Paddling into the *hongs* is truly an incredible experience. Often there is just a tiny entrance visible from the outside that opens into a huge "otherworld". Tidal lagoons open to the sky, filled with jungle flora, birds and monkeys.

Sea Canoe's success has spawned a dozen or so copycat operators offering kayak tours to the bay. The most popular trip is the one-day paddle and due to the huge demand to go on these trips there are often hundreds of boats visiting the best caves. Typically tours pick up guests at their hotels and drive to Ao Po, where boats piled with canoes and tourists head out into the bay. Cave visits are dependent on the tides and are done with a guide, the rest of the time guests paddle themselves behind a guide. There have been a number of complaints from tourists that some the guides have been damaging the caves and frightening the wildlife. Another point is that groups of 20 to 30 paddlers have no chance of seeing anything. So stick to a tour company that guarantees a maximum of 12 persons. Better still, join an overnight trip or multi day paddle. Sea Canoe runs a range of tours and kayaking workshops (see seacanoe.com for more details) from overnighters to 6-day expeditions (but they don't come cheap at costs up to $990). Some other day-tour operators are beginning to see the future in raising standards, but most prefer high volume (and profit) tours. It is worth making the effort to find a reputable operator like Sea Canoe or German run Santana Diving and Canoeing. South East Asia Liveaboards also runs kayaking adventures to the Similan islands and even Burma.

Sea Canoe
367/4 Yaowarat Rd. Phuket.
☎ 212 172, 📠 212 252,
email: info@seacanoe.com
Tours must be booked directly with Sea Canoe. 1 day tour costs **B**2,970.

Santana Diving and Canoeing
6, Sawatderak Rd. Patong Beach.
☎ 294 220, 📠 340 360, email: discovery@santanaphuket.com
1 day tour costs $70 (approx **B**2,800).

Ocean activities...

PHUKET ISLAND

THE KINGS CUP REGATTA

Organised by the Phuket Yacht Club, the Kings Cup Regatta is held annually over the King of Thailand's birthday weekend on December 5. This year will be the 12th and the event attracts yachts from all over the world. Competition is spread across a number of classes to ensure that all types of boats have an interest in the race. 1999 saw the competition spread beyond its traditional homeland of Nai Harn and Kata to Krabi and Phi Phi and over 100 yachts attended the five-day spectacle.

For information on Kings Cup 2000 check out www.kingscup.com

STANDARD BOAT TOURS

There are a variety of tours available from all the travel agents and counters. The two main choices are a bus and boat tour, or a boat tour. Bus and boat tours will pick you up at your hotel around 08.00 and drive to Phang Nga, stopping at some tourist attractions along the way. Then a two-hour longtail ride will visit Koh Ping Kan (James Bond island), Koh Pan Yi (the Muslim fishing Village) and Tham Lod (the natural tunnel). Then back by minibus stopping at one or two points along the way. Some take you through the mangroves and elephant trekking before going out into the bay, others stop at Lumpee Waterfall at Tai Muang National Park or take in a rubber plantation. The boat tours are marginally less frantic as a large boat carries around 100 hundred passengers into the bay, and then you transfer to smaller boats to visit the islands. All these tours are designed to get as many people through Phang Nga bay as efficiently as possible and they tend to treat tourists like cattle on a never-ending conveyer belt (which is what it must seem like to them). However you do get to see the famous islands, even if it is in the middle of the day when its too bright for decent photography, and if you are tight on time and money and this is the only way you can do it, then do it. James Bond Island and Phang Nga tours can be purchased from any travel agent. The cheapest minibus tours start at **B**600 and spiral up to **B**1,200 depending on what is included. Sim's half-day sunset tours, which is a straight drive to Phang Nga plus a short boat trip, is also popular with late risers in Patong. Boat tours cost **B**1,200 to **B**1,200 and are a far better bet if you just want to visit the bay.

The Travel Company ☎ 340 232

CRUISES

A much more enjoyable way to visit the bay is aboard a traditional Siamese junk. East-West Siam Co. operates two beautifully reconstructed sailing vessels that cruise Phang Nga Bay every day. They also take you round the islands by Longtail boat and you will probably rub shoulders with the rest of the crowd, but you get there and back in far better style and with a much higher level of service. East-West Siam ☎ 340 912, 📠 341 188.

After 3 days of fishing!

PHUKET ISLAND

Ocean activities...

CORAL ISLAND TOURS

There are a number of packaged day trips to islands just off Phuket. Koh Hae, or coral island, is the most popular. Here the two pretty sandy beaches have been blessed with a shallow coral reef ideal for snorkeling. However due to its close proximity to Phuket the island is swamped with tour groups every day and becomes a teaming mass of squabbling families. Not really recommended. To get there rent a long tail from Rawai beach (**B**500 return) - more if you want to spend longer. There are restaurants on the island and plenty of vendors so you don't have to worry about food and drink. Tours can be booked from any travel agent and cost **B**500 to **B**1,000 per person including a speedboat transfer, but are far from relaxing.

GAME FISHING

Phuket is ideally situated for big game fishermen. It is close to the migratory paths of a range of fish, including that classic fighting fish the black marlin. Other species that abound in the deep blue waters of the Andaman Sea are wahoo, mahi mahi (dorado), tuna, sailfish, king mackerel and sharks. There are also numerous species of light-tackle gamefish such as sea bass, barracuda, giant trevally and mangrove jack. At certain times of the year sailfish fishing here is as good as anywhere and Phuket is known as one of the world's top three queenfish sites.

The most popular fishing grounds are around the Racha Islands, just a couple of hours boat ride south of Phuket. This is where nearly all the trophy fish are caught and game fishing boats usually head to the waters around Racha Noi and Racha Yai, while longer charters often go as far as the Similans. Game fishing is popular all year round, but the best months for sailfish are August and September, when the seas can get rough, while the calm of November is usually the best month for marlin tuna and a whole host of fighting fish.

The Phuket International Sportfishing Classic is held in November and draws teams from all over the world. A number of operators now offer serious game fishing tours from Phuket. They all now practice catch-and-release, which is the international standard of catching, recording and releasing alive all billfish and sharks, in an attempt to sustain the populations of these magnificent fish. They also refrain from fishing in marine wildlife sanctuaries such as Shark Point.

There are also charter companies offering multi day tours on fully

41

PHUKET ISLAND

Built in what were tin mines, and connected to the sea with a kilometer-long channel, the boat lagoon is a well protected place.

equipped and purpose built game fishing boats as well as day trips. Groups can charter boats or individuals can join a day trip. Game fishing is not a cheap sport and a boat such as "The Andaman Hooker" or "Wahoo" will cost around **B**15,000 a day including equipment and lunch.

It is cheaper to rent a boat for light-tackle inshore fishing; **B**6,500 for 6-8 people for five to six hours of fishing.

Renting a Longtail boat and trailing hand lines is also a fun way to spend the day and there are dozens of boats off Ao Chalong, or Rawai beaches that will take you out for **B**500 an hour.

FISHING CHARTERS
Aloha tours
44/1 Viset Rd. Ao Chalong
☎ 381 215, ☎ 381 592.
Andaman Fishing
69 Phuket Rd, Phuket town
☎ 211 752.
Blue Water Anglers
35/7 Sakididet Rd, Phuket town
☎ 391 287.
Phuket Sport fishing Centre
Thaweewong Rd, Patong
☎ 214 713, email:
wahoo@phuket.loxinfo.co.th
Short time Fishing charters
59/2 Moo 9, Ao Chalong
☎ 280 654.
Thai Marine Leisure
Phuket boat lagoon ☎ 239 111.

SAILING AND BOATING
The Andaman Sea is a sailor's dream. Calm clear waters, deep blue skies, warm water temperatures, fair winds and the wonders of Phang Nga Bay to provide the scenery. Naturally Phuket is the base for yacht companies and Phuket Boat Lagoon provides a fully equipped harbour and boat yard comparable with any in Europe or America. Visiting yachts either take advantage of the facilities at the boat lagoon or head for the public moorings in Ao Chalong, the preferred haven and hunting ground for "yachties" the band of nomadic boat owners who sail across the world's oceans, sometimes picking up crews, hitchhikers or taking charters. This is the place to head to if you are looking for a passage to Malaysia, Singapore or beyond.

If sailing across the Andaman Sea is your idea of a perfect holiday you will need to contact one of the charter companies listed below. There are three types of cruise available: bareboat charters, crewed

PHUKET ISLAND

charters and joined crews. Bareboating means that you hire the bare boat and then you fuel, provision and crew it yourself. The charter company supplies the boat, back up and sailing information. On crewed charters they also supply a qualified skipper and a cook if required. Sunsail is the specialist at providing such charters and has a wide range of different boats from Oceanis 320s and up. Prices run from U$2,000 to U$5,000 a week. They also offer royal association accredited five-day sailing courses for B16,000. Joining cruises are an excellent way to enjoy a sailing experience. Thai Marine Leisure can offer cruises on boats ranging from Catamarans to junk rigged schooners at prices from U$461 for a 4-day cruise to $1,100 for a 7-day cruise. Join cruises are on fixed itineraries usually taking in Phang Nga, Krabi and Phi Phi.

A number of smaller companies offer cruises and one interesting alternative is to join Southeast Asia Liveaboard sailing cruises to Burma, as they run a mix of sailing, diving and canoeing on their trips.

CHARTER COMPANIES

Asian-Adventures
237 Rat-U-Thit Rd, Patong
t 341 927, f 341 798,
email: asian-adventures.com

Asia Yachting
59/2 Moo 9, Chaofa Rd, Ao Chalong t 381 615

Chinese Junk Cruises
East-West Siam at Paradis complex, Rat-u-Thit Rd, Patong
t 340 912,
email: philippe@samart.co.th

Marmas
The Boat Lagoon, 22/1 Thepkrasttri Rd, Phuket.
t 239 055

Sunsail Yacht charter
Phuket Boat Lagoon.
t 239 057, f 238 940, email: sunthai@phket.loxinfo.co.th

Siam Dive n' Sail
121/9 Patak Rd. Karon.
t 330 967, f 330 990,
email john@siamdivers.com

South East Asia Liveaboards
225 Rat-U-Thit Rd, Patong.
t 340 406,
f 340 586,
email:
info@sealive-aboards.com

Thai Marine Leisure
Phuket Boat lagoon. t 239 111,
f 238 974,
email: tml@loxinfo.co.th

The Yacht Haven
57/5 Moo 2, Mai Khao, Amphoe Talang. t 206 705, e-mail: marina@yacht-haven-phuket.com

GOLF COURSES

Phuket is home to some of the best golf courses in Asia, created by world famous course designers and set amongst beautiful scenery. Although by Thai standards they are relatively expensive, internationally speaking they are good value when one considers the high standard of the courses and level of service. Golf in Thailand is a very civilized sport and all the courses have plenty of refreshment stops and cheerful caddies to carry your bags and keep score for you. But remember Phuket has a hot tropical climate so it is advisable to schedule games for the early morning, or late afternoon.

Blue Canyon Country Club
Green fees B4,000
This world-class golf course has hosted the prestigious Johnnie Walker Classic twice and was rated by Tiger Woods as one of the best he has ever played on and by Ernie Els as "the best". An additional nine holes has been added to the original 18, providing a test for the golfer that lies somewhere between difficult and impossible, but with the blue limestone mountains and lakes providing a striking setting it is quite an experience to play. A comfortable 48 room hotel overlooks the golf course with room rates running between B4,000

Sailing, golfing...

PHUKET ISLAND

and **B**7,000. The course is located off Highway 422 just south of the airport and is the most expensive place to play in Thailand. You need to be either a member or a guest to get on.
☎ 327 440, ☎ 327 449,
email: blucares@samart.co.th

Banyan Tree Phuket Golf Club
Green fees **B**1,800 for Laguna Guests, **B**2,250 for visitors

This course is attached to the Laguna development at Bang Tao Beach and is good value for guests of the hotels there. The course is fairly flat and not as interesting as some, but provides a reasonable test and is well looked after. ☎ 324 350,
☎ 324 351,
email: info@lagunaphuket.com

Loch Palm Golf Club
Green fees **B**2,400

A pretty course in the center of Phuket with some challenging holes, featuring plenty of palm trees surrounding a huge lake. Located on highway 4020 near Kathu. ☎ 321 930.

Phuket Country Club Old Course
Green fees -**B**2,140

This was the first championship standard golf course on the island and as such remains a firm favorite with residents and regular visitors. Set amongst hills and lakes, it is a mature course so there are more trees and some unusual holes, which make for an exciting round. Located on highway 4029 between Patong and Phuket town. ☎ 321 038-41,
email:
info@phuketcountryclub.com

Phuket Country Club New Course
Green fees **B**900 (18-holes) **B**500 (9-holes)

This is a new 9 hole course and is exceptionally good value. It is quite tight with lots of water and out-of-bounds and is a good test for any golfer.
☎ 321 365-71,
email:
info@phuketcountryclub.com

Diving in PHUKET

SCUBA DIVING

Phuket is an international standard, world-class dive destination. Some of Asia's – and indeed the world's - top dive sites are within reach and many people come here just to visit the reefs.

There are dive sites in the Andaman Sea, all along Thailand's 750 km coast, which stretches from Malaysia to the Mergui Achipelago in Burmese waters. This is a vast area, much of which is still being explored and there are already over 80 recognized dive sites providing truly world class diving.

It is also a great place to learn how to dive; there are dozens of dive schools offering all the Professional Association of Diving Instructors (PADI) approved courses. PADI is an American based association that has become the industry's most widely known and accepted governing body. All PADI instructors have completed an Instructor development Course (IDC) with a certified IDC training center and all PADI dive centers comply with PADI requirements.

Many schools have reached 5-star status, which generally means they have successfully trained a large number of divers without any complaints over a number of years – a good gauge that the school has been around for a while and that their instructors are consistently competent.

Prices for dive courses tend to be informally fixed by the operators in each area. In Phuket, because there are so many operators, it can vary between ฿8,000 and ฿12,000 for an open water course. In Krabi, Phi Phi and Koh Lanta it costs around ฿10,000 and in Khao Lak it is as low as ฿7,800.

Phuket has the biggest choice of dive operators with some very experienced, high quality operations. The other areas also have some good operators, but you will find that standards are higher on Phuket.

Learning to Dive

The PADI open water diver course is a combination of theory, pool training and four open water dives. It takes four days, which consist of a day in a classroom, a day in the pool and four open water dives. Upon successful completion of the course you will receive the PADI open water diver certificate which is recognized practically anywhere in the world. It covers the basics and takes you to 18 meters below the surface, but does not turn you into an experienced diver and you will find that the best sites are deeper than this. If you intend to do a lot of diving or visit deep sites, it is a better idea to complete the PADI advanced diver course. This takes you close to 40 meters below the surface (the maximum depth recommended for recreational divers) and provides thorough training, including teaching useful skills such as underwater navigation and night diving. A course will last 3-days and include 5 dives. If you really want to get serious about diving then there are a whole load of specialist courses to choose from before becoming a divemaster, which is the first step towards becoming a diving professional. The PADI divemaster course is a comprehensive training program designed to shape and develop the skills and attitudes required to become a divemaster and instructor. To qualify for divemaster training you need to have 20 logged dives, be qualified as a PADI advanced and PADI rescue diver or equivalent and hold a PADI MFA certification or equivalent (not older than 2 years). A divemaster course can be completed in 10 days, however a longer apprenticeship, including spending some time working with a dive shop is recom-

DIVING

mended for anyone interested in becoming an instructor.

Many schools in Phuket are also instructor development centers (IDCs) and offer the instructor Exam (IE). Because it is so easy - relative to other professions - and reasonably cheap to become a diving instructor, Phuket has become a production line churning out hundreds of new instructors every year. Many of them will get jobs on the islands teaching, which means you may find that your instructor has little if any experience elsewhere – something to bear in mind if you plan to go on and dive in places with different conditions.

Conditions & seasons

The West Coast of Thailand - including the Similans, Surin, Hin Daeng, Burma Banks and Mergui - should normally be dived from October until May with the first part better for clear waters (i.e. visibility) and the second half better for spotting large Pelagic. From June through September the monsoon blows in from the Indian subcontinent in the west and many boats will not go out. Diving from Phuket is possible through the wet season and most dive companies stay open through the whole year. During this time they will dive in sheltered sites such as Koh Doc Mai. Some companies still go to the Similans and the diving can be good, but the rough seas can make it more of a tumultuous experience.

LIVEABOARDS

Many of the best dive sites in the Andaman Sea are out in the deep clear waters that lie beyond the continental shelf. The Similan islands, Hin Daeng and Hin Muang are all out of the range of even the fastest daytrip boats operating out of Phuket. To access these sites you need to take a liveaboard dive cruise. These large boats are a combination of hotel and dive platform – usually purpose built – and cruise comfortably to dive sites as far as the Andaman Islands (in Indian waters) and the Mergui Archipelago. There are now scores of liveaboards operating out of Phuket, Krabi and Phi Phi ranging from very basic converted fishing boats to luxury yachts to big spacious steel hulled cruisers. Liveaboard diving cruises are usually all inclusive and generally. involve four or five dives

DIVING

Andaman Islands sites...

a day, with breaks for meals. They are designed for serious divers and non-divers or snorkelers should carefully consider whether they want to be locked up with a bunch of mad-keen divers for days on end before booking. Prices range quite dramatically and are dependent on the level of comfort on board as well as the length of each cruise. Below is a list of reputable liveaboard operators that we have checked out and can recommend.

Asian Adventures
Very good value 4 day and longer cruises to Similans and Burma. ☎ 341 927, email: info@asian-adventures.com

Fantasea Divers
Very experienced and reputable operator; cruises to Hin Daeng, Similans and Burma. ☎ 340 088, email: info@fantasea.net

Andy Herrich Dive Expeditions
High service standards and well-organized cruises to Similans and Burma. ☎ 330 969, email: genesis@andy-herrich,com

South East Asia Liveaboard
First class operator with a range of boats and yachts cruising to Similans, Burma and The Andaman Islands. ☎ 344 022, email: info@sealiveaboards.com

Scuba Quest
Good value cruises to the Similans. email: kamala@phuket.ksc.co.th

Phra Nang Divers
Very good value and the main operators to Hin Daeng and Hin Muang. ☎ (075) 637 064.

Siam Dive 'n' Sail
Very experienced liveaboard organizers representing a wide range of boats. ☎ 330 967. email: info@siamdivers.com

Dive Sites

THE SIMILANS

The Similan Islands are a group of nine granite outcrops that lie in deep clear water 90 kilometers northwest of Phuket Island. With snow-white beaches and a tropical jungle above the water and spectacular dive sites in crystal clear water below, it's not surprising that the Similans are ranked as one of the top 10 dive sites in the world. They are easily accessible and are visited by a number of boats through the season, however the variety and quality of the diving makes sure very few divers are ever disappointed. There are 19 sites ranging from shallow bays and coral gardens located in the sheltered bays that form in the protected lees of the islands to the tunnels, caverns and swim-throughs that are formed by the sometimes strong currents on the unprotected western faces. The deepest sites go below 50 meters, whilst the average depth of most sites runs between 10 and 30 meters. Visibility is usually best during the first half of the season and can be as good as 30-40 meters (although 15m to 25m is more likely). Whilst the second half of the season is better known for large pelagic visitors. The higher temperatures cause plankton blooms, which can reduce visibility and attract whale sharks, manta rays, white tip and other sharks to the area in abundance.

SOME SIMILAN DIVE SITES
Breakfast Bend
Conditions: Expect calm conditions and visibility up to & above 25m. Maximum Depth: 34m
The site is so called as it is generally the first dive of the excursion, funnily enough after breakfast! The western section is relatively shallow, averaging 8m. Southeast of here are the beginnings of a reef of staghorns, which eventually achieve garden-like proportions. They are bigger but less frequent on the steep reef slope. There are lots of sargeant majors darting in and out making it an ideal site for snorkelers. The reef slope drops to 18m then steeply sloping sand-banks descend to 34m. Often octopus are present around this site.

Christmas Point
Conditions: Excellent visibility often exceeding 25m.
Average Depth: 20m.
Maximum Depth: 34m.

The west and northern quarters reach 30m and the south and east 18m. The south-western section features triangular boulders at 22m, these continue down to depths greater than 25m where you'll find leaning boulders, offering mazes of swim-throughs. The walls are highlighted by radiant soft corals with parrotfish, dog faced pufferfish and clown triggerfish in abundance. The overhangs and caves offer a home to schools of lion fish. Traveling northwards you'll see many more soft corals, leafy, brain, slipper and lip corals to name but a few, as well as groups of schooling pennant and Indian bannerfish alongside butterfly, wrasse and, if lucky, manta rays.

Elephant Head
Conditions: Visibility is good ranging from 15-25m plus. Currents can be strong flowing north-south with possibility of strong surges.
Maximum Depth: 70m+

The underwater terrain is breathtaking. The dive takes you around huge boulders sitting individually or stacked high to form daring swim-throughs comprising arches, caverns, gullies and tunnels at all depths. There is plenty of marine life and hard and soft corals. Southwards the boulders take on a different formation. Around these boulders are emperor and imperial angelfish, titan triggerfish and sheltering schools of yellowtail fusiliers and juvenile yellow snappers. The southern-most point of the site is a tiny group of submerged pinnacles in very deep water. A great place to observe small reef sharks.

Deep Six
Conditions: Visibility ranges between 15-25m. Currents can be strong.
Maximum Depth: 40m.

This is another deep dive following a ridge that features large sea fans in its deeper sections. Turtles and leopard sharks can be found on the sand. The diversity of fish life is average with bannerfish and angelfish making their presence felt.

Shark Fin Reef
Conditions: Visibility ranges from 5m (bad day) to 25m. Again currents can be strong.
Average Depth: 16m.
Maximum Depth: 40m.

The north-eastern side features a sloping reef, the south-eastern side a more dramatic sheer dropoff. Rocks resembling fallen hexagonal pillars are the highlight of this site. At the south-eastern end of these formations at about 16m is a large swim-through that provides an almost purpose built opening to the sites' other side. The marine life is much more intense and diverse, comprising schools of batfish, surgeonfish, Moorish idols and bannerfish alongside Napoleon Wrasse. This section is also a good place to spot passing sharks and large rays.

OTHER SIMILAN DIVE SITES

Chicken Hair Reef
One of the best sites in the Similans. Great visibility, caves, gullies, a wide range of fish and colorful coral.

Boulder City
Diverse corals, including sea fans on a collection of submerged boulders are the attraction here.

Barracuda Point
A deep dive going down 34 meters to see lots of batfish and colorful corals.

Stonehenge
Another deep dive – 40 meters – and sometimes strong currents. Worth it to see sea sponges, lobster and leopard sharks.

KOH SURIN, KOH BON AND RICHELIEU ROCK

North of the Similans and West of Ranong lie the five granite islands that form Mu Surin Marine Park. These provide some of the most outstanding sites anywhere in the world for sighting whale sharks, the harmless giants that feed on the rich plankton and are abundant in this area. Slightly outside the boundaries of the park are the other popular sites of Koh Bon and Richelieu Rock. These outcrops reach 40 meters and although strong currents can be encountered, they are fantastic places for whale shark and manta action. Other highlights in this area include the spectacular three-tiered reef at Koh Tachai. The Surin islands are a breathtaking journey for more experienced divers.

Richelieu Rock
Conditions: As the rock is in open seas there can be strong currents. Visibility ranges from 5m to 30m+.
Average Depth: 19m.
Maximum Depth: 45m

This is among the world's top listed locations for sighting whale sharks. One of Thailand's best sites, this is a wall dive around the main outcrop which is surrounded by smaller submerged pinnacles whose peaks range from 3m to 10m below the surface. The pinnacles have numerous shelves and ledges at all depths. The three southern pinnacles are at 22m and you'll find orange gorgonian sea fans immediately below radiant hermetypic corals. Around the corals is the usual abundance of marine life including snappers, shovelnose rays, scorpion fish, stone fish, moray eels, sea horses, shrimps and crabs. As this is the only food source in the area all the pelagics congregate there.

Koh Bon
Conditions: Visibility is good often reaching 30m.
Maximum Depth: 34m

This submerged pinnacle lies

DIVING

18m from the surface. The main attraction is the healthy number of whale sharks, other sharks and manta rays which for some reason are attracted to this otherwise plain site.

Koh Tachai

A series of three reefs around two submerged pinnacles with great swim throughs. Lots of marine life – a wonderful dive site.

Phuket Dive Sites

Shark Point (Hin Musang)

Conditions: Good and reliable visibility. Currents can be strong.
Maximum depth: 24 meters

Also known as Hin Musang, this is a protected area and is consistently ranked as one of Southeast Asia's top sites. It is home to a large number of leopard sharks as well as moray eels, lionfish and pelagics. You will always see a lot of marine life here.

Koh Doc Mai

Conditions: moderate currents with fair to good visibility.
Maximum depth: 27 meters.

Phuket's top Wall Dive where leopard sharks, schools of fish, hard and soft corals can be seen. Some caves to explore and as it is an island there is always shelter for beginners.

Anemone Reef

Conditions: Usually moderate currents, but be warned it can get rough on the surface. Visibility fair to excellent.
Maximum depth: 24 meters.

Lying less than a mile north of Sharkpoint, this dive site is a single large submerged rock. True to its name it is covered in a living carpet of sea anemones. Add to this scenery a constant parade of reef fish and you have a very colorful dive site. Anemone Reef is also noted for its lionfish - sometimes 12 or more in a group. Beginners should dive with a divemaster.

The King Cruiser Wreck

Conditions: Visibility is good, often reaching 20m.
Maximum Depth: 32m.

DIVING

This is an interesting wreck dive. The King Cruiser is a Japanese car ferry which collided with anemone reef in 1997 and sank in just over 30 meters of water, providing Phuket with a new, if unplanned, dive site. With an overall length of 85 meters the wreck offers some challenging diving for the experienced diver.

THE RACHA ISLANDS

Racha Yai
Conditions: Moderate to strong currents, visibility fair to excellent.
Maximum Depth: 24 meters.
A very popular local dive site due to its magnificent diving conditions and sheltered bays. Enjoy an exciting drift dive in the right tidal conditions over vast staghorn coral beds. A great dive for beginners or for rusty divers to get back into the swing of things.

Racha Noi
Conditions: The south tip can experience strong currents and is sometimes rough. Visibility is usually good and often excellent.
This is the most accessible place to see whale sharks, manta rays, leopard sharks and yellow tailed barracuda.
There are plenty of corals and sea fans.
The south tip is for experienced divers only, but the north side has great multilevel diving and is suitable for open water divers.

Phi Phi Dive Sites

There are a number of dive sites around the Phi Phi islands; most dive centers in Phuket will offer trips to some of these sites. There are more than a dozen sites around the islands, but the best ones are concentrated around the south of Phi Phi Leh and the Bida islands.

Hin Bida (Shark Point)
Conditions: Usually good with visibility up to 20 meters.
Maximum depth: 21 meters
A small rock, surrounded by an oval reef under the water. leopard sharks can nearly always be seen on the bottom as well as sea snakes, golden sweetlips, sea turtles, blue spotted stingrays, barracudas and whale sharks.

Bida Nok
Conditions: Good with visibility up to 20 meters.
Maximum depth: 30 meters
A wall dive with lots of coral and the chance of seeing whale sharks and mantas. At 20 meters there is a cave and an overhang. leopard sharks can usually be spotted on the bottom.

THINGS TO CONSIDER BEFORE DIVING

Apart from the obvious consideration of price you should bear a few things in mind:

→ How many people will be on the boat - some of the big companies will have up to 30 divers on board, so if you are going to a small site there will be a lot of bodies in the water.

→ What sort of boat will you be going on - if you are going the long way (say from Krabi to the King Cruiser, or Koh Lanta to Hin Daeng) you will not want to be on a small, slow boat.

→ Speed boat trips to Hin Daeng from Phi Phi or Lanta are great when the weather is good, but can be just as slow and a lot more uncomfortable if the water is rough.

→ How many people will be doing your open water course - small groups are much better for learning.

→ How much experience does your instructor have - especially if you are doing an advanced course and plan to go wreck diving in the English Channel, an instructor with experience beyond Thailand is preferable.

DIVING

Bida Nai
Conditions: Good with visibility up to 20 meters.
Maximum depth: 30 meters
Another impressive dive site with walls running down off the outcrop, caves and swim throughs. Lots of marine life and the chance of seeing large pelagics.

Hin Pae
Conditions: Good with visibility up to 20 meters.
Maximum depth: 16 meters
A relatively shallow dive site - 10 to 15 meters deep – but rewarding as there are sharks sighted here.

Hin Dot (Chimney Rock)
Conditions: Good with visibility 15 to 20 meters.
Maximum depth: 34 meters
A fantastic multi-level dive. The dive site resembles three chimneys emerging from the bottom of the sea to close near the surface. These dramatic pinnacles have developed over several hundred years and consist only of clams and wing oysters. Maximum depth of these pinnacles is 30 meters, but they reach up to 3, 12 and 15 meters. These enormous towers are famous for their large schools of fish. Other fish populations include grouper, pufferfish, lionfish, squid and bearded scorpionfish.

OTHER SITES OFF PHI PHI

Wang Long Bay
A wall dive with overhangs and a chimney. Marine life includes corals, moray eels, lionfish and lobsters.

Turtle Bay
Only 15 minutes away from Tonsai Bay, this dive site is a popular hunting spot at night for barracudas as witnessed by our night divers.

Lobster Rock
Also called mushroom stone. A perplexing outcrop is the center of abundant marine life. Stingrays, huge shoals of reef fish, lobsters, leopard sharks. to name a few.

Viking Cave Corner
A gentle dive boasting a small cave and an assortment of odd shaped submerged rocks decorated with soft and hard coral.

Stingray Wall
At the sandy bottom of a steep wall one will be able to study blue-spotted stingrays. The wall itself is covered by thousands of coral colonies.

Pilem Wall
An exhilarating 1km drift dive when strong currents are present along Phi Phi Lae's east coast. Fabulous soft corals, and an abundance of marine life.

Maya Corner
Cose to Maya Bay, harbors colorful corals, swim-throughs and a sandy bottom with leopard sharks. At the overhang one can find lionfish, puffers, sea turtles and squid.

Overhang Spot
South of Phi Phi Lae, features a big cave, divable for 50 meters without having to use lights. But don't venture any further! It is not easy to find out in the dark.

Whaleshark Wall
Features a big grotto, a big room with side-grottos. Coral boulders form interesting swim-throughs. This is the place for big game, grouper, sharks, rays and, once in a while, whale sharks.

Wang Long Cape Cave
This system of caves can be explored by experienced divers under the guidance of a certified cave dive instructor. The Wang Long Cave is a very exciting cave with two extensions into the rock.

Krabi Dive Sites

There are 15 dive sites off Ao Nang, all reachable with a 20 to 60 minute boat ride. Most Krabi based companies will also run trips to Shark Point and the King Cruiser wreck and to many of the sites off Phi Phi.

DIVING

South Andaman coast...

Koh See
Conditions: *Calm with visibility up to 20 meters.*
Maximum depth: 20 meters.
Excellent dive site with a number of caves and swim-throughs. A good place to see blacktip sharks and sting rays.

Koh Maeurai
Conditions: Good with fair visibility.
Maximum depth: 20 meters.
Lots of soft corals and marine life. Turtles and sea horses are often seen here.

Koh Wayasan
Conditions: Calm with up to 20 meter visibility.
Maximum depth: 20 meters.
Shallow coral garden, ideal for beginners.

Koh Door
Strangely shaped island – door is south Thai slang for penis – with fringing reef featuring caves and swim-throughs. Another good place to see blacktips and other reef sharks.

Koh Yawasam
A shallow site, but good for leopard sharks and sometimes blacktips and grey nurse sharks. Occasionally a strong current makes it challenging.

Koh Yawabon
Caves and swim-throughs make this an interesting site.

KOH LANTA NATIONAL MARINE PARK

Off the coast of the southern province of Krabi are multitudes of islands running from Ao Nang, south of Koh Phi Phi to Koh Lanta and beyond. They offer some of the best diving in the country and due to their distance from Phuket some of the least crowded. The farthest sites of Hin Daeng and Hin Muang are world class, with Hin Daeng home to a spectacular wall dive, which drops off to 70 meters.

Hin Daeng
Conditions: Can experience very strong currents. Visibility ranges from 10 up to 40 meters.
Maximum depth: 35 meters.
This is a spectacular dive site worth making the long journey to. It comprises a series of wall dives with intermittent shelves. Lots of coral and marine life, but the main attraction are the large pelagics that come to feed here.

DIVING

Whale sharks and mantas are regukar visitors and large schools of grey reef sharks are virtually guaranteed. Nurse sharks often loiter around a cave at 10 meters on the southwest wall.

Hin Muang
Conditions: Similar to those at Hin Daeng.
Maximum Depth: 35 meters.
Another fantastic dive site, perhaps the best in Thai waters. A series of submerged pinnacles covered in purple anemones. A feeding ground for many large pelagics, including the mighty whale shark. This site features a 70 meter drop off, the deepest in Thailand. Highly recommended.

Koh Ha
Koh Ha is a small group of islands almost directly West of Koh Lanta. These tiny islands, separated by channels over 50 meters deep, jut straight out of the Andaman Sea. The water here is quite clear and visibility frequently exceeds 25 meters. The highlight of diving here is a series of caves or caverns on the largest of the islands.

Koh Ha Yai
Conditions: Generally good visability and a weak current.
Maximum depth: 25 meters
The caves are safe to enter, even without a light, as the entrances are large and there is only one way in and one way out. The best part of entering these caves is that you can surface inside the island to view stalactites hanging down from the ceiling over 30 meters above the surface. The quality of light filtering through the water from the entrance is magical.

Koh Ha Nua
Conditions: Calm with good – sometimes excellent – visibility.
Maximum depth: 34 meters.
An unspectacular site, but some nice marine life and a small cave off the south west wall.

Koh Rok
Koh Rok, about 25 kilometers South of Koh Ha, are two sister-islands separated by a narrow channel about 15 meters deep. These islands, Nok and Nai (outside and inside) have some of the prettiest beaches in Thailand and are completely devoid of inhabitants. The islands are named for a small, furry mammal called a Rok in Thai, and this animal, along with monitor lizards, can be observed on shore with a little patience and a bit of luck.

Koh Rok Nok
The diving here is relatively shallow, with the best coral and fish life living above 18 meters. The bottom is composed of mostly hard coral, with small areas of soft coral at deeper depths. Black tip sharks patrol the reef shallows and Hawksbill turtles are sighted regularly.

Koh Rok Nai
Nice dive site with a range of coral, a good place for night dives with plenty of barracuda and tuna.

DIVING

BURMA

A NEW FRONTIER FOR DIVERS

As the dive industry in Phuket grew in size and confidence supicion began that there could be some great diving in the forbidden waters north of Surin National Marine Park. The existence of the Burma Banks had been known for a number of years but a paranoid government in Myanmar (Burma) would not allow foreign vessels entry to its waters. After many years of lobbying some of Phuket's dive operators were eventually granted entry to the Mergui Archipelago and Burma Banks. The pioneers of diving in Burma have been Southeast Asia Liveaboards and Fantasea Divers, the first companies allowed to dive in Burmese waters. More recently the military government in Rangoon has realized that there are profits to be earned from allowing Thai based boats access to their waters and now several operators have been granted licenses to enter Burma.

All tours to Burma must be conducted by licensed operators and there is an entry fee of around US$130, which includes a 30 day visa. Some trips depart from Phuket and stop at the Similans and/or Surin on the way. Others depart from Ranong on the Thai-Myanmar border.

The Mergui Archipelago consists of 10,000 square miles of virgin waters containing over 800 islands and is now open for marine exploration. Most cruises to this area are complete adventures, combining island discovery treks as well as incredible diving. Underwater highlights are found off Clara Island at North Sentinel, which is awash with sharks. Black Rock, a pinnacle dropping to over 250 feet and Western Rocky Island where whale sharks, reef sharks, manta, eagle and even devil rays can be seen around four submerged pinnacles. Shark and manta action is outstanding in Burmese waters and over 100 mantas in a single dive have been recorded. Another byword on Mergui cruises is exploration and a part of every trip is the discovery and search for new and exciting reefs, you can be almost sure you will get the chance to dive sites that nobody has ever dived before. You also get to step into a land that has been lost in time for over 50 years, islands covered by thick rainforest, bird life and fauna in abundance, as well as clear blue waters that are home to a seemingly limitless treasure.

SOME DIVE SITES
Western Rocky
Located 80 km off shore, Western Rocky offers a sloping reef, great wall diving and several surrounding pinnacles. A tunnel leads right through the island, with lots of crayfish and usually some large sleeping nurse sharks. Western Rocky is one of Mergui's best spots for shark sightings. Encounters with whitetips, gray reef sharks, blacktips and bull sharks are fairly common.

Barrcudas catching light.

Burma dives sites...

DIVING

Black Rock
This pinnacle is one of the most spectacular dive sites in the Mergui Archipelago with excellent reef life and an abundance of large pelagics including whitetips, silvertips, gray reef sharks, blacktips, bull sharks, eagle rays and mantas.

Burma Banks
The Burma Banks are a collection of seamounts located some 180 km north west of the Similans. With surrounding waters exceeding a depth of 300m, the top of the banks rise to within 15-24m of the surface and have a fairly high proportion of coral cover. However this is not what people go to the Burma Banks for. The reason for visiting is sharks, sharks and more sharks. Resident reef sharks include silvertips, whitetips, grey and nurse sharks, while oceanic visitors include tiger sharks, hammerheads and whale sharks. There are four banks currently being dived between the months of November and May. Visibility can range anywhere up to 30 meters and there are sometimes strong currents, but for shark spotting it can't be beaten.

Typical laid-back street life in Phuket town.

PHUKET Town

Phuket town was founded at the end of the 19th Century by the Chinese immigrants who had been prospering from the tin mining industry. It soon transcended Thalang. and become the capital of the island. It still retains much of its Chinese character with traditional architecture more reminiscent of Sino-colonial Penang than other Thai cities. The town is compact, but has never stopped expanding and is now an amalgam of old and new. The downtown area around Phang Nga road is full of old buildings influenced by the Portuguese, Malay, British and Chinese and lends Phuket town an ambiance and character that is unique in Thailand. The Chinese influence is further evident by the proliferation of Taoist temples throughout the town. The people are still very conscious of their heritage and every october they celebrate Taoist Lent with a fervor that defies explanation, and in February Chinese New Year is greeted by the sound of a thousand firecrackers.

For tourists Phuket town is often only of interest as a gateway to the island's abundant beaches, or as an historical place of interest. However those who take the time to spend a few days here discover a charismatic town with plenty to offer. It is close enough to all the southern beaches to bring them in range for daytrips. It is overflowing with authentic Thai restaurants and some of the hotels and guesthouses are excellent value and do not inflate their prices during peak season.

ORIENTATION

Phuket town is a big bustling place with a confusing one-way system and lots of traffic at rush hour. If you stick to the old center – which is the main area of interest – it is easy to navigate by foot. Most of the temples, shops, restaurants and bars are in the Phang Nga Rd/Ranong Rd/Krabi Rd vicinity. There is a modern alternative center in the south of town along Tilok Uthit Rd. This is where Ocean shopping Mall

An old Phuket mansion: Sino-Portugese style.

PHUKET TOWN

THE VEGETARIAN FESTIVAL

For nine days in October Phuket town is transformed into a celebration of ascetic excess. The vegetarian festival of Phuket is unique to the Thai Chinese of south Thailand. Although it coincides with Taoist lent, the people of Phuket take their abstinence further than other devotees of Kiu Ong Iah.

According to Taoist beliefs, Kiu Ong Lah controls the fate of individuals and is the embodiment of the nine emperor gods now enshrined in the heavens as stars. As an outward sign of devotion, his followers wear white clothes for nine days during the ninth lunar month.

The thousands of Chinese coolies who arrived in Phuket to work the tin mines also brought their customs and beliefs, but it seems that a strange combination of circumstances led to Phuket's version of the festival coming into being. In 1825, malaria was rife in Phuket and when a troupe of Chinese entertainers came to visit the island they inevitably succumbed to the disease. To fight off the evil spirits that had afflicted them, the actors invoked the rites of Kiu Ong Lah and his nagas, following a strict vegetarian diet combined with physical penance. The treatment was spectacularly effective and has been repeated every year since.

Although there are many aspects to the festival, most of the attention is now focussed on the nagas and the physical rites of purification they undergo in order to free themselves of evil spirits. Young men work themselves into a trance before piercing their bodies – normally their faces – with a bewildering array of sharp implements. They then join processions through the streets to demonstrate their piety. The processions are spectacular displays of pageantry and wind through the streets on every day of the festival. In the evenings there are demonstrations of fire-walking and razor ladder climbing. The acts of self-mutilation appeal to a large proportion of Phuket town's young men – and sometimes women – and have become as much a part of adolescent self-assertion as tradition. The nagas allegedly feel no pain and their wounds do not bleed, and although many of the shamens are expert piercers, many young men walk through the streets with spears, bottles and other objects protruding from bleeding wounds. Apart from the perverse spectacle of the nagas, the festival is a wild, colorful event full of firecrackers and dancing dragons. The processions start early each morning from any of the five Taoist temples in Phuket town, or from Kathu temple – which is where the festival is said to have originated. The streets are alive with white clad devotees and lined by some of the most innovative vegetarian food stands you will ever find.

The food is one of the highlights of the festival as chefs prepare fantastic offerings for the spirits, which are also on sale all over town. Nearly every restaurant in Phuket town offers a vegetarian buffet and the curries and stir fries made from pumpkin, mung beans, lentils and other vegetables and pulses have to be tasted to be believed.

PHUKET TOWN

and Robinson Dept store and some newer shops are located.

GETTING AROUND

The main bus terminal is on Phang Nga Road just east of the town center. This is where buses from outside Phuket terminate. Buses and *songtaews* to the beaches and other points on Phuket congregate on Ranong Rd. The easiest way to get around town is by motorcycle taxi - easily found on nearly every street corner.

Bars, Restaurants

Bee Bop Bistro
A buzzing' little bar/restaurant on Takuapa road. Often the scene of jam sessions as musicians from the island's many 5-star resorts like to hang out here. Jazzy décor and a cool place to while the night away.

Kajok See B50–100
With no English sign, this small place can be hard to find, but just ask anyone in Phuket and they will point it out for you. It is one of the island's best-loved Thai restaurants. Occupying an untidy shophouse with jazz music in the background it has a romantic charm, but it is the piquant southern curries that have given it its reputation. 26 Takuapa Rd. ☎ 217 903.

Sawasdee B100–200
A delightful restaurant set in a fine old wooden town house. Serves exquisite Royal Thai cuisine. 8/5 Maeluan Rd.

Mala B30–80
Opposite Sawasdee is a great daytime one-plate-meal restaurant. Interesting interior is decorated with all sorts of household artefacts. Try the *masaman gai* or *kaow yam*, a herbal rice dish with dried prawns that is supposed to be good for the health.

Thammachat .. B20-100
Serves *khao gaeng* and other one-plate-meal dishes as well as exotic local favorites such as pigeon fried in garlic. 62/5 Soi Puton.

Tungka Café .
B100–200
On the top of Rang Hill with sweeping views of the town, serves good Thai food.

Thai Naan B100–200
Claims to be the largest restaurant in south Thailand and occupies part of the last tin mine on Phuket. Live music while you eat good Thai and seafood. 16 Wichitsongkhram Rd.
☎ 226 164.

Laem Thong B200–500
Large Chinese/Thai restaurant specialising in shark fin soup, Peking duck and seafood. Expensive, but very good. 31-39 Chana Charoen Rd. ☎ 211 269.

Nai Yao
Occupying an old building on Phuket Rd. Very good and inexpensive seafood. The *tom yam* is especially good.

Mae Porn Restaurant ....
.... B40–80
A simple but excellent Phuket restaurant serving *khao gaeng* and other favorites. They speak good English and are used to tourists. Opposite On On Hotel.

Kanda Bakery B50–100
For freshly baked bread, pastries and sandwiches. located on Phang Nga Road.

Metropole Hotel ... B150–300
Has an excellent buffet lunch with food from all over Thailand. Good value at B159.

FOOD CARTS

Food Vendors B20–40
There are food vendors and small restaurants all over Phuket town serving phad thai, khao man gai, khanom jin etc, all at absurdly low prices. The best places are along Ranong Rd and at the night market behind Robinson's department store.

Hotels in Phuket...

Accommodation

BUDGET

On On Hotel B150–400
Located in large shophouse building that was once a well-known Chinese brothel. High ceilings and a fading grandeur lend it a certain character. The rooms are basic fan or air-con and there is a spittoon in each. 19 Phang Nga Road.
☎ 211 154. Recommended.

Wasana GH B150-400
Clean and good value. Fan and air con rooms, monthly rates available. 159 Ranong Road.
☎ 211 754. Recommended.

Pengman B100–300
Clean and basic single and double rooms above a Chinese restaurant. Some with shared bathrooms. 69 Phang Nga Road.
☎ 211 486.

Holiday Plaza B200
Directly opposite TAT office on Phuket Road. Clean rooms with private bathrooms. Good value

MID RANGE

City Hotel B500–800
Good quality hotel with air-con rooms each with TV, phone, minibar etc. Excellent value. Located on the corner of Dibuk and Thepkasatri. ☎ 216 910.

Pure Mansion B600–700
Brand new hotel with very clean air-con rooms with TV, minibar etc. Located south of town on 3/7 Chao Fa Road.
☎ 211 709, 📠 214 220.

Sinthavee B400-800
Hoary old hotel that just manages to retain some of its fading elegance. It has a good location and the rooms are large, but becoming musty. The massage parlour behind is of very dubious repute. 89 Phang Nga Rd.
☎ 211 186, 📠 211 400.

Phuket Crystal Inn B750
Brand new hotel near Ocean shopping mall. Very clean rooms with air-con, TV, minibar etc.
☎ 230 071, 223 527.

Thavorn Hotel B300–700
Fan and air-con rooms are available in this old well-located hotel. The museum downstairs makes it worth staying at with a good display of Phuket's history. Try to get a room at the back, as the front section is very noisy. Rasa Road.
☎ 211 333-5. Recommended

FIRST CLASS

The Metropole Hotel ....
.... B3,000–4,000
Well situated in the heart of town. Elegant rooms with nice finishing touches, swimming pool and a fitness center. Ask for a discount and you can usually get 30-50% off the rack rate. Montri Rd.
☎ 215 050.

Novotel Phuket City ....
.... B3,000–6,000
There are 251 superior and deluxe rooms in this plush upmarket hotel. Facilities include a large pool, fitness center and many other amenities. Located on Phang Nga Road.
☎ 233 402, 📠 233 335.

Arts & Crafts

Phuket town has developed into quite an art center. With many foreign residents and visitors interested in collecting Thai and regional art, textiles, furniture and handicrafts there is a ready market and the entrepreneurs of Phuket have been quick to recognize it.

Ban Boran Antiques
At 39 Yaowarat Road. An interesting selection of art objects, including imported gold jewellery from South India, Buddha images from Sri Lanka and Burma, and silver from Pakistan and Egypt.

Ban Boran Textiles
At 51 Yaowarat Road. Features fabrics from six countries in the region. While most of the textiles are in long pieces, some have been made into stylish shirts, trousers and scarves.

88 Ancient Art Gallery

PHUKET TOWN

On Yaowarat Rd. Displays a variety of ceramics, including Vietnamese celadon, Chinese Ming vases and Cambodian Buddha images from the Bayon period.

The Loft,
At 36 Thalang Road. A smart gallery and home decorating retailer. Also a restaurant with excellent Italian food. Good selections from Vietnam, Burma and Thai celadons, and Chinese porcelains

Touch Wood Antique
At 27 Yaowarat Road. A furniture shop selling colonial antique furniture mainly from neighboring Burma, Laos and Vietnam.

Puk Shop
At 7-9 Phang Nga Road. This wonderful old shop is a Phuket institution and a true treasure hunter's dream. An eclectic mix of Chinese and Thai antique ceramics acquired mainly on Phuket.

Antique Arts
At 68 Phang Nga Road is another reliable Phuket institution with an exquisite collection of Chinese porcelains, brass and lacquerware.

Royal Gallery
At 154 Phang Nga Road. A regular exhibitor of Thai artists. Usually up and coming painters, but sometimes well-known artists, always worth a look.

Practical info

SHOPPING

Apart from the art shops listed above, cheaper handicrafts can be purchased along Ratsada Road. Otherwise the main shopping areas are along Phang Nga Road or at Ocean Shopping Mall and Robinson's.

There is a huge lotus Supercenter on Route 4020. The best bookshop in town is The Books on Phuket road near the TAT office.

CARS FOR RENT
Pure Car Rent
75 Ratsada Road. ☎ 211 002. email:purecar@phuketdir.com

Practical Phuket...

At the 'Vegetarian Festival' of Phuket, not for the faint hearted.

email:purecar@phuketdir.com
Phuket Atipong Co Ltd
58/23 Mae Luan Road, behind Surakoon stadium. ☎ 212 543.

COMMUNICATIONS
Phuket telecommunications center
For overseas phone calls. Phang Nga Road. ☎ 216 861.
Phuket Post and Telegraph Office
For postal services, EMS and poste restante. On Montri Road near the corner with Thalang road. ☎ 211 020
In touch Worldwide
For worldwide express courier service. ☎/📠 343 024, email: itww@loxinfo.co.th

Internet
There are Internet offices all over the center.
Usually B2-3/min to log on.

HEALTH
Phuket International Hospital
Large modern facility with accident and emergency facilities comparable with many in Europe. Also dental clinic, plastic and cosmetic surgery, E.N.T. 44 Chalermprakiat Road,
☎ 249 400,
email: info@phuket-inter-hospital.co.th.
24 hour telephone 210 935.
Bangkok Phuket Hospital
International standard hospital with very modern facilities. Dental clinic, cardiology, kidney dialysis. 2/1 Hongyok Utis Road.
☎ 254 421-9,
email: adminbpk@bgh.co.th.
Emergency call out telephone 1060.
Phuket Ruampaet Hospital
340 Phuket Rd.
☎ 212 578, 📠 212 950.

Patong Beach

PATONG BEACHGUIDE

Patong is where all the action is. Located on the west of the island just 9 km from Phuket town, it is Phuket's busiest beach, a cosmopolitan international tourist center that has grown out of a banana plantation in 20 something years. It is brash and noisy, vibrant and lively, yet surprisingly well ordered with everything you could ever want to buy or entertain yourself with. Tranquillity is the notable exclusion. It is a cultural crossroads where western leisure demands collide with Thailand's ever-imaginative entertainment industry, and creates a kind of Disneyland for hedonists. There is far more concrete and neon than there are banana trees and coconut palms and there is very little peace and quiet - nightlife is a much stronger feature than the beach. Yet Patong is unashamed and unpretentious and its popularity is due to its ability to cater to the demands of a wide range of tourists – most of who come to Patong, because it is exactly, or close to, what they want. The bars, girls, discos, shops and entertainment are the essence of Patong. If you want relaxing beaches then go to Surin, Bang Tao or Krabi. That is not to say Patong does not have a nice beach. Its wide 4-kilometer sweep of sand was once regarded as the most beautiful beach on the island. Even now that it is almost completely covered in sunbeds, slowly baking bodies, hawkers and traders it is still a pretty beach in a deep cove, surrounded by green forested hills. The land space behind the beach is packed full of resorts and hotels, some of which were built before the height restrictions were imposed, giving it a municipal skyline. There is very little free space in downtown Patong and the roads that run back from the beach are crammed with shops, restaurants, bars, hotels and guest houses.

At night there are lights and neon everywhere and the beer bars blast out a cacophony created from outdated disco music and shrieking bar girls. Patong at night is not for shrinking violets or the faint hearted - loud and messy it may be but has never been accused of being boring, and it must be noted that the thousand or so girlie bars, go-go bars and discos that flourish around Bangla Road are the main attraction for many tourists.

There is a vast selection of accommodation ranging from simple guesthouses to 4-star hotels. The

Patong has the largest choice of beach activities.

PATONG BEACH

beach is bordered by Thaweewong Road and all the accommodation is behind this road. As a general rule, the closer to the beach you are the more you should expect to pay. Most of the larger resorts border the road but good value can still be found at the southern end. Many cheaper hotels can be found tucked down the sois running back from the beach or along Rat-U-Thit road. Wherever you stay on Patong you have to cross the road to get to the beach Most of the resorts on Thaweewong road cater to European package tourists and if booked from abroad can be surprisingly good value. The bigger resorts are definitely the way to go for families or anyone who wants the craziness of Patong, but would like some respite every now and again. Otherwise there are plenty of hotels and guesthouses costing from ฿1,000 upwards, although many of them have an almost exclusively single male clientele with Thai bar girls wandering in and out at all hours.

The beach is ostensibly public but in reality has been staked out by vendors who will rent you a beach chair and umbrella for ฿50 a day. There are also a myriad of food and drink vendors, so once you have found your spot you hardly need to move except to take a dip in the ocean every now and again. The flip side to the convenience factor is of course that you have to spend half your time turning down unwanted hawkers. However Thai beach traders are not as pushy as those in Bali or East Africa and everything is done with a laugh and a smile and many tourists and beach sellers become great friends. The northern section is the quietest as there are large sections where there are no resorts. This area is also popular with the local Thaïs who like to eat, drink and make lots of noise, especially at the weekends. A little further north yet still connected to Patong is Kalim Beach, which is scattered with boulders and is free of hawkers, providing an alternative for those tiring of Patong.

ORIENTATION

It's pretty easy to find your way around Patong. It is compact and most of the accommodation, shops and restaurants are between Thaweewong Road - the beach road – and Rat-U-Thit 200 Year Road. In between are a number of sois, which are crammed with more shops, eateries and all types of accommodation. The main ones being Soi Kebsub, Soi Pempong and Soi Post Office. Half way up the beach road and connecting to Rat-u-Thit is Bangla Road, which is where most of the nightlife is. North of Bangla it is quieter and there is even some wide-open park space - this is

PATONG BEACH

where the X-Games and Patong Carnival take place. At the far north of Patong is Kalim beach, which is quieter and has some great restaurants.

Beachlife

DIVING

There are dozens of scuba dive tour operators on Patong. Most offer instruction and daytrips to the local dive sights (see diving section for description) and some also run regular liveaboard tours to the Similans, Burma and Hin Daeng (see page 54 for liveaboard operators.)

Andaman Divers
Reputable PADI dive center with local and liveaboard dive trips.
☎/📠 341 126.

Asia Adventures
Offer all PADI courses and daily tours to all the local dive sites, including Phi-Phi islands. Good quality dive boat and level of service. Main office located on Rat-U-Thit Road.
☎ 341 799, 📠 341 789, email: info@asian-adventures.com, www.asian-adventures.com

Fantasea Divers
One of the longest established dive operators in Phuket and has an excellent reputation. Very professional, high service and safety standards and very good dive boats. Highly recommended for instruction and dive tours. Main office on Rat-U-Thit Road with booking office on the beach road near Holiday Inn. ☎ 340 088, 📠 295 510, email: info@fantasea.net, www.fantasea.net

Ocean Divers
On the beach road.
☎ 341 273.

Santana
Another long established dive school with a good reputation and a good quality boat. Daily excursions to all local sites.
☎ 294 220, 📠 340 360, email: info@santanaphuket.com, www.santanaphuket.com

Scuba Cat Diving
Offering all PADI courses and daily dive tours.
☎ 293 120, 📠 293 122, email: bro@scubacat.com www.scubacat.com

South East Asia Divers
Long established PADI 5 star center with a central location on the beach road.
☎ 344 022, 📠 342 530, email: info@phuketdive.net www. Phuketdive.net

South East Asia Liveaboards
Not to be confused with South East Asia Divers.
Offer PADI courses as well as live-aboard cruises. Good reputation and high service standards - technical diving specialists.
☎ 340 406, 📠 340 586, email: info@sealiveaboards.com, www.sealiveaboards.com

Warm Water Divers
Located on Rat-U-Thit Road. Operate liveaboard tours to Similans and Burma aboard a converted Chinese Junk.
☎ 294 150, 📠 342 453, email: info@warmwaterdivers.com, www.warmwaterdivers.com

West Coast Diving
PADI dive shop with all courses and daily tours. ☎ 341 673, email: info@westcoastdivers.com

SPORT FISHING

Phuket sport Fishing Center
With a fleet of three fully equipped sport-fishing boats this is the place to go for serious fishermen. Two of the boats have accommodation for one-day, overnight or longer tours, while a speedboat takes day trips into the Andaman Sea looking for gamefish. All the boats have all modern equipment and tackle. To charter a boat for the day costs around **฿**15,000 (max 8 persons), or to join daily trips costs

Sport on Patong beach...

PATONG BEACH

B3,000 per fisherman. The office is off Thaweewong Road near Soi post Office.
☎ 214 713, 📠 236 182, email: *wahoo@phuket.loxinfo.co.th*

Sea Dragon
A 40 ft British owned fishing boat available for fishing charters.
☎ 296 311.

WATERSPORTS

Patong beach is a hive of activity with all kinds of watersports available all along the beach. Different operators have claimed separate patches and it really isn't that hard to see what is going on. Sports available are;

   Jetskis – 1 hour for B700
   Parasailing – B500
   Windsurfing – B300-500
   Hobicats – B500–700
   Water-skiing B500
   Kayaks – B300–500

SHOPPING

Shopping is one of the Patong visitors' major pastimes and you don't have to walk far to find items for sale. Sarongs, woodcarvings, paintings, silks, T-shirts, fake watches and a wide range of souvenirs spill out onto the street all along Thaweewong Road and Bangla Road. Along these roads and on the sois leading off them are also literally hundreds of tailor shops offering made-to-measure suits; a number of boutique and fashion shops; some antique shops; dozens of convenience stores and 7-elevens; and a few gem shops offering jewellery and precious and semi-precious stones. Hard bargaining needs to be done as prices in Patong tend to be higher than elsewhere in Thailand, but if you work hard you can get a good price in the end. There are also lots of CDs, VCDs and computer CD ROMs and playstation games on sale. Prices are very low compared to the west as these are flagrant copyright violations, and although they are on sale quite openly they are actually illegal. The quality is often somewhat dubious and as a very general rule expect up to one in two discs to be faulty in some way. Video CDs are especially liable to be poor quality while playstation games are usually better. There are two major shopping centers with department stores and designer brands like DKNY, Calvin Klein, Addidas etc. There is also a lot of diving equipment on sale and most of the dive shops are well stocked with big name brands,

---

KHATOEYS

A colorful and visable part of Patong's nightlife is its transvestite and transsexual population. Known locally as khatoeys, or ladyboys, these girls who used to be boys are an endless source of fascination for foreign tourists. Many are able to transform themselves so convincingly into females that some visitors cannot tell them apart from the surrounding girls. There are stories in almost all the bars of Patong of unwitting tourists who took what they thought was a girl home with them, only to find out that they were getting a little bit more for their money than they bargained for. Many, but by no means all, Khatoeys have had surgery to further transmutate their bodies. Some have breast implants and some go further by having a full sex change.

The Thai philosophy of *mai pen rai* – or never mind – and a liberal attitude towards homosexuality, stemming from Buddhism's adherence to tolerance, means that khatoeys are accepted in Thai society. In wild and way-out Patong the khatoeys have become an integral part of the scene and Soi Crocodile on Bangla Road has been dubbed Soi Khatoey after its most prominent tenants.

A word of warning:.many khatoeys are expert pick pockets and will lift your valuables whilst pretending to grope and fondle you.

PATONG BEACH

although if you are heading through Singapore or Hong Kong you will find better prices there.

Ocean Shopping Center
At the Rat-U-Thit end of Bangla Road, has a variety of brand names on sale as well as cosmetics, a supermarket and a bowling alley.

Patong Shopping Mall
A large center on the beach road near Holiday Inn, has a number of designer clothes shops, KFC and a supermarket.

Andaman Plaza
On Thaweewong Rd north of Bangla, has a lot of cheap clothes (mostly copies of name brands) and Adidas and Nike outlets.

Evening Market
A market sets up on Rat-U-Thit Road every evening with lots of cheap clothes and second hand jeans - very popular with the locals.

Corto Maltese trading
Interesting garment and souvenir shop on Rat-U-Thit Road.
☎ 344 730.

Aloha Surf shop
Just behind Bai Thong Restaurant - stocks Quicksilver and other brandname surfboards and accessories.

Entertainment

In terms of nighttime entertainment Patong has got it all - everything you could possibly image and then some. It is a lively 24-hour party place with something for all creatures of the night. It is trying to clean up its image of a sex and sleaze center, but there are still plenty of young upcountry girls offering their company for the night, week or lifetime in return for some kind of financial security. Many of the go-go bars try to lure in couples as well as single guys, and on the surface it seems to be little more than harmless titillation that is on sale rather than obvious prostitution, however most of the young girls are more than willing to sell themselves and do so regularly. All the real action takes place up and down notorious Bangla Road, which is lined with beer bars, shops and restaurants. There are a number of Sois branching off Bangla which are packed with literally hundreds of bars all full of high volume Thai hookers ready to help innocent - and not so innocent - tourists spend their holiday cash as quickly as possible. Across the road from Bangla is Soi Sunset, which is the late night entertainment sector, and the action here often goes on until the early hours, with drunken farangs, lustrous bar girls and glitzy transsexuals cavorting amongst the bars and go-go bars of this den of iniquity. If hard drinking and easy sex is your poison Patong is the place to get infected.

NIGHT CLUBS

THE NIGHTCLUBS OF PATONG

Banana Disco
Located on the beach road just around the corner from Bangla Road it is handily placed to pick up the late drinking buzz. The dance floor is small but crowded and the sounds are a loud mixture of Europop and mainstream dance tunes. It is always busy and is usually full of single western men and young Thai girls, it hardly needs to be said that it is something of a meat market. **B**100 entrance fee includes one drink. ☎ 340 541.

Shark Club
Newer, bigger and at the other end of Bangla Road from the Banana Disco, but otherwise the same product in a slightly different package. It does have an upstairs area overlooking the dance floor which serves as a chill out area and seems to be open later than its rival - it does-

PATONG BEACH

n't get going after 02.00 when all the bar girls start flooding in. It is really a glitzy pick-up bar trying to pass itself off as dance club but still good fun. B100 to get in, including one drink.

Safari Club
About a kilometer south of Patong on the road to Karon beach. Safari is easily the most innovative and interesting club in Phuket with assiduous DJs spinning the latest dance tracks and an exotic safari-esque interior. Unfortunately its location often keeps the crowds below the necessary number required to create an atmosphere and it can be woefully empty at certain times of the year. However when it's busy it is the best club in town.

PUBS AND CLUBS
Paradise bar
One of the original beach bars and a Phuket landmark. A hassle free drinking bar with good snacks available and live sport on big screens. Good location in the middle of the beach road makes it a popular sunset venue. Recommended.

Chicago Fun Pub
Opposite the top end of Bangla Road, this is a late-night venue that is always packed full of working girls. The action often goes on until dawn and gets fairly raucous - best to leave your principles behind. ☎ 344 437.

Crows Nest
One of a string of inside drinking bars on Bangla Road that provide a relatively safe haven for serious drinkers. A good meeting place, especially early evening.
☎ 341 602.

Faulty Towers Pub
A British drinking den on Soi Sunset, full of hard-core Patong regular visitors. Good place to find out what the score is around town. ☎ 344 061.

Molly Malone's
The owners have spared no expense and done an excellent job turning the basement at Patong Shopping mall into an Irish theme bar. Inside is a stain glass and hard wood interior and a long bar complete with draught Guinness and Kilkenny - but at nearly B300 a pint it doesn't come cheap. Live music every night from 21.00.
☎ 292 771.

Ned Kelley's
Aussie drinking bar on Bangla Road - popular with hard drinking Antipodeans and a good place to watch the evening's entertainment unfold.
☎ 340 711.

Q Bar
In front of the Ocean Plaza shopping center on Bangla road. A reasonably civilized place to sit and watch the world go by, with a better décor than most of the rest.
☎ 341 547.

Scene on a quiet day on the strip.

PATONG BEACH

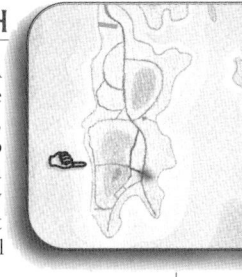

BEER BARS

The beer bars - or girlie bars - of Patong Beach are its most numerous and visited night spots. Within a 500m radius around Bangla Rd there are over 150 beer bars. The bars are usually not much more than a square bar with a roof, no larger than 3 square meters and butted right on next to each other. The bars are filled with young upcountry Thai girls trying to make some money any way they can. They are a friendly bunch and know how to entertain customers without going too far - anyone wanting to take these ladies out of the bar for whatever reason must pay a **B**200 "bar fine" to compensate the bar owner and then negotiate a fee with the girl (which she keeps all) depending on what or where you go. The main concentrations of bars are along sois that run off Bangla Rd. Over the years each soi has gained a name and particular character that most of the bars try to portray.

Soi Crocodile - Named after a nightclub that used to exist at end of the soi, however it is now more often called "Soi Khatoey" after the colorful transvestites and transsexuals who have taken over the first part of the street bordering Bangla. Every night a dozen or so girls who used to be boys cavort and display their new bodies for the tourists. They usually dress up in outlandish costumes and will eagerly pose for pictures - as long as you pay (Bt50 to **B**100 seems to be enough). They are obviously on to something because this is the busiest section of Patong between 22.00 and midnight.

Soi Sea Dragon - The middle section is all standard beer bars, whilst a number of go-go bars inhabit the shop-houses each side. Busy every night.

Soi Eric - Soi Eric's trademark is that it's very clean, that they only have one disc jockey for the whole street and that they have the best toilets in Soi Bangla entertainment area.

Soi Gonzo - A scruffy little street full of bars, however Gonzo Bar itself is a popular early evening hangout as it has a pool table.

Soi Sunset - At the end of Bangla Road across Rat-U-Thit is the street that should really be renamed Soi Sunrise because this is when the party finishes. Only for late night party boys and girls not easily shocked by some fairly seedy spectacles.

GO GO BARS

Go-go bars are a firm fixture in the Patong night scene and no matter what people say, they are most certainly part of its appeal for many. Most bars feature topless dancers but discourage nudity. Many have "erotic" shows featuring ping-pong balls, chopsticks and the many of the bizarre acts that seem to have become part of Thailand's eccentric tourist machine. The girls are not owned, controlled or pimped by any of the owners and are free to go whenever they want. However if they want to continue in work they must pay, or find a customer to pay, a **B**500 "bar fine" if they want to get off work or "go out" with a client. Go-go dancers consider themselves superior to bar girls and usually charge more money for their services.

Rock Hard A-Go-Go
At the top end of Bangla Road, this is one of the oldest bars in Patong and bills itself as the Number. 1 Go-Go bar with the most lively and attractive girls in Phuket, which is probably a fair appraisal.
☎ 340 409.

Playschool A-Go-Go
Small and seedy bar on Soi Sea Dragon. ☎ 344 260.

Extasy A-Go-Go
Located on Soi Sunset - a bit hit and miss, certainly not as popular

PATONG BEACH

as Rock Hard, although it can have its moments during peak season. ☎ 341 510.

Flash A-Go-Go
At the far end of Soi Eric, this upstairs go-go bar is the raciest spot in town. Outrageous shows and friendly staff ensure that it is usually busy.

CABARET SHOWS AND THEATRES

Phuket Simon Cabaret
The ever-popular transvestite extravaganza is Phuket's answer to the Moulin Rouge. Lots of feathers and sequins and formation dancing. Certainly a spectacle and a pretty good evening's entertainment. ☎ 342 011-5.

Pirate's Cove
Located behind Holiday Inn. A large mini golf course with a Pirate theme and a surprisingly good restaurant. It has two different courses and is a good place to take the kids - open 10.00 to 23.00. ☎ 342 951.

Horror
This is a haunted house of the very scary kind. Actors, electronic gimmicks and lighting contrive to produce a heart stopping tour. At B400 it is probably overpriced, but is definitely recommended for diehard horror movie buffs. ☎ 293 123, horror@phuket.kse.co.th

Vegas Beer Bar
Live Muay Thai every night (19.00-03.00) at the Rat-U-Thit end of Bangla Road. ☎ 341 632.

MASSAGE

As with everything else Patong has the full range - from a revitalizing foot massage, through traditional Thai massage, to special erotic body massage. There are also some dedicated health centers with a range of therapeutic massage and sauna and of course plenty of beach masseurs on hand during the day.

Boo's Original Thai Massage
A good honest traditional massage for B200 per hour.

Christin Massage
A full body massage parlor where the girl uses her naked body to massage your naked body and then offers extra services (wink, wink). In other words a brothel. Located on Rat-U-Thit Road. ☎ 340 369.

The Hide Away
Part of a chain of health centers offering massage, sauna and herbal treatments. With properly trained staff, this is the best bet for an authentic Thai massage. Located on Soi Na Nai Road. ☎ 340 591.

Paradise Herbal Sauna
Located behind Paradise bar this is another one worth trying, where you can get a thorough rub down with a range of aromatic oils. An hour massage will cost B300 to B350 and a sauna is B200 to B350. Ask for discounts in the low season.

GYMS AND SPORTS FACILITIES

Holiday Inn Fitness Center
A big well equipped gymnasium inside the Holiday Inn complex and open to the public with daily, weekly and monthly rates available. Open 09.00 till 21.00. ☎ 360 608 ext. 8123.

Patong Gym
Gym and fitness center on Soi San Sabai. Reasonable range of training machines and free weights.

Thai kick Boxing Gym
Located on Na Nai road near the Hideaway Spa, this is where many local fighters train; they will happily accept farang fighters with some Muay Thai or kick boxing experience.

Restaurants

Patong has an enormous range of restaurants and is truly a gourmet's dream come true. As you would expect from Thailand's most popular holiday island there are some outstanding Thai and Seafood restaurants. Add to that some very

PATONG BEACH

good representatives of all the corners of the earth and nobody could possibly ever tire of eating out in Patong. There are eateries to suit all budgets and some of the best Thai food can be found in the cheaper places, while at the top end there are some genuinely world-class restaurants. It also needs to be mentioned that as a general rule restaurants in Patong dilute the local cuisine to cater for the tastes of foreigners - which is quite understandable seeing as 90% of their customers are tourists. So if you are expecting the ferociously spicy Thai cuisine you will need to ask for your food '*pet pet*' (spicy) or "*baep Thai*" (Thai style) - but be careful.

Argentina Grill & Steakhouse . . . . B500 and up
North of Patong on Kalim beach Road. This is a carnivores only restaurant with lots of steak and imported meat on the menu. Recommended. ☎ 340 571.

Bai Thong Restaurant B250–300
Popular seafood restaurant in front of Patong Resort. Excellent setting, thoughtful décor and good service make this a good choice. The seafood is fresh and very good - the menus come with color pictures to make ordering easier.

Baan Rim Pa B300–600
A Phuket institution, superbly situated above Kalim Beach overlooking Patong Bay. No holiday is complete without getting dressed up and spending an evening soaking up the atmosphere in this beautiful piano bar and restaurant. The ambiance is second to none and the food is pretty good too. ☎ 340 789. Recommended.

Buffalo Steak House B250–400
The Patong branch of this popular Scandinavian chain can be found on Soi Patong resort off Bangla Road. The steaks are excellent and very good value (local beef), although the restaurant lacks ambiance. ☎ 340 855.

Casanova B100–300
Good Italian fare and seafood at Patong Resort arcade. ☎ 340 417.

Da Maurizio B300–600
On Kalim Beach Road, overlooking Patong Bay (just past Ban Rim Pa). Superb Italian cuisine and world class seafood in an unbeatable setting. Recommended.

Hawkers Food Center
Towards the north end of Thaweewong Road. A large Singapore style food court with dozens of different restaurants offering special dishes - a great place to sample every day Thai cooking. Recommended.

Kuba Restaurant . . . B100-400
A very special Thai and seafood restaurant that does a superb set dinner. You need to order 24

A typical open air seafood restaurant.

PATONG BEACH

hours in advance as they only cook to order with the freshest ingredients. Located at the far south of Thaweewong Road, continue along the dirt track and you will see it before the Amari Resort. ☎ 292 191

Navrang Mahal B100–200
One of the better Indian restaurants on Phuket and reasonably priced. Located on Soi Patong Resort. ☎ 292 280.

Papaya B150–250
Classy Thai restaurant behind Bai Thong and part of the same complex.

Potpourri B200-300
The Indian restaurant in the Horizon Resort is well worth trying. A little more expensive than the others but easily the best in town. Recommended.
☎ 292 526

Lai Mai Restaurant
Open-air seafood restaurant in front of Patong Shopping Mall. Live music every night.
☎ 340 460.

Pizzadelic B100–200
Interesting square pizzas are the specialty here as well as email and some of the hottest sounds in Patong. Good place to hang out early in the evening.

Patong Seafood . . B200–300
Still the best seafood restaurant on the beach road.

Roma Pizzeria Ristorante . . . .
. . . . B200–300
Very good Italian restaurant on Soi Post Office.

Saloniki
The only Greek restaurant in Patong offers a range of Greek dishes and salad. Worth a try.

Sam's Steak House . . . .
. . . . B300–500
Part of Holiday Inn complex and very highly regarded. Good décor, excellent service and top quality steaks make this a great choice if you are in the mood for western cuisine. ☎ 340 608. Recommended.

Sabai Sabai B50–150
Another local favorite and long established café. Their trademark is bad service and great food at reasonable prices - which is just about right although the waitresses some times let their guard slip and can be quite friendly. Located on Soi Post Office.

Savoy Seafood
The biggest seafood market in Patong where you choose your own fish and crustaceans to be cooked to order. Pretty good value and very good.

The Islander B100–300
For a good square meal at a reasonable price, this British-style restaurant is hard to beat. All the usual favorites from roast dinners to fried breakfasts. On Soi Patong Resort. ☎ 342 685.

The Royal Kitchen . . . .
. . . . B100–300
Chinese restaurant with a fantastic view. On the 25th floor of The Royal Paradise Hotel. Try the Peking Duck. ☎ 340 666.

Viking Grill Garden . . . .
. . . . B150–250
Huge open air Scandinavian garden with barbeques and buffets, where home sick Vikings can eat as much as they want for B180. Just off Bangla road.
☎ 341 775.

Vallhalla B100–300
Scandinavian theme restaurant on Soi Sunset with a buffet feast every night. The setting is supposed to resemble the ancient Viking home of the gods but looks more like the set for a surreal Swedish soap opera.

Zum Schlawiener . . . .
. . . . B100–200
Austrian, German and Thai foods specializing in imported meats and cold cuts. ☎ 324 062.

Accommodation

There is so much available accommodation on Patong Beach that it would be futile to try and list it all here. Below is a list of hotels and guest houses that we have inspected and can recommend or feel compelled to comment on. It should act

PATONG BEACH

as a good guide for where you should stay and what you can expect for your money. The first figure is the low season price of the cheapest room, while the second figure is the high season price for the best rooms.

FIRST CLASS

Amari Coral Beach Resort
High quality and well maintained with a nice quiet location at the far south end of Patong with it's own private beach. Highly Recommended.
☎ 340 106, 340 115, email: coralbea@phuket.loxinfo.co.th

Baan Sukhothai B2,000–7,000
A delightful resort right in the middle of Bangla Road, but tucked away unobtrusively. Behind kinaree fountains are "nipa" style cottages and a hotel with traditional Thai interior design. The hotel has all amenities and is the most stylish place to stay in downtown Patong.
☎ 340 195, ☏ 340 330.

Club Andaman Beach Resort B2,000–5,000
Located on the quiet northern end of Patong Beach in 15 acres of secluded tropical gardens and coconut palms. A very nice resort, ideal for families and still in reach of Patong and Kalim beaches. Recommended.
☎ 340 361, ☏ 340 530, email cabrhkt@sun.phuket.ksc.co.th

Holiday inn Resort $80–150
Centrally located on Thaweewong Beach Road. A very tidy and well-run package holiday resort. Excellent facilities, good size pool, reasonably priced bar and restaurants - yet very unpretentious.
☎ 340 608-9, ☏ 340 435, email: holiday@sun.phuket.ksc.co.th

Thavorn Beach Village . $100+
A few bays north of Patong on the way to Kamala, this impressive locally owned luxury resort has a large secluded beach all to itself. It also boasts the largest swimming pool in Thailand and a cable car to help guests to their hillside villas. The owners harbor ambitions to rival the Amanpuri and the Thai style villas come complete with jacuzzis. Very nice.
☎ 290 334-42,
☏ 340 384, email: info@thavornbeachvillage.com

MID RANGE

Horizon Beach Resort Hotel B1,500–5,000
Good standard resort in the heart of Patong on Soi Kebsub. Has a good swimming pool and all the standard hotel amenities. An excellent Indian restaurant too.

Patong, along the beach.

PATONG BEACH

Good value. ☎ 292 526. 📠 292 535, email: *horizonbeach@phuket.com*

Royal Palm Resort B1,100–2,500
Good location on the beach road at the end of Soi Kebsub, but pretty ordinary rooms.
☎/📠 292 510-12, email: *kris_royalpalm@hotmail.com*

Thara Beach Resort B1,500–3,000
☎/📠 292 510, email: *kris_royalpalm@hotmail.com*

Patong Penthouse B1,000–3,000
Located just on the outskirts of town on the northern end of Rat-U-Thit Road. Rooms and bungalows are set in a very pleasant garden with a pool. Good place for families. Rooms range from standard fan rooms to deluxe rooms with air-con, TV & VCR, fridge etc. Recommended.
☎ 340 350

Phairin Hill Hotel B850–5,000
At the far south of the beach road well away from all the noise. Range of rooms from fan cooled to suites with all amenities. Well run hotel with a swimming pool. Recommended.
☎ 340 743, 📠 340 522.

San Sabai bungalows B500–1,500
Located at the end of Soi San Sabai. Large and reasonably priced resort. Very good rates for long stays and in low season. Fan and air-con rooms. ☎ 342 948, 📠 344 888.

Thara Hotel ... B1,300–6,000
Another good value resort with a swimming pool and all the usual features. Well located on Thaweewong Road just north of Bangla Road.
☎ 340 135, 📠 340 446, email: *thara@sun.phuket.ksc.co.th*

BUDGET

Adventure Inn ... B700–1,400
Formerly the Dive Inn. This is a clean and friendly guest house run by Asian Adventures. there is a bar with a pool table downstairs with well appointed air-con rooms above. Recommended.
☎ 341 799, email: *info@asian-adventures.com*

Azzurro Village .. B700–1,400
Good clean rooms with fridge, TV and air-con. Located on Rat-U-Thit Road just north of Bangla. Recommended.
☎ 341 811, 📠 341 812.

Expat Hotel B700–1,500
An old Patong favorite located at the end of Soi Sunset. Popular with regular night owls. The place is looking a little run down now, but there is a swimming pool. Fan and air-con rooms. ☎ 342 143, email: *expat@loxinfo.co.th*

Paradise Bungalows B350–1,400
Centrally located on the beach road with either air-con or fan rooms. Facilities are minimal and the rooms are getting a little shabby but still a reasonable deal for the location. ☎ 340 172.

Sandy Mansion .. B600–1,400
Small hotel on Soi Kebsub with decent rooms. All with air-con, TV and fridge. ☎ 344914

PS Hotel B850–1,700
On Rat-U-Thit Road at the end of Bangla. Good value rooms with air-con, TV and fridge and very popular with single western men.
☎ 340 184.

2000 Mansion .. B600–1,500
On Rat-U-Thit road at the end of Soi Kebsub. Reasonable rooms with air-con, TV and fridge. Good value.
☎ 294 032, 📠 345 027.

Practical info

BANKS
Most of the major Thai banks have branches in Patong.
Thai farmers Bank is on Rat-U-Thit Road with exchange facilities and an ATM. ☎ 340 447.
Siam Commercial Bank has a branch on Thaweewong Road also with foreign exchange and ATM. There are also many exchange

PATONG BEACH

booths all along Thaweewong and Bangla Roads where you can change cash and travellers cheques at bank rates.

TRAVEL AGENTS

There are small agencies offering bus, boat and plane tickets, as well as tours and tickets for shows around the island about every 50-meters along the beach road. They are all pretty much the same and commission driven, but usually reliable and good for booking cheap boat trips, Phuket Fantasea or Simon Cabaret.

The Travel Company
On Rat-U-Thit road, English run with good service and range of products.
☎ 340 232, 📠 344 668, email: travelco@loxinfo.co.th

COMMUNICATIONS AND INTERNET

There are now dozens of Internet cafes offering a range of communication services. Prices for web surfing should be 2 to 4 baht a minute. Many places charge less in the mornings and will discount for regular users.

Connect
Located in the Paradis Complex on Rat-U-Thit Road. Comprehensive range of internet services. ☎ 294 195, email: connect@patong.com

In Touch
On the second floor (up the escalator) just south of Soi Post Office. Good and knowledgeable service. Facilities include Internet (**B**2-3 a minute), fax, overseas calls (**B**49 a minute to the UK), photos, scanning, mobile phone rental (**B**485 a day + cost of calls). ☎/📠 343 024, email: itww@loxinfo.co.th

Pizzadelic
The funkiest place to get on line. Good service and surfing costs **B**2-3 a minute.

POST OFFICE

The main Patong Post Office is now on Thaweewong Rd. This is where mail arrives to be sorted and they have EMS and packing facilities.

The old and best known post office is still PO83150 on Thaweewong Road and has the full range of services plus Patong Communication Center upstairs (open 08.00 to 23.00) where calls to Europe cost **B**46 a minute. PO84320 (open 08.00 to 15.00).

Lodging on Patong...

Rentals along the beach front.

HEALTH

Wattana Clinic
Modern facility with 24-hour doctor on call. Good for cuts, bruises and ailments, but for anything serious go to one of the big hospitals. ☎ 340 690, ☎ 341 178.

Patong Inter Clinic.
Just off Thaweewong road on the way to Patong Resort. Good standard clinic.

Arin Clinic
Half way along Soi Kebsub - clinic open until 11.00.
☎ 341 159.

BIKE AND CAR RENTALS AND TAXIS

Avis
In the Holiday Inn hotel.
☎ 340 608.

Budget
Reputable car rental company with offices all over Thailand. Reasonable prices and they deliver to your hotel - all rental cars carry full insurance. They also have an office at.the airport.
☎ 427 188,
☎ 427 189 and a reservation free call number:
088-220 310,
website: www.budget.co.th.

Hertz
In Patong Merlin Hotel.
☎ 340 037.

Patong Big Bikes
Located next to Azurro Resort, the longest established and most reliable place to rent big bikes.
☎

Via Rent a Car
On Rat-U-Thit Road. Reputable rental company with a reasonable range of vehicles and competitive prices.
☎ 341 660, ☎ 341 661,
email: via.cars@phuket.com

There are cars and bikes for rent all along Thaweewong Road. They offer unbeatable prices but no insurance (see page for tips on renting cars and bikes).

Karon Beach

KARON BEACH GUIDE

Karon beach is Phuket's second most popular beach. It is a marvellous 3-kilometer stretch of golden sand on the west coast of the island, between Patong and Kata Bays. The bay is wide and open and the beach is superb.

Although Karon is well developed as a tourist resort it is not nearly as packed as Patong. There are a few big hotels that have huge grounds and one or two high-rise developments. The rest of the accommodation, shops and bars are packed around the lively Patak Road (East) - near the roundabout – or Luang Pho Chuan Road and Patak Road East. Some of the architecture is dated and unattractive, but the beach makes up for the town's insipidness. Karon is far less frenetic than Patong and should appeal to those seeking an "all-round" destination. There is plenty going on at night, a great beach, good restaurants and enough space to find a bit of peace and quiet.

One of the delights of Karon is that it still retains much of its character as a Thai beach. There are always masses of food vendors and some great alfresco eating opportunities on the promenade overlooking the sea.

In the rainy season a strong wind blows in from the west and the surf really gets up, making it a challenging surfing destination for a few months each year (usually August and September).

ORIENTATION

The town of Karon lies about halfway down the beach and stretches into neighboring Kata Bay. There are several pockets of activity. At the north end around the roundabout and up East Patak road there are a number of bars, restaurants and shops - this is probably the liveliest area at night as well as being the main shopping area. Further south is a second mini center where several girlie bars and a few restaurants are located. Then there are a number of big resorts including the very big Thavorn Palm Beach Resort, the road runs around the bend into Kata beach at the far south. At the fusion of the two bays is another lively section with several dive shops, restaurants and some bars.

Beachlife

WATERSPORTS

A range of watersports is available on the beach: Waterski (**B**500); wakeboards (**B**500); bananaboat (**B**300); windsurf (**B**250-300); hobiecats (**B**500-700); jetskis (1/2 hour for **B**700).

Karon Bay, a 6 km stretch of sand, but few trees.

KARON BEACH

DIVING

Aquatic Adventures
☎ 396 326; email:
aquatic-adventures@usa.net

Dive Asia
Located on Patak Road east just after the roundabout. One of the best-known dive companies on Phuket. ☎ 396 199, email:info@diveasia.com

Kon Tiki
Well-established Scandinavian diving school with daily dive tours and liveaboard trips to the Similans. Located on Patak Road. ☎ 396 312, ☎ 396 313.

Marina Divers
Marina Divers - Phuket. Phuket's largest PADI 5 Star IDC center and dive resort with over 11 years experience in the local diving industry.
☎ 330 272, ☎ 330 516.

Siam Dive n' Sail
Dive and boat charter company who organize dive and sail expeditions and liveaboard diving and instructor training courses. Very experienced and knowledgeable staff. ☎/☎ 330 990,
email: john@siamdivers.com

Entertainment

Karon's nightlife is not very sophisticated. There are no nightclubs or smart pubs, but plenty of bars - mostly beer bars and girlie bars, but couples are welcome and most seem to enjoy the fun.

There are two bar areas. One between the beach and Soi Bangla –known as Karon Strip and the other off Patak Road. There are also several Thai style karaoke bars on the main road at the top of Soi Bangla.

Skylight Bar
British run pub with pool table and satellite TV – live football. Good music and always lively. Just off Patak Road.

Dimensions Bar
Close to Skylight Bar with a similar setting, but not as good.

Dino Park
A small-scale dinosaur theme park, with a cavernous bar and restaurant as well as mini golf. Looks a bit tacky, but seems to attract a reasonable crowd especially at night. Located at the south end of the beach, next to Marina Cottages - golf costs B240 and it's open from 10.00 to 24.00.
☎ 330 625.

Kon Thai Pub
Huge western-style Thai folk pub and restaurant. Live music and good Thai food and seafood and great beer munchies. Mainly Thai clientele.

Rock Café
Is a two-story pub in the plaza in front of Central Waterfront. Some good music, but not much of an atmosphere.

Restaurants

Al Dente B200–400
Italian restaurant in front of Central Waterfront. Not bad but overpriced.

Buffalo Steak House . . . .
. . . . B200–500
Part of the Scandinavian chain offering excellent steaks at reasonable prices. Located in the plaza in front of Central Waterfront.

Curry House B50–100
Popular Thai restaurant specializing in…curries. Small, unpretentious and very good.

Jao Nang B200–400
Offering beautifully prepared Royal Thai cuisine - small portions, but very good - nice ambiance. Located in front of Central Waterfront.

Karon Cafe B100–500
Extensive Thai and western menu and it's all good. Really good steaks, excellent value breakfasts. Probably the best restaurant in Karon - check out the tamarind duck. ☎ 396 217.

Dragonheart B200–400
Chinese and seafood restaurant

KARON BEACH

in front of Central Waterfront. Good food - worth trying.

Old Siam **B300–700**
Impressive restaurant in Thavorn Beach Hotel. Has a "Khantoke" Thai buffet with classical dance 20.00-21.00 every Wednesday and Sunday. Good range of Thai cuisine, very well presented for **B**695 per person.

On The Rock **B120–200**
Wonderful setting at the far south of Karon with views across the beach. Food is really good and the atmosphere is great.
☎ 330 625.

Food Stands
Along the beach there are some excellent food stalls where you can get Thai and Isaan favorites, such as som tam and grilled chicken and kway tiaw (noodle soup).

Karon Viewpoint
At the far north of the beach with great views across the bay. Good menu with Thai and international fare.

Accommodation

Arcadia . . . . **B3,000 up**
One of the original hotel/resorts built in the 70s; now a little rough round the edges but still OK. Nice rooms and facilities, but the building is an eyesore.
☎ 396 038-44, ☏ 396136.

Central Karon Village **B2,500-4,000**
64 luxurious villas designed to fit into a unique "back to nature" atmosphere.
A very original resort overlooking Karon Beach at its northern end. The villas, which are decorated to the highest modern standards with classic Thai fabrics, are equipped with hot and cold showers, air conditioning, mini-bar, and satellite TV and IDD telephone. Each villa has a large balcony which opens out on to the gardens and all are facing the sea, which gives a special sense of space and freedom
There are also two terraced swimming pools featuring a falling water cascade.
☎ 286 300-9, ☏ 286 316, email: ckvpp@samart.co.th

Central Waterfront Suites **B3,000–7,000**
This huge 20-storey tower spoils Karon's skyline, but provides great views for its guests. It has one and two bedroom vacation suites, a pool, tennis courts and a fitness center, as well as a very central location.
☎ 396 498, ☏ 396 793, email:
waterfront@resort-hotels.com

Food in Karon...

Karon, a village atmosphere in some areas.

KARON BEACH

Felix Karon Hotel B1,000–4,000
The low-rise buildings curve around two swimming pools. The resort has 121 rooms and suites with private balconies, some of which are a bit too close to the road, but it is a high quality resort with good facilities and the hotel is deservedly popular with holidaymakers from all over the world.
☎ 396 666, 📠 396 853
email: felix@phuket.com

Karon Beach Resort B2,800–5,000
At the far south of the beach. Nice location as it is one of few resorts that actually fronts on to the beach. All rooms are deluxe and have a seaview.
☎ 330 006, 📠 330529

South Sea Resort B3,000–5,000
Very nice Mediteranian-style resort with 100 rooms and bungalows around a pool. All facilities and amenities. Located on the beach road north of Thavorn Beach. ☎ 396 611-5

Thavorn Palm Beach Resort . . . . $80–$430
The largest complex on Karon and it takes up a huge 20-acre chunk of real estate right in the center of Karon. It boasts 210 rooms, five swimming pools and four restaurants.
☎ 396 090-3

MID RANGE

Karon Silver Resort B500–1,500
Located on Soi Bangla, a clean and comfortable resort with fan and air-con bungalows. Good central location and helpful staff.
☎ 396 185, 📠 396 187.

Karon View B700–1,500
New hotel/guest house on Soi Bangla, very clean with decent rooms with air-con and TV. Good value.

Karon Café B700–1,200
Small guesthouse above the restaurant with nice air-con rooms that are better than most hotels. Satellite TV, fridge and friendly service make it great value if you don't need the trappings of a resort.
☎ 396 217, 📠 396 745,
email: karoncafe@loxinfo.co.th

Marina Cottage . . . . B3,000 to B4,000
Very nice resort in a jungle environment, close to the beach at the Kata end. Beautiful Thai style rooms in green, lush gardens Highly recommended.
☎ 330 493-7, 📠 330 516,
email:

The bays: Kata Noi, Kata and Karon at the back.

KARON BEACH

info@marina-cottage.com
www.marina-cottage.com

Phuket Ocean Resort . . . .
. . . . B1,500–2,500
Sprawling up the hill at the north end of the beach. Good standard hotel with 3 swimming pools and reasonably modern rooms.

P.P. Villa Hotel . . . B600–1,200
On Patak Rd with 22 fan and air-con rooms, some with TV. Good value if you don't mind staying in town. ☎ 396 461, 📠 396 461.

Southland Inn . . . B800–1,200
Just off Patak Road with only eight rooms but clean and well looked after. ☎ 286 131, 📠 396 867.

BUDGET

Happy Inn B200–500
Cheap and cheerful guest house on Soi Bangla.

Anne House B100–400
Cheerful little terrace rooms with fans - just off north Patak Rd, but still close to the beach. A good deal if you are on a budget.

Lume & Yai Bungalow . . . . . .
. . . . B300-500
Up the hill beyond Anne House. Accommodation in small but comfortable huts. ☎ 396 096

My Friend Bungalow . . . .
. . . . B200–500
Basic rooms for rent on Patak Road West.

Practical info

SHOPPING

The main shopping area is on Patak Rd. where all sorts of souvenirs and essentials are available. There is a Kodak shop, supermarket and various other stores.

BANKS AND EXCHANGE

The Siam City Bank is located in front of Central Waterfront and has an ATM. Otherwise there are plenty of exchange facilities on Patak Rd and along the beach road, especially at the south end.

COMMUNICATIONS AND TRAVEL AGENTS

There are a number of Internet outlets on Patak Rd. it costs **B**2 to **B**4 a minute to surf the web. Karon Communications center is located next to Dino Park (open 08.00 to 23.00) and calls to Europe cost **B**46 a minute.

TAXIS

Taxis ply the road all day running between Kata, Karon and Patong or to Phuket town. Private hire taxis hang around by the roundabout on Patak Rd. Fares are negotiable.

KARON BEACH

AUTO & MOTORBIKE RENTAL

There are cars and bikes for rent from Patak Road near the roundabout, but be careful on the conditions and the condition of the vehicle. Otherwise big bikes are available from a shop on Patak Road near the temple. (it has no name but has bike for rent signs and lots of bikes). This is the best place for big bikes and choppers.

Phuket Karon Corner

At Karon Corner Inn, on the roundabout on Patak rd, has plenty of Honda Dreams and Suzuki Caribian Jeeps for rent.
☎ 396 930.

Budget Rent a Car

Has an office in South Sea Resort. A choice of models with full insurance and back up.
☎ 205 396

CLINICS

Santi Clinic close to the roundabout can look after cuts and ailments.

KARON NOI BEACH

Also known as Relax Beach. This white sand crescent beach is the exclusive home of Le Meridien Hotel.

Le Meridien B3,000–20,000

A super luxury resort with excellent facilities (including tennis courts, scuba diving, watersports, gymnasium, squash courts and a spa). The rooms range from swish to fantastic and the service and ambiance exude class. One of the top ten hotels on Phuket.
☎ 340 480-5, 340 479, email: *info@meridien-phuket.com*

Karon Noi...

Le Meridien and its secluded beach.

Kata Beach

KATA BEACH GUIDE

Kata and Kata Noi are two scenic beaches just south of Karon. Kata, the larger of the two, is one of the nicest beaches on the island. It is a small bay, not much more than a kilometer long wrapped in green mountains. Although the beach is public it is dominated by the huge Club Med Resort, which has taken practically all the prime landsite. Kata village runs behind Club Med, with most of the development concentrated at either end of the bay. The cheaper accommodation, bars and many restaurants are located at the north of the bay where Kata spills into Karon. At the southern end of the bay is the elegant Boathouse Hotel and Lobster Square and a host of shops and restaurants catering for a more up-market clientele. Kata has a nice balance, with a fair portion of nightlife places combined with good amenities to go with a relaxed atmosphere, and natural beauty in abundance. It is a refreshing alternative to Patong; ideal for those who don't like everything right in their face, yet with enough going on to keep most people happy. It is more scenic and compact than Karon, and has more of a village atmosphere, some good restaurants and a lively little bar scene Further south is Kata Noi Beach, another beautiful bay, but this time dominated by the five-star Kata Thani Hotel. The beaches are great for families, there is good snorkeling and the water is usually calm.

Beachlife

WATERSPORTS

A range of watersports is available on the beach: Waterski (**B**500); wakeboards (**B**500); bananaboat (**B**300); windsurf (**B**250-300); hobiecats (**B**500-700); jetskis (1/2 hour for **B**700). Surfboards are available for rent from Kata Seasight restaurant at the south end of the beach.

DIVING

Andaman Scuba Venture
Reputable outfit offering courses and liveaboard dive tours.
☎ 331 006, ☎ 330 591, email: andamanscuba@hotmail.com, www.Andamanscuba.com

Calypso
Long established, German run PADI dive center. Good reputation. ☎ 330 869,
email: info@calypso.com

Nautilus Divers
Swiss run dive school with PADI courses and daily dive tours.
☎/☎ 330 174

Scuba Cat
Branch of the Patong based school. ☎ 293 120,
email: bro@scubacat.com

The Dive Center
PADI dive center with full range of courses and daytrips and Similan liveaboard tours. ☎ 330 802,
email: scuba@phuket.com

MASSAGE

Hideaway
A delightful alternative to sitting on the beach is to while a way a few hours in the sauna, steam bath or plunge pool. Friendly and well run and good for your health. Prices are very reasonable with a.massage costing around **B**300 and saunas for **B**100. They also do specialist massages and skin rejuvenation and there is a Thai massage school run by Graham Stapleton. ☎ 342 475.

Nightlife

Kata is not a wild nightlife area, but there are plenty of places to sit and drink. Most of the bars and restaurants are on Thai Na Road. There is

KATA BEACH

the obligatory strip of girlie bars on Patak Road offering all the same services as those in Patong at marginally lower prices. Or at the other end of the scale you can sip fine wines and smoke Cuban cigars at the Boathouse Wine and Grill.

Blue Fin Tavern . . . .
Wonderful bar and Tex-Mex restaurant on Thai Na road. Great place for local information and damn good fajitas

The Frog Club
A friendly little bar with a pool table – a bit of a divers hangout, but not a bad place for a drink.

The Bounty
Pleasant hassle free bar opposite The Boathouse. Has a pool table and is pretty friendly.

3 Fishes
Aussie run bar on Thai Na Road. Pool table and live Aussie rules football.

The Anchor Bar
Hassle free bar on Thai Na Rd. with a pool table. Does a big English breakfast and great fish and chips. A good place to pick up local information.

Restaurants

Gallery Grill B400–600
Superb restaurant with classic Thai and innovative international cuisine and seafood. A bit pricey, but worth pushing the boat out for. ☎ 330 123, email: info@baankata.com

Gung . . . . . .
. . . B200–400
A very trendy (bordering on pretentious) seafood restaurant and wine bar in Lobster square.

Island Restaurant . . . .
. . . . B100–200
Large open fronted international restaurant with barbeque seafood. Never disappointing, but nothing really special.

Flamingo Bar and Restaurant .
. . . . B100–200
Located opposite the Boathouse. This is THE place for pizza. Made in a traditional wood fired pizza oven, they are great. Good atmosphere, but some indifferent live music.

The Boathouse Wine and Grill .
. . . . B300–800
Bills itself as the best restaurant on Phuket and has a pricelist to match. The food is always excellent and the setting (overlooking the beach) is wonderful. An impressive wine list can easily push a meal for two into the several thousands of baht range.
☎ 330 015.

Kompong Kata Hill . B100–200
Garden restaurant on Thai Na Road. Nice setting, but the food is no more than average.

Siri's Kitchen B20–60
One of the best places for cheap and cheerful Thai food. On Patak Road behind Club Med.

Food in Kata...

Originality on Kata's sidewalk.

KATA BEACH

Pizzadelic B100–200
Big brightly colored bar, restaurant and Internet center on Thai Na Rd. Good tunes, tasty pizzas and friendly service – worth a try.

Helvetia Restaurant and Bakery
.... B100-150
Clean and friendly. Good bread and pastries. Located on Thai Na Road.

COOKING SCHOOLS

Gallery Grill Cooking School
☎ 330 123.

Kata Thani Cooking School
☎ 330 914.

Accommodation

FIRST CLASS

The Boathouse Inn ....
.... B5,000–20,000
Exquisite small "boutique hotel" with 36 rooms and suite facing the sea. A superb restaurant, a large pool and fantastic location right on the beach. Everything here is done with style. Very, very nice and very, very expensive. Regular cultural events, including art exhibitions.
☎ 330 557, 📠 330 561, email: *theboathouse@phuket.com*

Kata Thani ... B3,000–12,000
Huge five-star resort that covers most of Kata Noi Beach - 465 rooms and all the facilities you would expect and then some. Four swimming pools, five restaurants, tennis courts, fitness center etc. The rooms are functional rather than luxurious and the hotel lacks the character of some of its rivals. However the location is excellent as Kata Noi is a beautiful quiet bay, while Kata village is easily within range.
☎ 330 124-6, 📠 330 127
e-mail: *katathani@phuket.com*

Club Med
Part of the worldwide chain of "all-inclusive" resorts. Great location covering most of the prime real estate in Kata. Facilities include watersports, tennis courts and a nine-hole golf course. If you like the "Club Med Thing" then this location is hard to beat. ☎ (076) 330 456.

MID RANGE

Peach Hill B1,500–4,000
Located on a hill at the north end of Kata overlooking the beach with 44 rooms and 21 bungalows. Nothing flash, but very comfortable and well run hotel. Nice pool and a quiet, peaceful atmosphere.
☎ 330 603, 📠 330 895.

Pop Cottages ... B800–3,300
On the hill at the south end of Kata beach. A clean and modern hotel with air con rooms, TV etc, and nice pool with views across the beach.
☎ 284 146-7, 📠 330 794,
email: *popcott@loxinfo.co.th*

Full Moon Resort ....
.... B800–2,500
Air-con rooms with TV and fridge above a bar/restaurant. Friendly service but maybe overpriced. At Centerpoint on Patak Rd.
☎/📠 330 980,
email: *fullmoon@phuketdir.com*

Marina Cottage, a small forest by itself.

KATA BEACH

Smile Inn B650–1,200
Central location at the Center point where Patak road runs into Kata. Reasonable quality air-con rooms with TV and fridge.
☎ 330 926, 📠 330 925.

Kata Plaza B500–1,000
Serviced apartments with studios and one bedroom apartments available for daily or monthly rent. ☎ 330 511, 📠 330 513.

Kata Happy House ....
.... B600–1,500
On the back road near the school and temple. Clean air-con rooms available. Shuttle bus to the beach, nice atmosphere.

Kata Delight Villas ....
.... B1,500–3,300
Great location right on the beach at the south of Kata Beach. Rooms are nice, but not great, but the hotel is well run and a very pleasant place to stay.
☎ 330 636, 330 342,
📠 330 481,
e-mail: psg@loxinfo.co.th.

BUDGET

Charlie Guesthouse ....
.... B250-350
Basic but clean rooms on the back road. ☎ 330 085

Cool Breeze B250-750
Big simple fan rooms on Kata Noi beach. ☎ 330 484

Little Mermaid ... B300–1,000
Big bright blue building on Thai Na Road. Has excellent value rooms, clean and well looked after. This is a really good budget option.
☎ 330 730, 📠 330 733.

Kata Guesthouse ..B300–800
Small clean rooms at the southern end of Pak Bang road

The White House Inn ....
.... B500–1,600
Very nice bungalow resort that manages to retain a peaceful garden atmosphere on Patak road right in the heart of Kata. Big air-con rooms are exceptional value.
☎ 330 405, 📠 330 404.

The Center Inn .. B400–1,200
Clean and functional hotel near the central crossroads. Well run and reasonable value although the prices tend to increase dramatically in peak season. ☎/📠 330 631.

Practical info

SHOPPING
Good Earth Book Shop
A great little second hand bookshop full of interesting local information as well as dog-eared best sellers. The place to find out what's new in and around Phuket.

Kata Plaza
Convenience store, souvenir shops, a Kodak shop and tailors shop at Kata plaza.

CARS AND BIKES FOR RENT
Tommy Big Bikes
On Thai Na Road.
☎ 01-891 6826.

Budget
The well known chain have an office at Kata plaza. ☎ 205 396.

Tuk's Bike Shop
Best place to rent bikes, good service and support Located in front of Little Mermaid Guesthouse.

HEALTH AND FITNESS
Dr Chusak's clinic is right opposite Scuba Cat on Thai Na road.
Kata Gym is just off Thai Na Road. It has many free weights and machines - old but in good order. B100 a day to work out.

TAXIS AND BUSES
Buses to Phuket town and Karon and Patong leave from Kata Plaza.

COMMUNICATIONS
The Post Office is located on Patak Road (East). There are Internet offices on Thai Na road and at Kata Plaza.

Lodging on Kata...

87

South Phuket

NUI BEACH

Between Kata and Nai Harn there is a signpost to Nui Beach. If you follow the dirt track for about 2-kilometers you will eventually arrive at a beautiful secluded beach. The road is pretty rough and very steep in parts and best reached by walking. It can be navigated by 4WD or motorbike – but not by tour bus – but you need to be a confident driver. The beach is sheer paradise and there is a restaurant and bar. Food and beverages from outside are not allowed on the beach, but fortunately the food is good and reasonably priced. They can also arrange for a taxi back again later. Worth the effort. Recommended.

NAI HARN BEACH

Nai Harn village is sleepy and clean with blooming bougainvillea and pretty houses; it is no wonder that this is where many of Phuket's expatriate residents choose to live. The palatial Meridien Yacht Club takes up the northern section of the beach and there is a clutch of restaurants and souvenir shops close to its restaurant. Otherwise development on the beach itself has been restricted by the Samnak Song Nai Han monastic order that claims most of the beachfront land. There are beach vendors and sunbeds available on the beach, which is a perfect powdery dune, either side of a large lagoon. The lack of development makes it one of the best spots on the island.

Warning: Swimming is dangerous there in the monsoon season

Le Royal Meridien Phuket Yacht Club . . . . $125 up
Another very classy 5-star hotel on a beautiful beach. Great facilities, top class service and a beautiful setting.
☎ 381 156, 📠 381 164. email: info@phuket-yachtclub.com

Nai Harn Villas $100-140
Luxury holiday homes available for rent. The compound has a

Nui beach, real exclusivity.

SOUTH PHUKET

large swimming pool, ideal for families. Monthly rates are a better deal and start at $750.
☎ 381 959, 📠 381 961,
email: nhvilla@phuket.com

RAWAI

Accommodation

Romsai Bungalows . . . .
. . . . B400–600
Behind the lagoon on the way to Rawai. Standard no-frills bungalows with fans. ☎ 381 338.

Nai Harn Resort . . . .
. . . . B500–1,000
In Nai Harn village on the road to Kata, well back from the beach. Nice big fan and air-con bungalows. Friendly and good value. Recommended.
☎ 381 810.

Yanui Beach Bungalows . . . . .
. . . . B300–800
Beautifully situated in the bay just beyond Nai Harn. Simple huts and a restaurant, a great place to get away from it all. Recommended. ☎ 288 982.

Restaurants

Jintana B30–50
Tasty home cooked Thai food.
Coconut Restaurant . . B50–70
About the best of the restaurants in front of Le Meridien.
Yanui Bungalows . . . B60–150
Regarded as the best Thai food in the area.
Le Meridien . . . . . . B200++
For a guaranteed gourmet treat try any of the restaurants at the Yacht Club.

AO SANE BEACH

A scenic little bay just north of Nai Harn Bay and only accessible by passing through Le Meridien. Very quiet and very beautiful. One of Phuket's best kept secrets.

Accommodation

Jungle Beach Resort . . . .
. . . . B1,500–3,000
Superior class resort with 44 rooms and cottages and a small pool. Rooms have air-con, TV etc. Fantastic location.
☎ 381 108, 📠 381 542.

Ao Sane Bungalows . . . .
. . . . B300–500
A variety of simple beach huts, good value, great location.
☎ 288 306.

The southern beaches...

Nai Harn, still untouched by concrete.

SOUTH PHUKET

Le Meridien Yacht Club, exclusive and bonding to the slope.

RAWAI BEACH

Rawai is just around the Promthep Cape on the south west of the island. The beaches on this side are not nearly as pretty as they are on the west, because they are bordering shallow coral bays. Rawai is no exception, but as it is close to Phuket town it is a popular spot with the locals. The best things about it are the seafood restaurants that line the beach road. Here you can get superb authentic Thai seafood at unbeatable prices. There are also Thai style snack bars with mats on the floor specialising in barbequed meat on sticks and delicious *som tam*: which is all bliss when washed down with a few glasses of Thai whiskey.

Rawai fishing village is at the T-junction at the north end of the beach and is a scruffy collection of vendors and boatmen offering trips to Koh Hae. Big tour buses trundle in and out depositing babbling groups of camera-laden tourists into speedboats for their snorkeling trips. There is a Sea Gypsy village close by, but it is a poorly maintained novelty attraction for the tourists to snap pictures of before their boat trip.

To get to Rawai, take a bus from Phuket town, Kata or Karon for **B**15 or charter a tuk-tuk from Patong (**B**100 to **B**150).

Rawai Beach, more like a fishing village.

SOUTH PHUKET

Bars, Restaurants

Salaloy Restaurant
Excellent seafood restaurant attached to the bungalow resort.

Rimley Seafood
Tremendous seafood carried across the road to tables right on the beach. The sort of place you can just sit and eat all day. Highly recommended.

Food Vendors
Just pick one and take a chance, they are all pretty good.

Nikita Bar
Easy going beach side bar – the only place to drink if you stay in Rawai. Recommended.

Accommodation

Salaloy Bungalows B300–1,000
On Wisit Road across from the beach. Pretty good fan and air-con bungalows. ☎ 381 370.

Siam Phuket Resort B1,300–2,100
Tidy little resort with rooms and bungalows and a pool, which is open to all as long as you buy drinks. Air-con bungalows with TV, telephone, minibar etc. Good value. ☎ 381 346, ✆ 381 347, email: spresort@phuket.ksc.co.th

Phuket Island Resort
The large self-contained resort on Lae Kha, north of Rawai. 290 air-con rooms in a large park with a lake and a private beach. They also have rooms and a restaurant on Koh Bon and run a shuttle boat to the beaches on that island. The hotel is old and fading, but still comfortable.
☎ 381 010-7, ✆ 381 018.

AO CHALONG

This sheltered bay has become a favorite mooring point for visiting yachts and is the jumping off point for tour boats and dive boats heading out to the islands south of Phuket. It is a hive of activity during the day as it is home to a number of boat yards and tour buses come and go. It is a scruffy working set of docks and not a pleasure beach. As the home to wandering yachts it has become a yachties hangout and there are some interesting bars and restaurants in the village behind the pier.

Bars, Restaurants

Don's Barbecue
On Saiyuan Road opposite the mosque. A favorite haunt for res-

Fishermen in Chalong bay.

SOUTH PHUKET

lighthouse. Jimmy's Lighthouse has gained a legendary reputation amongst the seafaring community and is THE meeting place and hangout for anyone interested in boats. The food is great, with an interesting and varied, mainly western menu.
Recommended.

Tang Mo Restaurant and Bar
The scene of many wild parties and exhibitions of excess. This is where visiting yachties look for deep beer bottles and shallow love. Friendly girls and tasty Thai food. On the road leading to the pier.
Recommended.

Poo's Beach Bar
A good snack bar near Chalong Circle. Offers free book loan and has an email service. Occasional live music.

Wandee's Garden & Country
Big garden pub near Chalong Circle with very good Thai food, some western selections and Korean barbeque. Live Rock and folk music.
☎ 280 256.

ident expatriates and visitors in the know. Mouth-watering barbequed ribs and other meats cooked over charcoal, American style. Worth going out of the way for. Recommended.

Kan Eng Seafood
Big semi-open seafood restaurant near the pier. Fast service and good Thai and seafood. Recommended.

Jimmy's Lighthouse
On the seafront under a fake

Accommodation

Father Bungalows
Motel type affair near the pier. Comfortable rooms with air-con and TVs. Helpful and friendly.
☎ 281 282, 🖷 281 283.

Phuket Fishing Lodge
On the.beach next to the pier with beachfront rooms for rent. Clean and convenient.
☎ 281 005, 🖷 281 007.

SOUTH PHUKET

Practical info

POLICE AND IMMIGRATION OFFICES

The Immigration offices are located in the large building next to Jimmy's lighthouse, providing Immigration formalities for yachts arriving from overseas. The large Chalong police station is on Chao Fa Road.

BIKE RENTAL

Bikes can be rented from Marlin bar near the pier.

BOAT SERVICES

There are a number of Palm Sails Canvas work and awnings. On the road to the pier.

SECOND HAND MARINE SUPPLIES

On Visit Rd going towards Rawai.

HOT WAVE

Wetsuit wholesaler near Chalong Circle.

TOURS & BOAT RENTAL

Contact Aloha Tours near the pier for every kind of excursion and private boat charters.
☎ 381 215, ☎ 381 592.

KOH HAE (CORAL ISLAND)

CORAL ISLAND RESORT B1,800–3,300

On Koh Hae or Coral island. Secluded resort with deluxe bungalows surrounding a large pool. Would be a great place to get away from it all if the island wasn't invaded by group tours every day. However there are some nice walks and good snorkeling. The booking office is on Viset Road going towards Rawai.
☎ 281 060, email:
coral_island@phuket.com

CAPE PANWA

At the end of the southwestern tip of Phuket is Cape Panwa. A peaceful and scenic area covered in coconut groves.

Cape Panwa Resort B4,000–11,000

The smart and exclusive 5-star

Cape Panwa, a favorite for local tourists on weekends.

SOUTH PHUKET

resort has a private beach, hilltop swimming pool and all other facilities. It has been the choice of many visiting celebrities including filmmaker Oliver Stone and actor Leonardo DiCaprio.
☎ 391 123, 📠 391 177, email: gmcph@phuket.ksc.co.th

Bay Inn Hotel B2,400–6,600
If your budget doesn't quite stretch to the Panwa resort, but you like its style, the Bay Inn is a little more affordable and almost as good –just less swanky.
☎ 391 5145, 391 208.

MAITON ISLAND

Nine kilometers southeast of Phuket island is a pretty island with one resort complex (on a nice stretch of sand) that caters almost entirely to package tour groups, Japanese in particular.

Maiton Resort . . . .B8,000 up
75 luxury Thai villas on a large sandy beach. Excellent facilities including watersports and diving.
☎ 214954, 📠 214959, email:sminfo@maitonisland.com

RACHA YAI ISLAND

Another idylic island 20 kilometers south of Phuket. Located in deep water, it is famous for scuba diving and game fishing.

Ban Raya B1,000-2,000
22 fan and air-con rooms on a secluded beach. A back to basics retreat with electricity at night only. Comfortable rooms and a good restaurant.
☎ (01) 677 7914,
📠 (076) 274142,
email: banray@phuket.com

Kamala Beach, not long ago the quietest on the island.

North of Patong

PHUKET'S NORTH WEST COAST

KAMALA BEACH

Just 15 minutes north of Patong is the pretty little village of Kamala. Basking in the shade of tall casuarina trees is a 2-kilometer crescent beach with low scale development and a quiet, prosperous village of tidy cottages and bougainvillea. There is only one large-scale resort – the unobtrusive Kamala Bay Resort – and a string of smaller places. For anyone thinking of staying on Phuket for a month or more there are several Thai houses for rent at reasonable prices. This is a wonderful place to base yourself, with a real village atmosphere and conveniently close to Phuket town and the madness of Patong when you need them.

Beachlife

The Beach Club
Watersports center set up by Kamala Bay terrace.

Scuba Quest
Friendly dive company that has Kamala Bay pretty well sewn up. Offers reasonably priced courses and dive tours and has a good liveaboard boat. ☎ 271 113, email: kamala@phuket.ksc.co.th

Bars, Restaurants

Paul's Place B200-400
Beautifully located on the southern headland on the way to Kamala Bay Terrace. A classy restaurant with great views and exotic eastern and western offerings.

Kamala Beach Pavilion B60-150
At the southern end of the village and right on the seafront. Good Thai food, seafood and cocktails.

Bank's bar
A friendly little pub next to Kamala Beach Pavilion. Also has food.

Kamala seafood B60-150
Right on the seafront. Pretty good Thai food and seafood barbeques.

Nanok Seafood B30-60
Pretty little restaurant at the north of the beach. Great place to sit and eat simple Thai food.

Mamas and Papas . . B30-100
At the far north of the beach down a dirt track. Basic Thai beach restaurant. They have sunbeds and keep that end of the beach tidy. A quiet place to spend the day.

Mama Farang B50-150
Breakfasts and bakery on the main road behind the village.

Café Java B100-300
Big, bright Mediterranean style café with satellite TV and occasional live music.

Accommodation

Kamala Bay Terrace B2,000–5,000
4-star resort located on the sloping hills at the far south of the bay. 123 rooms and Thai style bungalows, large pool and fitness center. The beach is rough coral and not ideal so guests are shuttled to the beach club further up the shore. Well run and very comfortable.
☎ 270 801, ☎ 270 818, email: aoy@kamala.co.th

Nanok B300–1,000
At the north of the village with some very nice rooms for rent.

Phuket Kamala Resort B1,500–2,500
At center of the beach with 30 air-con rooms and a swimming pool. Lacks character but comfortable enough. ☎ 324 396.

PHUKET WEST COAST

Laem Sin, no more the secret beach of Phuket.

Malenee House
Rooms and houses available for rent all over the village.
☎ 271 365.

Bird Beach B400–600
Small cottages on the beach close to Bank's Bar. ☎ 270 669.

There are always several "rooms for rent" signs up around the village and these often prove to be the best deals. Just enquire where you see a sign.

Practical info

There are bikes available for rent from Malenee House and a minimart and several laundries close to Bank's Bar. Otherwise there are some shops on the main road.

LAEM SINGH BEACH

A beautiful secluded cove between Kamala and Surin. It is well signposted and can be reached by following a footpath down to the beach. There are a couple of basic restaurants and sunbeds for rent, but nothing else. During high season bus loads of Asian tourists arrive for an hour or so, but if you come early in the morning you invariably get the beach to yourself.

SURIN BEACH

Surin beach has always been popular with the locals and the Thai Royal family have been coming here since Rama VII visited in 1928. There is very little tourist development and it really feels like a Thai beach, with food vendors and small restaurants stretched out beneath the shady casuarina trees. Unlike most of Phuket's beaches, Surin Beach has a steep sand shelf, making it less suitable for swimming. Big waves are common on Surin beach during the monsoon season and can create dangerous undertow conditions. The waves during this time attract serious surfers, in spite of the dangers.

Restaurants

Hui Xain Thai Restaurant B100–200
Clean and tidy Thai restaurant and wine bar occupying one of the new shophouses close to the

PHUKET WEST COAST

Toto Italian restaurant B100-300
Excellent Italian food in a nice garden setting, rated as one of the best Italian restaurants on Phuket and a very pleasant place to spend the evening. On the road leading to the Chedi Resort. Recommended.

Gecko Bar and Restaurant B100–200
Small bar near Toto's. Clean and friendly and drinks are a lot cheaper than the big resorts nearby.

Food Vendors
All along Surin Beach are small Thai restaurants and food vendors. You can have a delicious seafood meal for B100 per person as long as you don't mind sitting on plastic seats. Recommended.

Accommodation

Pen Villa B2,500–5,000
This is a very nice family run resort with 15 excellent air-con rooms. There is a swimming pool and some family rooms. Recommended for those seeking a relaxed ambiance. Located a kilometer inland from Surin Beach. ☎ 271 100.

Surin Sweet Apartment B600–800
Despite the dreary external appearance there are 30 clean and comfortable rooms with air-con and TV, plus a small swimming pool.
☎ 270 863.

Sabai Guesthouse . B400–800
Simple modern rooms for rent.
☎ 231 146-7.

Practical info

There is a tourist information office and police box in the car park behind the beach and a minimart close to Toto's with motorbikes available for rent and a taxi service.

PANSEA BEACH

The northern extremity of Surin beach has been renamed "Pansea Beach" by the developers of the super luxury resorts that have made it their private domain.

Indisputably one of the most beautiful spots on the island, the only way you can spend any time here is by checking into one of the two most exclusive resorts in Phuket.

Smaller beaches...

Surin beach, usually quiet on week days.

PHUKET WEST COAST

Accommodation

Amanpuri Resort . . . .
. . . . .US$400–6,000
This is the choice of those for whom money is not an issue. Where the very rich and often famous come to seek privacy and high class pampering. Accommodation is in private pavilions and palatial villas, complete with a personal swimming pool, cooks and butlers.
☎ 324 333, 📠 324 100,
email: amanpuri@phuket.com,
www.amanpuri.com

The Chedi . . . . .US$160–520
A visual treat, this 110 room resort is an exotic blend of Balinese and Thai architecture fronting Pansea beach. The facilities and service are exceptionally good and the rooms are the height of luxury, full of thoughtful little touches, such as telephones on the balcony.
☎ 324 017/20, 📠 324 252.

BANG TAO BEACH

North of Surin is a majestic 8-kilometer beach of white sands, which is home to the Laguna Phuket complex. A unique hotel development built around disused tin mines that have been flooded and turned into a series of coastal lagoons. This combination of five hotel resorts and a golf course occupies the northern section of Bang Tao and there are several shops, restaurants and other businesses scattered around the area aiming to feed off the five star clientele. Otherwise the southern part of Bang Tao bordering Surin village is very quiet and undeveloped. Muslim fishermen still mend their nets in shacks on the beach and a large Mosque dominates the pretty village. There are still one or two more reasonably priced resorts enjoying a piece of the beach, but very little else going on here. The Laguna complex was cleverly designed to remain as unobtrusive as possible and its presence is undoubtedly the reason that the roads are so good and the whole area is spotlessly clean.

Restaurants

The Ruen Thai – Dusit Hotel . .
. . . . B250–350
Excellent Thai cuisine served in an old teak house beside one of the lagoons.

The Saffron @ Banyan Tree Hotel B300–500
Superb food from all over Southeast Asia; Vietnamese, Indonesian and Sri Lankan as well as Thai. The curries are superb and the décor exquisite.

Tatonka Café B200–300
An innovative restaurant close to the Laguna complex serving Asian and international cuisine.

Toto's B100–300
Another branch of the excellent Italian restaurant. Delicious pasta and very good value.

Lanna restaurant . . B150–250

NUAD PAEN BORAN

Ancient or traditional Thai massage is based on the concept that invisible energy lines run through the body - 10 important sen or lines have been identified which are concentrated on as acupressure points. Applying pressure to these points, which act as windows to the body, enables the exchange of cosmic energy through which the body maintains its energy balance with the energy of the universe. Congestions or disturbance of these flows can lead to sickness and working on the energy lines through massage can help break these blockages and stimulate the free flow of prama, restoring well-being.

PHUKET WEST COAST

Classy Thai restaurant located close to the entrance of the Laguna Complex. Not as expensive as the hotel restaurants, but just as good – if not better.

Sasha's Barbeque and Grill
Opposite the Hideaway Spa. Excellent evening barbeques should be tried at least once.

Beach restaurants
South of the Laguna complex are a number of beach restaurants serving good 'honest' Thai food at a fraction of hotel rates.

Accommodation

Bang Tao Beach Cottage
Seven beautiful cottages at the southern entrance to Bang Tao Beach. Beautifully designed with patios and small gardens.
☎ 271 167,
email: pattkhor@hotmail.com

Bang Tao Laguna B1,800
Established 18 years ago as the first resort on Bang Tao Beach. Very well-run and friendly with many regular guests. 60 bungalows ranging from fan to air-con, some with fridge and hot water. All in lots of space and only separated from a large empty beach by casuarina trees. ☎ 324 260.

Phuket Laguna Complex
These five luxury hotels are all managed separately but guests are allowed to enjoy the amenities of all the others. For example you can sign for a meal in any one of the 24 restaurants. All the resorts are up-market hotels, very professionally managed with high service standards. The Allamanda is the smallest and least expensive and is more family oriented, offering a kids club and babysitting services. The Laguna Beach resort aims at sport and leisure with a water park and watersports as well as tennis, squash and badminton courts.

The Dusit is very chic, combing luxury with tasteful Thai interior design at reasonable prices. A new spa has just been added offering a wide range of not-too-expensive services. The Sheraton is a huge 323 room complex surrounding one of the lagoons, with a business center, conference facilities and suites with private jetties. The Banyan tree is the most luxurious of the lot, with a super spa facility and a level of indulgence only surpassed by The Amanpuri.

Laguna world...

Laguna. The Sheraton on-the-lake.

PHUKET WEST COAST

An area built on old tin mines. Now tourism 'a la carte'

The Allamanda . . . .
. . . . **฿2,800–5,600**
☎ 324 359, 📠 324 360.
e-mail:
allamanda@lagunaphuket.com

Dusit Laguna . . . . . **฿4,000+**
☎ 324 320, 📠 324 174,
email: yaowaluck@dusit.com

The Sheraton Grande Laguna Beach . . . . **฿5,000+**
☎ 324 101-7, 📠 324 108,
email: Sheraton@samart.co.th

Laguna Beach Club . . . .
. . . . **฿5,000+**
☎ 324 352, 📠 324 353.
Reservations ☎ (66-76) 270 993
e-mail:
rsvn@lagunabeach-resort.com

The Banyan Tree . . .**US$400+**
☎ 324 374, 📠 324 375.
Fax to Spa: (66-76) 271 463.
e-mail:
banyantree@lagunaphuket.com

Practical info

Hideaway Spa
A much cheaper alternative to the expensive hotel spas is this Bang Tao branch of the popular Phuket Spa chain. Excellent sauna and massages for under ฿1,000.
☎ 271 549, 📠 342 553,
e-mail:
info@phuket-hideaway.com

The Lakeside. Village fit for foreign tourists.

PHUKET WEST COAST

Canal Village
Over 40 shops affiliated to the Phuket Laguna Group. Lots of reproduction handicrafts, silks – including a branch of Jim Thompson's, and other high quality souvenirs. You won't find many bargains, but everything is high quality. ☎ 324 453-7 ☎ 324 065.

Jungle Gym and Fitness
Fitness center located in the row of shophouses before the entrance to the Laguna complex.

H2O Sports Divers
5 star dive shop located next to Jungle Gym. ☎ 270 562.

Quest
Outdoor training center with a climbing wall specialises in team-building and other corporate training programmes.
☎ 324 062-3, ☎ 324 058, email: quest@lagunaphuket.com

National Car Rent
Cars for rent with full insurance. Next to H2O divers.

NAI THON BEACH

A 1-kilometer crescent beach In the remote north-west of the island between Bang Tao and Nai Yang bays. Flanked at either end by rocky headlands, a road runs the length of the beach with a few quiet bungalow resorts offering rooms for rent. It is a great beach for swimming and there is some snorkeling at either end of the bay.

The area is very green with pandanus, cashew and rubber trees among the casuarinas and coconut palms.

Laguna world...

Accommodation

Naithon Beach Resort B800–1,500
The main resort in Nai Thon only has 14 wooden chalets. Well constructed and comfortable enough with fan or air-con. Located opposite the beach at the southern end of the bay.
☎ 205 379, 214 954.

Phuket Naithon Resort B500–1,000
Offers concrete bungalows of various sizes facing the beach.

Nai Thon Bay, very secluded indeed, away from any road.

PHUKET WEST COAST

NAI YANG BEACH

Nai Yang. literally translates as "in the rubber" and the roads leading to this scenic beach are lined with rubber plantations. The northern section of the beach has been declared a national park due to its important and diverse flora, including coastal mangrove forests.

The southern section is occupied by a number of mid range resorts and the whole beach is a favorite spot for Thai daytrippers who come to enjoy the clean air and swim in the protected waters.

There are great clutches of food vendors and a string of small restaurants giving Nai Yang a vibrant atmosphere. Obviously not as tranquil as some of the quieter bays.

Accommodation

Pearl Village .. B2,500–3,000
Large resort at the south of Nai Yang. Air-con bungalows and cottages, swimming pool, good watersports facilities.
☎ 327 006, ☎ 327 338.

Crown Nai Yang Suite . . . . . .
. . . . B1,500–3,500
Big unattractive hotel resort next to Pearl Village. ☎ 317 420.

Garden Cottage . . . .
. . . . B500–1,500
On the road leading to the beach. 14 spotless rooms with fan or air-con, fridge, hot water. Well run, friendly with a good restaurant. Recommended.
☎ 327 293.

Nai Yang House .. B400–800
Opposite the temple. Nine fan and air-con rooms. Clean and good value.

National Park Bungalows . . . .
. . . . B400
12 large simple wooden bungalows are available for rent in the grounds of the National Park.
☎ 327 407.

Nai Yang, the beach under the casuarina trees.

Koh Phi Phi

PHI PHI ISLANDS

The Phi Phi islands were once voted the third most beautiful island group in the world and for our money they are the most beautiful places in Thailand. Phi Phi Don and Phi Phi Leh are two large rocky islands in the deep waters of the Andaman Sea, about 50-kilometers southwest of Krabi town. Phi Phi Don is the better known and consists of two amazing limestone mountains connected by a double-sided white sand beach – it is also where all the accommodation is. Phi Phi Leh is a huge monolith south of Phi Phi Don and is uninhabited apart from a few Sea Gypsy settlements. It is home to beautiful Maya Bay, which has recently gained international fame as the location for the movie "The Beach". The Phi Phi islands are part of the Haad Noppharthara/Koh Phi Phi National Marine Park, but its jurisdiction is difficult to describe and authority is inconspicuous - to say the least. Phi Phi Don has become horribly overdeveloped in parts, but its awesome natural beauty is sufficiently strong to allow it to remain one of Thailand's most popular beach destinations. Phi Phi Leh is left to the bird's nest collectors and only day-trippers are allowed to visit beautiful Maya Bay.

PHI PHI DON

The larger of the islands really is a fantastic and unique place. The two beaches that connect the awesome cliffs are blessed with powdery white sands and the waters that surround the island are crystal clear. Such beauty cannot go unnoticed and Phi Phi Don is seriously in demand as a tourist destination. The land in between the two large bays is where most of the development has gone on over the years and it has been done at break neck speed. Legal land ownership ambiguities arising from the island's supposed status as a national park and as a home for the nomadic Sea Gypsies have meant that much of the construction has also been done outside the law. The end result is that the western end of Ton Sai Bay has become a ramshackle shantytown of half built guesthouses and businesses all piled on top of each other in an ugly heap. Waste collection is disorganised and inept and open rubbish piles are everywhere. In contrast, the eastern end is home mostly to upscale resorts and is much cleaner and tidier. Ton Sai Bay is where the boats from Krabi and Phuket dock and a pier stretches out into the bay. The beach is usually clogged with longtail boats waiting to take tourists on all kinds of tours. Loh Dalam Bay is where everyone does his or her beach thing and consequently is very busy, especially during the high season. However even when it is jam-packed with sun worshippers there is no denying it: Loh Dalam is an exceptionally beautiful bay. Phi Phi Don has long been home to a "travelers scene" and most of the inhabitants of Phi Phi's shantytown are young backpackers who enjoy the island's compact and noisy nightlife far more than its natural beauty – goatee beards and body piercing are *de rigueur* on Phi Phi. The outer rim of the island has a number of scenic bays that can only be reached by boat. They are much quieter and more exclusive than Ao Tong Sai.

GETTING TO AND FROM PHI PHI

If you are travelling to Phi Phi from anywhere outside the region you will come via Phuket or Krabi. The easiest way to get there is by plane or bus to Krabi and then take the boat from Krabi town. You can go via Phuket, but this requires longer additional journeys from Phuket airport or town to the boat. Traveling during the monsoon season (June to September) can be risky and boats

PHI PHI ISLANDS

BIRDS NEST SOUP

The Chinese dish of bird's nest soup is considered such a delicacy that people will pay dearly for the tiny swift's nests that constitute its main ingredient. It is a popular western misconception that the soup is made with unpalatable twigs and feathers. The *Aerodrames fuciphagus*, the white nest swiftlet, and *Aerodremus maximus*, black nest swiftlet, discharge a viscous solution from two glands beneath their beaks and carefully build nests as it dries on contact with the air. These birds spend most of their lives in caves and can fly in the dark, using a sophisticated natural method of navigation. They also make their nests in caves and tunnels, often high up out of reach of any predators. Collecting this vital ingredient for such a popular soup is often a dangerous and difficult task. Special climbers risk their lives scaling the cliffs using bamboo ladders and ropes to reach the inaccessible nests.

As the nests are rare and difficult to collect they command very high prices. A kilo can go for U$2,000 in Bangkok and twice that in the markets of Hong Kong. Given the value of this "white gold" it is not surprising that the right to gather them is highly sought after and extremely lucrative. Concessions are awarded by the government to the highest bidder – in practice this usually means the most influential bidder – and are protected by heavily armed guards.

As the prime bird nest sites are in the tourist areas of Phang Nga Bay and Phi Phi there are inevitably conflicts of interest between the concession holders - who prohibit entry to their caves - and the tour operators – who would like to take tourists into the caves. An uneasy peace usually exists between the two sides with the collectors allowing operators access to some of the sea hongs in Phang Nga Bay. However last year a dispute involving one of Phuket's Sea Canoe operators ended with a near fatal shooting and limits being put on the number of visitors allowed into the caves.

to Phi Phi have been known to sink (how do you think the King Cruiser wreck got there). Schedules are dependent on the weather, but boats will run when they really should not, so exercise extreme caution if you want to experience Phi Phi in low season. It should be noted that the boats from Phuket are bigger and more stable.

Express boats to Krabi town; 09.00, 13.00, 14.15. 1 hour 20 minute journey; cost **B**150.
From Krabi town; 10.00, 11.00, 14.30, 16.00, **B**150.
Express boats to Ao Nang and Railey; 15.30, 1 hour 30 minute journey; costs **B**250.
From Ao Nang/Railey 09.00, **B**250.
Express boats to Koh Lanta; 09.30, 11.30, 14.00, 1 hour 30 minutes; costs **B**180.
From Koh Lanta; 08.00, 13.00; costs **B**170.
Express boat to Phuket; 09.00, 14.30, 1 hour 30 minute journey; costs **B**250.
Jet cruise to Phuket; 15.00, 40-minute journey; costs **B**450.

GETTING AROUND

There are no roads on Phi Phi so if you want to go to the outside beaches or Phi Phi Leh you take a longtail boat. Longtails are everywhere on the island and you can rent one for the day (**B**1,000) or as a taxi (**B**20 to **B**50 per trip).

Beachlife

Loh Dalam Beach has an enclosed area for swimmers outside Phi Phi Princess Resort. This is the best area for sunbathing, there is a volleyball net and although it is a busy beach people don't seem to mind. In fact

PHI PHI ISLANDS

for most of the beautiful young crowd, the busier the better.

Micro bikinis and lithe tanned bodies easily outnumber the rest here. Deckchairs are available for **B**30 a day.

DIVING

There are about 12 dive operations on Phi Phi, most of them offer the same PADI courses and trips to the local dive sites. Phi Phi is perfectly positioned to make most of the best dive sites in the south Andaman Sea reachable on day-trips.

There are some good standard, experienced operators making it an ideal place for divers. Open water courses cost around **B**9,000 and 2 local dives around **B**1,800. Some companies offer speedboat trips to Hin Daeng including 3 dives for **B**6,000. Prices are fixed everywhere.

Moskito Diving
Experienced operator and dive center. They now have a new liveaboard boat and run trips to the Similans at reasonable rates ($640 for a one week trip) and Hin Daeng as well as to the local sites. Located behind Mama restaurant, opposite the post office. ☎ (01) 229 1361, ☎ (076) 217106

Barakuda Dive Center
A well-established school with a good reputation and a decent dive boat. Located on t main street.
☎/☎ (075) 620 698, email: dive@barakuda.com, www.barakuda.com.

PKK Diving
Located on the main street. A friendly operation with good equipment and a solid boat.
☎ (01) 229 2711, (01) 230 3138.

Sea Frog
Reputable company on the main street. PADI and NAUI courses. email: seafrog@psscomm.co.th

GAME FISHING

There are now some specialised operators with all the equipment offering game fishing trips around Phi Phi. The deep waters are ideal for game fish; especially sail fish, which are in season from September to December. Shops in Phi Phi DO NOT practice catch-and-release, claiming that they do not affect the game fish population nearly as much as local fishermen.

Beach activities...

Maya beach life, less secluded now, but cleaner.

PHI PHI ISLANDS

Big Game Fishing
On the main street offers trips by longtail boat (B1,800), fishing boat (B3,000) or speed boat (B5,000) including equipment and lunch.

KAYAKING
Phi Phi viewpoint rents out kayaks for B400 for eight hours or B100 per hour. Great way to visit deserted bays. Phi Phi Watersports has higher quality ones for B250/hour and B1,250 for eight hours. Sunset kayak tours are available for B600 (3 hour paddle) from any travel agent.

PARASAILING, WATERSKIING, BANANA BOAT
All available on Loh Dalam Beach for B500 a go.

SNORKELING AND BOATS FOR RENT
Round-the-island snorkeling day trips start at about B300 per person including equipment and lunch. Equipment is widely available if you want to go it alone. Longtail boats charge B600 for half a day and B1,000 for a whole day. Boats are available all over the island, especially by the pier.

ISLAND TOURS
All travel agents and most longtail boat owners offer day trips to nearby islands and beaches. Trips to the Viking Cave and Maya Bay ("The Beach") on Phi Phi Leh are the most popular and cost B200 to B300 per person.

Trips to Bamboo island and Mosquito Island are also pretty good as the islands really are beautiful, but you may have to share them with a couple of hundred East Asian package tourists.

WINDSURFING
Phi Phi Princess Watersports rents boards out for B250 per hour, B850 per half day and B1,250 per full day. Hobie cats and dinghies start at B300 per hour.

Nightlife

The ghetto of Phi Phi Don may be scruffy and unappealing during the day but at night it comes into its own and seems to transform itself into a brightly lit eating and drinking circus. Young travelers work as touts to entice the wandering crowds into the bars, and noodle shops sprout out of nowhere. Everywhere there are shops and restaurants all illuminated by blinding strip lights that hang precariously from electrical cables.

The bars blast rock, reggae and dance tunes out onto the streets to combine with the Thai pop melodies supplied by the food hawkers. Somehow it all seems to work to the delight of the young crowds that flock to Phi Phi searching for a good time in paradise.

<u>BARS</u>
Apache Bar
Big bar that staggers up the hill above the main street before it gets to P.P. Don Resort. Satellite TV (including live football) and fire shows on the beach are the specials here.

Carlito's Way
The bar with the attitude is locat-

PHI PHI ISLANDS

ed on the main street just past Chao Koh Resort.

Fatty's Inn
Nice looking bar between Tin Tin's and the Reggae Pub offering food and drink.

The Reggae Pub
The biggest and busiest bar in town. An open-air affair with a boxing ring that stages nightly Muay Thai bouts. The music is rock and reggae and the bar desperately needs a face-lift, but it is still always lively.

Rolling Stone
A scruffy bar full of hammocks and friendly bar staff. The scene of many tequila drinking sessions and drunken nights. A good place to meet fellow party animals.

Tin Tin Bar
Located down a dirty side street off the main street. This lively little bar is as close to a nightclub as there is in Phi Phi. Open until 04.00-ish and always very, very loud. Happy hour from 20.00 to 22.00 every night and often has free tequila nights - Thai tequila is basically raw alcohol.

Restaurants

Charlie Restaurant . . B50-200
In front of Charlie Resort is a great spot for lunch with a big open-air restaurant shaded by a big net. It is a real hangout and a perfect place to spot perfect (and not so perfect) bodies. The food is pretty good too.

Ciao Restaurant . . . B150-200
Italian restaurant right on Loh Dalam beach. A cool place to relax and eat pizzas. Pretty good food too.

P.P. Princess B200-300
A good restaurant right on Loh Dalam beach. Little bit pricey but a great spot.

Thai Cuisine B100-150
Good curries and tom yam. Located on the main street.

Pee Pee Bakery B50-150
Good place for breakfast. Tasty pastries and quick service. Has BBC world service on TV all day.

Mamas B100-200
Still one of the best places for Thai food and seafood. Good location on the main street.

Amico B150-250
Small Italian place opposite Pee Pee Hotel. Nice atmosphere and good food. Worth a visit.

Le Grand Bleu . . . B200-250
Small French restaurant near Pee Pee Hotel. Great 'moules marinière' and a friendly atmosphere.

Patcharee Bakery . . B100-150
Another good breakfast option. Tasty sandwiches and friendly service, located on the main street.

Ton Sai Seafood . . B150-250
Large seafood restaurant on the main street. Probably the best place for shark and mackerel steaks. Worth checking out.

Garlic House B100-150
Thai and Chinese food specially crafted to suit European tastes. Surprisingly good and always busy. Located near the Reggae Bar.

Captain Unico B100-200
Good Italian restaurant located near Rolling Stone Bar.

Vasana Seafood B50-150
Very good value Thai and seafood in a pretty basic but clean restaurant.

Took Barbecue B20-100
For great Isaan foods try this small restaurant just past Carlito's Way, they have an upstairs seating area and do a mean *som tam* and barbecued everything.

Viking Seafood B100-200
A busy little seafood restaurant near the Reggae Pub. Always busy, which is a good advertisement for seafood.

Lemongrass B50-100
Plain but good and honest Thai food.

Eating on Phi Phi...

PHI PHI ISLANDS

Food vendors
There are dozens of noodle shops and other street vendors all around the town. The phad thai next to the reggae bar is excellent, the khao gaeng (curry on rice) in the market is also very good, but if you are worried about hygiene give it a miss.

Accommodation

BUDGET
There are dozens of small guesthouses in the shantytown on Ton Sai and they provide the bulk of budget accommodation available on Phi Phi. During high season it is likely that this will be all that is available. Most of the rooms are partitioned spaces above a shop or restaurant and have very limited privacy. Some have showers attached but most share facilities. Prices range from B200 to B600 depending on the season and you will just have to wander around and see what is available.

Rim Na Villa Bungalow . . . . . .
. . . . B500–700
Big bungalows raised on stilts, in the middle but set back from the town with views across a water treatment plant. Pretty good value for Phi Phi. ☎ (01) 229 2520, 📠 (01) 229 2846.

Chao Koh Phi Phi Lodge . . . .
. . . . B400–700
Collection of small wooden bungalows right on the main strip. Very noisy at night and indifferent staff, but better than the guesthouses. ☎ (075) 611 313.

Chong Khao Bungalows
B300–900
Without doubt the best budget option on Phi Phi. They will not take bookings so you have to show up and take your chances. A range of fan bungalows of various sizes are available. Located at the far west end of Ton Sai in a large and shady garden that borders the mountain. The management is helpful and friendly and you feel as far from the madhouse as it is possible on Phi Phi. Recommended.

Lek's House . . . . B300+
One of the better guesthouses in the heart of town.

Orchid House . . . . . . B200+
One of the friendlier guesthouses. Small rooms, but cleaner than some others.

Phi Phi Don Resort . . . .
. . . . B500–1,500
Located at the east end of Thong Sai with small box-like bungalows near the beach. Very noisy due to the amount of longtails coming and going.
☎ (01) 228 4252,
📠 (01) 397 1038.

MID RANGE
Charlie Beach Resort . . . .
. . . . B600–1,000
Located in the middle of Loh Dalam Bay with 75 rooms and bungalows in a coconut grove. All the rooms are the same; you pay more to be near the beach. The rooms are clean but nothing special, yet the resort is well-run and friendly and still one of the best places to stay on Phi Phi. ☎ (076) 210 928, 📠 (076) 217 106. Recommended.

Tara Inn B500-1000
Located in the heart of town with large fan and air-con bungalows and rooms. Not a bad deal if you can stand the noise at night.
☎ (01) 476 4830,

PHI PHI ISLANDS

☎ (01) 907 3257,
email: patim41@hotmail.com

**Andaman Beach Resort . . . . .
. . . . B750–1,600**
Located towards the east end of Thong Sai Bay away from the sounds of the town, but still in range of the noisy longtail boats. Large fan and air-con bungalows and a pleasant section of beach, make this a pretty good option. ☎/📠 (075) 621 427.

**Pee Pee Viewpoint resort . . . .
. . . . B800–1,800**
Perched up on the hill above Loh Dalam Bay, this old but still nice resort stands aloof from the circus below. Reasonable value (for Phi Phi) fan and air-con rooms and one of the few quiet and secluded resorts on the island. Recommended.
☎/📠 (01) 477 6947,
☎ (075) 622 351.

**Phi Phi Pavilion Resort . . . . . .
. . . . B1,500–2,000**
Very well designed bungalow resort right in the heart of Loh Dalam Beach. 50 deluxe fan and air-con bungalows in a coconut grove. A little bit expensive but really very comfortable and nice to look at. Recommended.
☎ (075) 611 295,
📠 (075) 611 578.

**Phi Phi Hotel . . . .
. . . . B1,800–3,400**
Big multi-storey hotel on Ton Sai Bay near the pier that caters mostly for package tourists. Rooms are OK (air-con, TV etc) and some have great views, but it's a shame that the hotel building spoils everyone else's view.

**Tone Sai Village .
. . . . B1,800**
At the far west end of Ton Sai bay and owned by Phi Phi Island Cabana. A quiet and well-designed resort with 30 deluxe wooden air-con bungalows (TV, IDD etc) and friendly staff.
☎ (075) 620 634,
📠 (075) 612 132.

FIRST CLASS

**PP Princess Resort . . . .
. . . . B1,600–12,000**
Lovely deluxe bungalows with big decks and full of nice interior touches in a garden right in the heart of Loh Dalam Bay. If you can afford it this is the place to stay on Phi Phi.
☎ (075) 612 188, (01) 723 0504, 📠 (075) 620 615.

**Phi Phi Island Cabana Hotel . .
. . . . B1,800–10,000**
One of the oldest resorts on the island and now the most luxurious on Ton Sai Bay. It sits in huge grounds that cover most of the west side of the island and has a large pool, tennis courts and other facilities. Rooms are in the main building or deluxe bungalows. ☎ (075) 612 594-6.

Lodging on Phi Phi...

PHI PHI ISLANDS

OUTER BEACHES

All the outside beaches can only be reached by boat and are much more peaceful than the Inner island.

HAADAO

Lovely long sandy beach with clear waters, only a short boat ride from the entertainment on Tong Sai.

PP Long Beach . . . B300–600
At the east end of the beach with bungalows sprawling up the hill into the forest. In need of refurbishment, but not bad value.

Pee Paradise Pearl Resort B400–1,000
Wide range of clean new fan cooled bungalows spread along the mid section of the beach. Friendly staff and a good restaurant. ☎ (01) 723 0484, 📠 (01) 228 4370.

LOH BAKAO

Beautiful secluded beach with just one resort.

Pee Pee Island Village B800–3,000
A range of fan and air-con bungalows in a well run resort that nestles into its landscape snugly. Good restaurant and helpful staff can help organise trips to the inner island. ☎ (01) 211 1907.

LAEM TRONG

This is another secluded and beautiful beach that runs along the northern cape. Previously home to only a handful of Sea Gypsies, it is now inhabited by upmarket resorts. There is a pier and the hotels whisk most guests in without them ever setting foot on Ton Sai Bay.

Phi Phi Palm Beach B4,000–20,000
A very nice luxury resort separated from the other places by a Sea Gypsy village. Beautifully landscaped gardens with a big pool and deluxe cottages with all the facilities you would expect. For isolation and sheer extravagance this is hard to beat.
☎ (01) 723 0052.

PP Coral Resort B1,600–2,400
Large wooden air-con cottages right on the beach. A bit expensive for what you get, but still nice. ☎ (01) 214 056, 📠 (01) 215 455.

PP Natural Resort B2,000–3,500
At the north of the beach with nice views of the cape. Very comfortable cottages scattered around the beach and headland. ☎/📠 (01) 723 1250.

Practical info

SHOPPING

There are tons of souvenir shops all through Tong Sai, but don't expect any bargains. There are also several minimarts. Chao Koh minimart is open 24 hours.

PHI PHI ISLANDS

HEALTH

PP Hospital
Located just before Phi Phi Island Cabana on Ton Sai bay and is OK for superficial injuries and VD. For anything else you will have to go to Phuket.
☎ (075) 622 151.

BANKS

Krung Thai Bank
Right in the middle of the town changes travelers cheques and cash and does visa advances. There are no ATMs on the island.

COMMUNICATIONS
The Post Office is just off the main street and has EMS and poste restante services. Telephone calls can be made from any travel agent and there are literally hundreds of Internet outlets.

PHI PHI LEH

This craggy limestone island just south of Phi Phi Don is uninhabited as it is a prime bird's nest collection site. It has recently shot to prominence, as it was the primary location for the filming of the movie "The Beach".

MAYA BAY
Maya Bay beach is "The Beach" and is a popular spot with day-trippers and visiting yachts. It is a nice (although not better than many others in the area) sandy beach in a deep craggy limestone bay. It is the scenery of the bay that impresses most and Maya is a great place to spend a day on the beach. Snorkeling is excellent and no rogue sharks have been seen there. Expect more and more visitors as the movie has been released and the aerial shots of the island will not be left unnoticed.

VIKING CAVE
A cave on the northern rim of the island contains drawings of ships that some say are Portuguese Traders, but are more likely to be Asian junks. Somehow the cave got named after the Vikings, who almost certainly never got this far east. A popular stop on day trips and worth a look if you are heading round to Maya Bay.

Maya Bay -Crystal clear waters and a snorkeling favorite.

Phangnga Bay

Phang Nga (or Phangnga) Bay is one of Asia's greatest natural wonders. Powerful geological forces working over millions of years have created a shallow sheltered bay in the Andaman Sea full of steep sided sculptured limestone islands that rise dramatically out of the emerald waters.

Due to its close proximity to Phuket, Phang Nga Bay has become one of Thailand's most spectacular tourist attractions. The charms of Koh Tapu - Nail Island - better known as James Bond Island and the Muslim fishing village on Koh Panyi are well known and they receive hundreds of visitors every day. These sites and the fantastic limestone formations and cliffs that make the bay so extraordinary are mostly concentrated in its northern waters and this 400 square kilometer area has been declared a national park. Many of the islands are geological anomalies and all manner of strange shapes and sizes. Their names are reflections of this and you will come across Koh Khai – egg island; Koh Ma Chu – puppy island; and Koh Hong – chamber island. Hong is the name given to the caverns and caves inside the islands and it is possible to enter these mysterious chambers in a longtail boat, or better still a kayak.

Most tours take you to the main sites of Koh Panyi and James Bond Island and cruise around the northern section of the bay. Some tours go further to Tham Lawt (tunnel cave) and Khao Kian (where there are wall paintings). There are many ways to visit the park from Phuket (see page ? for more information). Otherwise you can charter boats from Tha Dan close to Phang Nga town for cheap longtail tours of the islands.

There are also many tour operators in Phang Nga town offering a range of tours.

BOAT TOURS AROUND THE BAY

Longtail boats at Tha Dan pier are available for charter if you want a private tour. Small boats – able to carry eight people – cost **B**650; larger boats – up to ten people – cost **B**1,500.

TOUR OPERATORS
Sanyan tours
A long established company offering good value tours of the bay. Prices are: half day (**B**150) and full day (**B**300) tours and overnight tours (**B**400).
☎ (076) 430 348.

Kean Tours
Also offers a range of tours around the bay.
☎ (076) 411 247

Sailing Phang Nga Bay ... in great old style.

PHANG NGA TOWN

This small town is set amongst fantastic limestone scenery and is the capital of Phang Nga Province. It is also the best – and least expensive – place to hire boats to visit the bay. If you get up early you can take a morning tour covering all the islands before the package tourists from Phuket arrive.

To get to Phang Nga town take a bus from Phuket (2 hours) or Krabi town (1 hour). Or from The southern bus terminal in Bangkok (VIP buses cost **B**515 and take 14 hours).

Accommodation

Ratanapong Hotel **B**150-500
An OK place in the middle of town with clean air-con and fan rooms. ☎ (076) 411 247.

Hotel Summit **B**350-600
A clean and friendly hotel near the center of town with 20 air-con rooms. ☎/📠 411 130.

Phang Nga Bay Resort **B**850-1,500
Large hotel near the pier with swimming pool and air-con rooms complete with TV, phone etc. ☎ (076) 412 067-70, 📠 412 057.

KOH YAO

Koh Yao Yai and Koh Yao Noi are two long islands – Koh Yao means long island – in the middle of Phang Nga Bay. The islands are a rocky land mass of karsts, hills and beaches and somehow seem to have remained largely untouched by the tourism of neighboring Phuket. Most of the population live on Koh Yao Noi, the smaller of the two islands, and fishing and coconut farming are the mainstays of the tiny economy.

There are only two resorts on Koh Yao Noi, which has some pretty beaches. If you want to see what Phuket looked like 30 years ago, then this will give you a pretty good idea. It is a very basic, rustic example of South Thai island life. For mountain bikers: there are some wicked off road trails winding through the hills, so bring your bikes and get away from it all for a few days.

GETTING THERE

There are two boats a day from the pier at Ao Po on Phuket. They leave at approximately 08.00 and 12.00. A return boat leaves Ta Khai at some time after 06.00. Fares are **B**45 each way and the journey takes about an hour.

When you arrive at Ta Khai just take a motorbike taxi to whichever place you want to stay.

Accommodation

Sabai Corner **B**300-700
An eco-lodge owned by Sea Canoe's manager and used by the Phuket-based kayak company as a base for many of their Phang Nga Bay paddles. It has some large thatched bungalows available for rent and can offer a range of kayak tours.

Tha Khao Bungalows **B**400-600
Large thatched roof bungalows for rent on Tha Khao beach.
☎ (01) 676 7726,
Phuket ☎ (076) 212 172.

Long Beach Village **B**500-1,500
Located on a quiet beach on the east of the island. There are almost 50 large wooden bungalows and a wonderful restaurant and beach bar. Rooms range from standard to superior bungalows with large decks in lots of space. There are some watersports facilities and the resort is well run and very friendly. An ideal tropical getaway.
☎/📠 (01) 211 8647,
Phuket ☎/📠 (076) 381 623.

KRABI

KRABI BASICS

Located on the mainland east of Phuket Island, Krabi province stretches south covering over a hundred kilometers of the Andaman Coast. It covers 5,000 square kilometers of mountains, hills, and jungle and encompasses over 200 islands including the Phi Phi islands and Koh Lanta. The main town is also called Krabi - or Krabi town to avoid confusion - and the primary tourist beaches are located to its north. It is this area that is commonly referred to as Krabi and includes the popular beaches of Railey, Phra Nang and Ao Nang as well as other adjacent beaches and a number of islands just off the coast.

The whole area is presently in the middle of a tourist boom and is now quite firmly entrenched on the international tourist map, having made the transition from a backpacker destination into the mainstream market. The airport has only recently opened and demand for rooms presently exceeds supply so developers are frantically building resorts and hotels all over the place. The reasons for Krabi's popularity are magnificently obvious as soon as you arrive. The coastline is studded with awesome limestone karsts that provide breathtaking backdrops for picture post card beaches. The Phra Nang peninsular is arguably the most beautiful place in Thailand, an opinion that is supported by the fact that *The Sunday Times* in England voted Phra Nang Beach the second most beautiful beach in the world a few years ago.

Apart from the beaches there is also lots to do and see in Krabi, the area has become an adventure sports mecca with world-class rock climbing, sea kayaking and scuba-diving, all well organised and easily available, as well as jungle treks out into the nearby national parks. Nightlife is not a prime objective for most visitors to Krabi and even the busy beach resorts of Ao Nang and Railey are tame in the extreme compared to Phuket. However Railey has always had a unique "travellers scene" that has developed as a fusion between hedonistic yachties, young fun loving backpackers and old Asia hands, and even its recent push towards up-market tourism has not diminished it too much.

The new airport has made Krabi much more accessible and therefore far more marketable for tour operators, and the package tourists are beginning to arrive in bigger numbers. But at the time of writing Krabi seems to be taking it fairly well. Although it is now difficult to find near empty beaches or enjoy deserted islands, there is still room for everyone – even during high season. However the pressure on room space has driven prices up and Krabi is no longer the inexpensive alternative to Phuket it once was - during high season prices can become close to unreasonable.

With Krabi's newfound fashionableness the fickle tourist market is currently still willing to absorb these increases though it is still frustratingly difficult to find rooms during December and January; anyone planning to visit during this time really should book well in advance.

GETTING THERE
BY AIR

Krabi Airport opened in November 1999 and is a small but efficient entrance to the province located just 15 kilometers northeast of Krabi town. Thai Airlines fly once a day from Bangkok (departs 10.15; costs ฿2,150), but expect that to increase later. Bangkok Airlines fly twice/week from Samui (฿1,770 each way).

From Phuket airport there are two choices. The cheapest way is to take the shuttle bus to Phuket town and then an air-conditioned bus to Baan Talaad Kao. This

KRABI

takes about six hours and costs B161 per person. The fastest way is to take a taxi from the airport – from either one of the two transport companies in the arrival hall – to anywhere in either Krabi town or Ao Nang. This takes about two-and-a-half to three hours and costs B2,000 per car.
Thai International - Krabi Office: ☎ (075) 612 888, Bangkok Office: ☎ (02) 628 2000.
Bangkok Airways: ☎ (02) 229 3456-63.

BY BUS

The bus station is at Baan Talaad Kao 7 kilometers north of Krabi town and there are regular daily air-con buses to Bangkok (B446), Phuket (B101), Surat Thani (110), Haad Yai (B153), Trang (B77), Satun and Nakhorn Si Thammarat (B110).

There are also VIP buses to Bangkok departing every evening at 17.00 (fare is B660). With only 24 seats, they are well worth the extra money as they are much more comfortable. From Bangkok, VIP buses leave the Southern Bus Terminal at 18.00 and 18.30.

Local non air-con buses also ply the same routes as well as going up to Ranong (B94) and cost just over half the price, but are only for hard core budget travellers as they take nearly twice as long. There are shuttle buses to Krabi town (depositing you outside New Hotel) every 2 minutes costing B10.

KRABI TOWN

The provincial capital serves as the main gateway to Krabi's beaches and islands including Phi Phi and Lanta and most travelers pass through without stopping for much more than a coffee. The town is located at the mouth of Krabi River and is pleasant enough, although aesthetically unremarkable. Recently it has been trying to market itself as a base from which to visit the various attractions of the province and if you plan to do a lot of day trips and prefer the character of a Thai town to tourist resorts then it does have something to offer. Like many Thai towns, what Krabi loses in looks it makes up for in eating opportunities and you will find the area's best and most authentic Thai restaurants here. There is a wide range of accommodation available all over town and along the river and during high season they pick up the overflow from the beach resorts. Everything is available from super-budget guesthouses to the luxurious Maritime Hotel. The town is small and friendly and if you have budget constraints it is a really good value alternative to neighboring Ao Nang with comparable rooms up to 50 percent cheaper.

ORIENTATION

The main part of town is a well-concentrated square block adjacent to the river. Its two main roads – Utarakit Rd and Maharad Rd - run parallel to the water. The two Chao

KRABI

Fah piers - express boats or longtails to almost everywhere - are on Kong Ka Rd, which runs off the south end of Utarakit Rd. There are lots of guesthouses, restaurants and tour offices around this area and if you want to get in and out, everything here is geared up to help you do it quickly. Most of the hotels, shops and restaurants are located either on these two roads or in between them and this whole area is easily navigable by foot. The Talaad Kao bus station – for buses to Phuket, Bangkok and elsewhere outside Krabi - is quite a way north of the town center but there are regular shuttle buses leaving from outside New Hotel.

Restaurants

Azzura Pizza and Spaghetti B100–200
Reasonable Italian fare in this small and friendly restaurant on Utarakit Rd.

Pizzaria Firenze . . . B100–200
A very good Italian restaurant on Kung Ka Rd with the usual pizza and pasta dishes, but in big portions. Good value.

May and Mark Restaurant B50-100
Small budget restaurant with big portions at reasonable prices. English breakfast and liver and onions on the menu - it is a favorite venue for hungry Brits. Located on Maharat Soi 2.

Ruen Pae Floating Restaurant B100–200
What was once a great restaurant is no longer worth eating at. The setting is still very nice - out on the Krabi River with lovely views and a pleasant breeze. It is still a cool place to enjoy a few beers or a bottle of Thai whiskey, but the food is really not very good.

Café Europa B100–200
If you have had enough Thai food this Danish owned restaurant has a wide range of really good European options, including great steaks and a really good breakfast. It has also become something of a Krabi institution – having been open for nine years – and the proprietor is a font of local knowledge. Located on Soi Ruamjit off Issara road. Recommended.

Kwan Café and Restaurant B50-100
Opposite the Chao Fa Pier. Serves real coffee, Thai and western food. With Internet access it is a good place to hang out.

Ruen Thai Restaurant B80–150
Located on Maharad town just outside the center, this excellent restaurant is the best choice for a real Thai feast. The setting is traditional Thai garden and the atmosphere is always great. The seafood is great, as is just about everything else – prices are very reasonable to boot. Recommended.

Jao Suow Mahachaon Restaurant B50-100
Located on Maharad Road just outside the center. Good choice for simple Thai food.

Rim Chaon B50-100
This great little restaurant is right on the river, near the piers – a superb place to eat really fresh seafood.

Hollywood Restaurant B100-200
New live music venue on Issara Rd. The music is nothing special, but the food is very good – an imaginative Thai menu, well worth checking out.

Ving Café B50-100
On Phuk-Sa-U-Thit Rd serves real coffee and snacks.

Nightlife

Krabi town's nightlife caters mainly for Thai tourists and is made up of live music bars and karaoke. There

Eating in Krabi...

117

KRABI

are bars areas on Maharad Soi 5 and Soi 7, where there are some open-air bars and Thai style country pubs. Maharad Soi 2 has the largest concentration of karaoke, where hostesses entertain groups of men while they drink and sing their favorite ballads., but they are not really much fun if you don't speak Thai. Gather Point next to Europa Café is a hang out for young trendy local teenagers, but there have been reports of drug taking and fights. Europa Café is a good place to go early in the evening and the owner will happily direct you onwards if you want to continue drinking late into the night.

Accommodation

BUDGET

Seaside Guesthouse B100–200
Located towards the south of Maharad Rd. with reasonably clean basic box-rooms with shared washroom/toilets or slightly bigger rooms with shower/toilets. Friendly and helpful. ☎ (075) 612 3571, 621 351

SBM Guesthouse B200–350
14 rooms above a shophouse all with inside shower and toilet, some with air-con. Tidy and well run – better than average.

Cha Guesthouse .. B200–500
Located on Utarakit Rd. just south of town this charming little guest house has a big garden behind an old wooden shophouse with a number of clean basic rooms at good prices. It is a very peaceful place to chill out for a few days and probably the best value budget option in town. Recommended.
☎ (075) 611 141.

Jungle Guesthouse B50–100
On the seafront in the middle of town on Utarakit Rd and has the cheapest and nastiest rooms in town. Small rooms with shared facilities and not very clean.

Café Europa B400-800
Five clean, comfortable rooms above the restaurant – tastefully decorated with en-suite bathroom. ☎/📠 (075) 620 407.

Chao Fa Valley ... B400-800
Located 500 meters south of the pier down Chao Fa Rd this place is worth the walk if you are staying for a few days or more. Big bamboo bungalows with fans and en-suite bathrooms in a quiet garden. Recommended.
☎ (075) 612 713.

K.L. Guesthouse .. B200-600
Another set of rooms above a shophouse ranging from small rooms with shared facilities to reasonable fan rooms with en-suites. ☎ (075) 612 511.

K.R. Mansion B200-400
Located down Chao Fa Rd. just past Chao Fa Valley, this big guest house has 40 fan rooms with shared or private bathrooms. Friendly and comfortable.

MID-RANGE

Boonsiam B700–1,400
Big new hotel on Jao Kun Rd, just off the Krabi to Phuket Rd about one kilometer from the town center. Slightly more expensive than the others in this category, but easily the best. Big clean rooms with all amenities. Recommended
☎ (075) 632 511-5.

City Hotel B350–700
Fan and air-con rooms with satellite TV – reasonably clean and not a bad deal.
☎ (075) 611 961, 621 280.

Grand Mansion Hotel B300–600
North of town on Uttarakit Rd. this clean and well run hotel has 58 air-con and fan rooms with satelliteTV – good value.
☎ (075) 611 371.

Grand Tower Hotel B300–600
Clean, quiet and modern hotel on Chao Fa Road close to the pier but has been gaining a poor reputation for security. Air con rooms with hot water and satellite TV. ☎ (075) 621 456-7.

KRABI

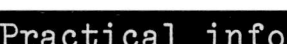

New Hotel B200–500
Run down and rough hotel with fan and air-con rooms, located on Maharad Soi 6.

Thai Hotel B300–600
Scruffy old Thai-Chinese hotel with fan rooms or air-con rooms with hot water and TV. It is now in desperate need of renovation and some of the rooms have become very tatty. If you do stay, insist on a room in the new wing. Karaoke and restaurant downstairs stays open late.

Vieng Thong Hotel ....
.... B600–700
Another scruffy Thai hotel with musty old air-con rooms with TVs that are rarely tuned in. Located across from the river on Uttarakit Rd. Does have a TV. ☎ (075) 620 020-3, 🖷 (075) 612 525.

FIRST CLASS

Krabi Meritime Hotel ....
.... B1,000–4,000
A big five star hotel on the river two kilometers north of town with views across the Andaman Sea as far as Phi Phi Don. It is in a lovely setting surrounded by limestone karsts and mangroves with well appointed rooms, a beautiful pool, fitness center and all other facilities. This is where Leonardo DiCaprio stayed - good value.
☎ (075) 620 028-46, or in Bangkok: ☎ (02) 719 0034-9, e-mail: Krabi@asianet.co.th

Krabi Royal Hotel ....
B1,000–2,000
Located north of town on the way to Talaad Ban Kao. Big old hotel that used to be the best in town but has fallen well behind. Has all facilities but now well over-priced.
☎/🖷 (075) 611 584.

Practical info

TOURS, TICKETS AND INFORMATION

There are dozens of travel agents and tour offices all over the town center. The best place to buy onward tickets is from any of the shops or cafes opposite Chao Fa Pier as they all speak good English and will give free information.

The places that have big signs saying "Tourist Information" are also tour and ticket shops and are nothing to do with the TAT, so do not expect them to be any more impartial than the others. Phantip Tours opposite Chao Fa pier operates an air-con bus to Surat Thani and Krabi Green Travel (☎ 075-630 171) also opposite the pier is a particularly helpful place. All agencies can organise buses to practically anywhere in Thailand as well as local tours and hotels. Songserm have an

Lodging in Krabi...

A typical inter-island boat. Services may be interupted at times during the monsoon.

KRABI

office south of the center on Kong Ka road.

All the guest houses also offer the same services and if you are staying in one you may as well get them to arrange tickets or tours for you.

KRABI TAT AND TOURIST POLICE

The official tourist office is just north of the center along Utarakit Rd and has a few maps and will give advice. The tourist police are also based here.

SHOPPING

Krabi town is not a great souvenir shopping spot and is mainly geared up to cater for local residents. There is a department store on Maharad Rd. and most of the shops are located between Maharad Rd and Utarakit Rd. There is a Kodak shop on Issara Rd.

Hot and Spicy
Sells souvenirs, local handicrafts and objets d'art from north Thailand. ☎ (075) 630 433

Tex Rock Climbing Shop
A well stocked climbing shop and booking office for rock climbing on Railey Beach. On Utarakit Rd. next to Jungle guesthouse.

BANKS

Most of the major Thai banks have branches in Krabi town and there are plenty of ATM machines and exchange booths (open until 17.30). There is a Siam City Exchange booth right by the Chao Fa Pier and the nearest ATM machines are just along Utarakit Rd.

INTERNET AND COMMUNICATIONS

The Telecommunication Office
Located one kilometer north of the center on.Utarakit Rd and is the cheapest place for overseas calls (B55-per-minute to Europe).

Post Office
Located just south of town on Utarakit Rd. (Open Mon-Fri 08.30-16.30, Sat 0900-noon) Has EMS, poste restante and packing service.

There are dozens of Internet centers all over the town center. Cha Guesthouse is currently the cheapest at B1-a-minute, most of.the others charge B2-a-minute. Nearly all the tour offices and guesthouses opposite the Chao Fa pier have terminals.

CAR & BIKE RENTAL

There are 100cc Honda motorcycles for rent all over town - prices range between B150 and B200 and it is well worth bargaining especially if you want one for a few days.

Budget Rentals
Located on Maharad Soi 2. Has a range of cars for rent with the full Budget back-up and insurance. The best bet if peace of mind is your main consideration. ☎

Thaimit Rental
On Utarakit Rd, with cars and vans for hire at reasonable prices. ☎ (075) 632 054.

Krabi Travel Co.
Minibus transport, cars and bikes for rent. Located at Seaside Guesthouse on Maharat Rd. ☎ (075) 612 3571, 621 351.

HEALTH

For accidents and emergencies go to Krabi Hospital, located on route 411 north of the town center on the way to Baan Talaad Kao. Facilities are OK, but for anything really serious go to one of the big hospitals in Phuket. ☎ (075)611203

TAXIS AND BOATS

There is a pick up service opposite the reclining Buddha on Maharat Rd, with *songtaews* to Ao Nang (B20) and Fossil Shell Beach (B40).

Longtail boats to Railey can be found all along the seafront north of Chao Fa Pier. The last boats leave at 17.00. The cost is B50 per person and they will not go until they have 3 or 4 people, unless you pay B100 to B150.

Ao Nang & Railey

AO NANG

Ao Nang is the most accessible of Krabi's beaches. Situated 16 kilometers from Krabi town it is the most developed in the area. It is a small seaside town in a pretty bay surrounded by looming karst scenery. The beach itself is better suited for building sandcastles than barefoot bliss, but just a short boat ride offshore there are some delightful tropical islands with some of the area's finest sands. Ao Nang is also the gateway to the Phra Nang peninsular and is ideally located to use as a base to explore its caves and beaches. Route 4203 from Krabi town runs right down to the coast and along the front, before looping round to Haad Nopparatthara, so most of the beach backs onto the road.

Most of the hotels and resorts are on the town side of the road. The town is still small and very pleasant with a warm atmosphere, plenty of cafes and restaurants, enough shops and a few bars.

Beach Guide

ISLAND TOURS

Longtail boat rides to Railey and Phra Nang headlands cost B20 per person each way. Otherwise the most popular day-trips are to the Poda islands or to Koh Hong. For beaches go to Poda, for caves and scenery go to Koh Hong. Travel shops in Ao Nang sell island tour tickets, which pool strangers into the one boat. This has brought two daytrips within reach of most pockets: 4 island tour (Phra Nang and Poda island group) for B190 per person, and 5 island (Koh Hong group) for B250 per person. The price includes snorkel, mask, and lunch of fried rice, water and fruit. Each boat leaves around 09.00 and returns about 16.00. Bookings can be made from bungalows and travel counters.

PHI PHI ISLAND DAY TRIP

Ao Nang Princess leaves Ao Nang at 9am daily, returning 5pm. A round trip ticket costs B670 including simple lunch, Viking Cave and snorkeling in Maya Bay.

OTHER TRIPS

Travel counters offer longtail boat tours on Krabi River (B190), Klong Tom hot spa & forest hiking (B500-550), Phang Nga cave temple, Panyi village and Koh Tapu, "James Bond" island (B420-590), Ao Luk waterfall and caves (B550). These are guideline prices which may vary slightly between travel agents.

SPEED BOAT RENTAL

An expensive game: Barracuda Tour on the beach front have a 5-seater boat for B6,000 per day, a 12-15 seater for B10,000.

Longtail boats are the fastest way to get from beach to beach.

PHRA NANG AREA

DIVING

Dive operators in Ao Nang mostly offer courses and local tours. A PADI openwater course cost around ฿9,000 and a two-dive-tour cost from ฿1,800.

Ao Nang Divers
Located at Krabi Sea View Resort, with another office at the front. German run operation with a good reputation offering all PADI courses and liveaboard dive tours. ☎ (075) 637 242, ☎ (075) 637 246, email: info@krabi-seaview.com

Phra Nang divers
One of Krabi's best-established dive operators, with an excellent reputation. They offer all PADI courses as well as regular day trips and great value liveaboard excursions to Hin Daeng and Hin Muang. ☎/☎ (075) 637 064, email: pndivers@loxinfo.com, www.pndivers.com

Kon Tiki
The Krabi booking office for the Phuket-based operator. Located on the beachfront Road.

Sting Ray Divers
PADI dive school on Moo 2 offering all courses and dive tours to local sites. ☎ 637 493.

Seafan Divers
Thai run NAUI dive school on Moo 2, offering local tours and all NAUI courses. ☎ 637 214.

Thai Nature Tours
The only dedicated eco and nature tour company worth its salt. They organise day trips and two or three day excursions to local sea caves (with a chance of seeing turtles), Khao Sok National Park, Koh Chon National Park and Patalong in Trang. Knowledgeable guides lead tours with a genuine interest in conservation. A day trip to Khao Sok costs ฿2,500 per person, three-day tours are ฿7,500 and a four-day excursion is ฿9,700. ☎ 637 470. Recommended.

SEA KAYAKING

Krabi companies typically offer three different day trips: canyon tours, which start from Ao Leuk, 50-kilometers north of Ao Nang (only available in high season); cave tours to Tam Lod, which include paddles through the coastal mangrove forests; coral tours to nearby islands which include snorkeling. All tours include lunch and all the companies follow similar itineraries, especially if they are visiting the tidal sea hongs. Tours through the 200-meter high limestone canyon at Ao Leuk are particularly good. Costs are: Krabi Canyon ฿700-1,200 (depends on tides); Ao Leuk ฿1,500; Krabi River ฿1,000; Koh Hong ฿1,800; beach rentals ฿100-150 per hour (reductions for half/full day). Daytrips include guides, lunch and transfer by road or longtail boat.

Princess Watersports
On the beachfront. Good tours at reasonable prices. Ask for Ray.

Sea Kayak Krabi

Massage right on the beach.

PHRA NANG AREA

Located on the seafront road – offers all the standard tours.
☎ (075) 637 301, 637 400.

Sea Canoe
Located next to Phra Nang Inn on the sea front. The original pioneers of sea kayaking from Phuket also have an office in Krabi offering all the local tours plus overnight excursions from Phuket. ☎ (076) 212 172.

Nosey Parker
☎ (076) 637 318.

Phra Nang Canoe Club
Located in front of Phra Nang Inn, they offer all the usual sea kayaking tours. Also kayaks for rent.

FISHING TRIPS

Game fishing trips are available with local fishermen in longtail boats. It is best to go early morning or late afternoon. A three-hour trip (06.00-09.00, 15.30-18.30) from Ao Nang costs **B**1,500, or all day (09.00-15.00) for **B**2,000.

ISLAND TOURS

Organised excursions to the beautiful beaches of Koh Poda, or Chicken Island are available from any travel agent and cost **B**280 to **B**380 per person. However if you can get a group of people together or don't mind swallowing the extra expense it is worth hiring a longtail for the day and seeking out the quietest spot. Longtails cost **B**1,500 a day and are found opposite Pra Nang Inn. All the owners know all the islands and will take you to the best spots as well as act as guides.

SNORKELLING

Dive shops provide mask/snorkel/fin hire at **B**150 a set per day (**B**500 deposit).

MOUNTAIN BIKING

Mountain bikes cost **B**80 per day from Coke Big Bike (637 099).

TENNIS

Krabi Resort has a tennis court at **B**150 per hour. Racquets & balls **B**100 a game.

FISHING

Line fishing with bait and soft drinks supplied costs **B**1,000 for each boat. The trips are around 150 minutes long. Departs 6am and 4.30pm. Max two people per boat. Money refunded if you don't catch anything! Book at Green Park bungalows.

MOUNTAIN BIKING

Mountain Bikes are available for rent at **B**200 a day from Sea, land and Trek near Krabi Resort.

Nightlife

Ao Nang is not really a late night place as most people come to enjoy the beaches and islands during the day. There are a few bars open late down on the front and now a small strip of girly bars on Moo 2 about 300 meters up from the beach on the right. There seems to be a stage in every Thai resort's development which calls for a girlie bar strip; sometimes they are successful, sometimes they fail, but you can be sure that sooner or later they will appear. In Ao Nang's case they seem to exist solely for the pleasure of local diving instructors. There is also a strange and honestly awful disco at the end of the girlie strip.

Lisa & Lottes Disco
This dismal disco is in desperate need of bulldozing. The best thing about it is the potential entertainment that could be caused by the bare electrical cables and a collection of CDs that they must have found on the beach. The question "why?" remains unanswered.

Full Moon Bar
In the middle of the front, this is the best and busiest bar in town. Open late most nights – satellite TV and live premier league football.

PHRA NANG AREA

In sight of the small inhabited island of Koh Hong.

Bernie's Place
Located about 200 meters up Moo 2 on the left-hand-side. Live music, pool table and a Thai/western buffet.

Luna Beach Bar
Located around the corner from Ao Nang on the way to Haad Noppharatthara. A big new open-air beach bar that aims to hold regular party nights. It has a good layout and if they get the music right could be the hottest spot in town.

Malibu bar
Small bar on the beachfront road. Has been known to stay open very, very late.

The Smoke House
Trendy looking bar on Moo 2, nice décor and decent cocktails – the only place in Ao Nang serving frozen Margaritas. Good burgers available for **B**50.

Restaurants

Ao Nang Villa **B**150–300
Great breakfast buffet.

Spicy Bar and Restaurant . . . .
. . . . **B**100–150
Good Thai and seafood catering mainly for tourists. Located in Ya Ya Plaza. Very nice location overlooking the water.

Ya Ya Beach Seafood . . . .
. . . . **B**100–150
Another nice restaurant in Ya Ya Plaza right on the waterfront. The best choice for fresh seafood. Recommended.

Baan Thai Seafood . . . .
. . . . **B**80–120
On the corner at the west end of the beach near Krabi Resort. Good Thai food at reasonable prices.

Fantasia Mediterania . . . .
. . . . **B**150–250
A new Italian place on the front road that is beginning to get a good reputation.

The Beach Restaurant . . . . . .
. . . . **B**100–200
Right in the middle of the front road. Offers a range of Asian dishes from Japanese to Indian to Thai. Great spring rolls.

Azzura Italian Restaurant . . . .
. . . . **B**150–250
About the best western food in Krabi. Good Pizzas, big portions. Recommended.

La Luna **B**150–300
Another Italian place that is worth a try. Nice location down on the front and a reasonable selection of wines.

Lottas Café **B**150–250
Located on Moo 2 just up from the beach. Specialises in

PHRA NANG AREA

Scandinavian fare, which is not bad but definitely overpriced.

Austria Hut B150–300
Reliable Germanic food. Pretty good if you are into cold cuts and sausages. Located on Moo 2 past Seaview resort on the opposite side of the road.

Lai Tai B150–250
A Mexican restaurant that may not be quite up to Californian standards, but makes a change if you need one.

Kolibri Coffee Shop ....
.... B40–150
Located opposite Bernie's place, has good coffee and snacks.

The Last café B60–100
At the end of the dirt road at the far eastern end of the beach. This is the best place to hang out during the day. The bar/restaurant is built with wood and bamboo and nestles amongst the palm trees. Good one plate Thai meals. Recommended.

N.B.: For really good and authentic Thai food head round to Haad Noppharattha (see page 129 for more details).

Accommodation

BUDGET

Ao Nang Village .. B300–800
Good value bungalows located along Moo 2 just past the Austria Hut.

Ao Nang Palm Hill . B400–800
Ten bungalows on the hill about a kilometer from the beach back up Moo 2. A friendly resort with good value fan cooled rooms.
☎ 637 207.

Cowboy Inn B300–600
Guesthouse located close to Lai Thai Resort on Moo 2 well back from the beach. Good value clean fan rooms if you don't mind a short walk into town.

Jinda Guesthouse ....
.... B200–1,800
Very friendly four story guesthouse next to Phra Nang Divers. Rooms are clean but unimaginative. Fan and air-con available.

Bernie's Place ... B300–500
Guesthouse above the restaurant of the same name. Clean fan rooms and friendly service.

MID RANGE

Ban Ao Nang ....
.... B1,800–3,200
A new resort at the west end of town not far from the beach. A three-story building with air-conditioned rooms overlooking a big swimming pool – very comfortable and centrally located.
☎ 637 072-3, ✆ 637 070,
email: baonan@loxinfo.co.th

BB Bungalows .. B850–1,300
Located behind Krabi Seaview

Lodging in Ao Nang...

Kayaking along the cliffs in Phra Nang Bay.

PHRA NANG AREA

Resort are 12 large fan-cooled bungalows. ☎ 637 542, 📠 637 304.

BB Inn Hotel . . B1,800–2,000
Next to BB bungalows a new hotel with 15 air-con rooms.

Beach Terrace . . . .
. . . . B1,800–2,400
Big multi-storey hotel at the west end of the beach that towers ostentatiously above the surrounding palms. Rooms are air-con and functional and some have splendid views, but the hotel really is an eyesore.
☎ 637 180-3, 📠 637 184.

Felix Phra Nang Inn . . . .
. . . . B2,900–4,400
Very centrally located opposite the beach on the eastern corner of the front road. An old three-story resort with swimming pool and all amenities. The building is designed to blend in with its surroundings and the rooms are decorated with local handicrafts and seashells.
☎ 637 130-3, 📠 637 134-5,
e-mail:
phranang@sun.phuket.ksc.co.th

Krabi Seaview Resort . . . .
. . . . B700–3,500
Well-constructed and professionally run resort set back from the road on Moo 2. Choice of rooms and bungalows ranging from fan to air-con. Recommended.
☎ 637 242-45, 📠 637 246,
email: aonang@loxinfo.co.th

Lai Thai Resort . . . .
. . . . B2,400–3,000
Located up Moo 2 well back from the beach, this very pretty and well-run resort has 20 air-conditioned Thai style bungalows.
☎ (075) 637 281,
📠 (075) 637 282.

Peace Laguna Resort . . . .
. . . . B850–1,900
☎ 637 338, 📠 637 347.

PK Mansion B450–2,200
Big 40-room guesthouse next to Phra Nang Inn. Well run and reasonably friendly. The fan rooms are particularly good value.
☎ 637 431, 637 471.

FIRST CLASS

Ao Nang Paksi . . . .
. . . . B2,000–5,000
Brand new hotel built by the Meritime Group. All the facilities you would expect, big swimming pool and a shuttle to nearby beaches.

Krabi Resort . . B2,900–8,400
A 40-room hotel plus bungalows. One of the original resorts and still one of the best, although it is almost always booked out through high season. Swimming pool, tennis courts, satellite TV. They also have bungalows on Poda Island.
☎ 637 030-5, 📠 637 051.

126

PHRA NANG AREA

Practical info

TOURS AND TICKETS AND INFORMATION
There are plenty of small agents all over town offering tours and tickets to everywhere – they are all much of a muchness.

SHOPPING
There are the usual collection of supermarkets and souvenir shops along the seafront and up Moo 2. Kolibri Coffee Shop has a book exchange service.

BANKS
There is an exchange booth on the seafront road near Ao Nang inn. There are no ATM machines in Ao Nang.

INTERNET AND COMMUNICATIONS
There are several Internet shops in Ao Nang, charging B3-4 a minute.

CAR & BIKE RENTAL
There are 100cc Honda motorcycles for rent at several places along Moo 2. Prices fluctuate according to the season. B150 a day in low season, B250 in high season and B200 in between.

Coke Big Bike
Has Honda Dream (B200), 400cc choppers (B500), 750cc (B750) and off-road DT 200cc Yamahas at B350. Suzuki Caribian 4-wheel drive jeeps with air-con rent at a pricey B1,200 per day.

TAXIS AND BOATS
Taxis to Krabi town congregate outside Phra Nang Inn and run from 06.30 until 18.30. They depart as soon as they have enough customers and charge B20 per person. Boats to Railey and Fossil Shell beach depart from the beach opposite Phra Nang Inn and charge B40 per person. Boats to Koh Lanta and Phi Phi depart from the small pier opposite Ya Ya Restaurant.

HEALTH
There is a clinic next to the Tourist Center on the seafront road.

HAAD NOPPARATTHARA

This two-kilometer long beach is part of the Haad Nopparatthara National Park and is a favorite spot for Thai picnickers especially on Sundays when the beach is lined with cars and Thai families eating, drinking and sleeping. There is a visitor's center and some park bungalows are available for rent. The beach is not particularly nice and the best thing about this area is the string of Thai restaurants that fringe the road just before the park headquarters. You can get delicious *som ta*m and other snack foods as well as fresh seafood at bargain prices. Most of the menus are in Thai, but there is usually something in English and some of the staff will speak enough for you to order some great food. The best thing to do is just point and shrug and hope for the best, as long as you are not too fussy about the ingredients you are more than likely to be impressed by the results. A great meal for two can be had for a hundred baht.

HAAD KHLONG MUANG

An isolated beach between Ao Nang and Haad Nopphararthara, which can only be accessed by boat, this is the place to go if you are looking for peace and quiet. Coconut palms and casuarina trees surround the beach and there are just three bungalow operators all providing an authentic back to nature experience. The beach is not the best in the area, but it is one of the most deserted.

Lodging on Ao Nang...

PHRA NANG AREA

Accommodation

Andaman Inn B150–600
Bamboo huts ranging from small rabbit hutches with shared facilities to spacious bamboo bungalows with balconies. ☎ 612 728.

Emerald Resort . . . B150–800
At the end of the beach are 36 bamboo bungalows of various sizes, well spaced out in a large shady garden. Very secluded and well-run resort – a refreshing throw back to the early days of tourism in Thailand. Recommended.
☎ 01-892 1072, 01-956 2566.

Bamboo Bungalows . . . .
. . . . B100–300
The cheapest deal on the beach with small wooden huts without electricity. The restaurant does superb pizzas from an old Italian wood burning pizza oven.

Ao Nam Mao

The next bay around from Railey East has a similar beach environment – mud beach and coastal mangrove forest. It is not a paradise beach but can be an interesting environmental getaway. The bay is accessible by road from Krabi and Ao Nang.

Dawn Of Happiness Beach Resort B400–800
This is an environmental, conservation and education resort project owned and run by Tom Henley, local conversationist and author of books on Krabi and Khao Sok. The bungalows are all constructed out of local materials and are scattered around the forest. The staff will help organise nature walks and excursions to local villages, creeks and waterfalls. If you want to get back to nature for a while or take time out to learn about the startlingly varied environment on the Isthmus of Kra then this is an ideal place. If you are after a lively time don't bother. The only thing against Dawn of Happiness is that it is often used by foreign adventure tour companies and their sometimes cliquey groups can dominate the resort for the two or three days that they stay. Recommended.
☎/🖷 (01) 464 4362.

RAILEY BEACH AND PRA NANG PENINSULAR

Phra Nang peninsular is separated from the mainland by a giant limestone rock that isolates it more effectively than any body of water could. With no roads, incredible white sand beaches, towering cliffs, caves and picturesque karst islands basking in clear blue waters, Phra Nang is Thailand's original Shangri-La paradise. It consists of three beaches, separated by the sheer cliffs that have become legendary amongst rock climbers. The

Chicken Head Rock.

PHRA NANG AREA

two west facing beaches – Railey West and Phra Nang are quite probably the best beaches in Thailand.

RAILEY BEACH

Railey has achieved mythical status amongst travelers in South East Asia as the ultimate beach paradise. There are actually two beaches – Railey East and Railey West – however Railey East is more of a mangrove swamp than a beach and functions as a pedestrian thoroughfare and entry point for longtail boats. Anyway the two beaches are only a hundred meters apart and Railey West more than compensates. It is a huge sandy playground protected by imposing palisades and fringed by easygoing beach bars nestling beneath a canopy of palms. A more perfect beach environment would be hard to imagine.

The local residents – who consist of little more than the original five families – have fiercely protected Railey's independence and there is still hardly any governmental presence on the peninsular. This meant that in its early years Railey became a Mecca for those seeking a truly free environment, including an eclectic mix of hippies, travellers and assorted fun seekers and it soon gained a reputation as a "party place" where marijuana was smoked openly and the beach bars stayed open until the last person passed out.

Over the last few years the resort owners in Railey have been consciously trying to push the area's reputation upmarket as they try to maximise the earning potential of an asset that is in great demand. The resorts on Railey West have gradually been upgraded and the room rates greatly inflated, meaning that Railey is not the cheap paradise it once was and causing it to be abandoned by some of the perpetual travelers who built its reputation. Although the outward look of the beach has not changed it is not as "love, peace and happiness" as it used to be, with more well-heeled and well-behaved visitors. Railey East has managed to retain more of its travelers allure and is still as popular despite the fact that room rates are considerably higher than those on Koh Lanta or the islands off the East coast of Thailand.

GETTING THERE

You can get longtail boats to Railey and Phra Nang from Ao Nang and Krabi town. The boat from Ao Nang takes about ten minutes and costs ฿20 per person or ฿50 if you want to go alone. If the weather is bad try to get to Ao Nang by land and then take the boat from there. Also if you arrive by plane in Krabi or Phuket, go to Ao Nang rather than Krabi town. The boat from Krabi takes 30 to 40 minutes and costs ฿50 per person or ฿200 for a boat on your own.

From late May to late September the boat service is entirely dependent on the weather conditions – which can be treacherous.

Beachlife

DIVING

Phra Nang Divers
The oldest dive school on Railey and still the best. They offer PADI courses, daily tours to local sites and have regular day trips to the King Cruiser Wreck, Shark Point and Koh Phi Phi. Also liveaboard tours to Hin Daeng/Hin Muang. Located on Railey West at Railey Beach Bungalows.
☎/📠 (075) 637 064,
email: pndivers@loxinfo.com,
www.pndivers.com

Krabi Divers
Located on Railey East at Viewpoint Bungalows. Locally run PADI dive school with a reputation as being somewhat lacksidasical.

PHRA NANG AREA

Railey West beach, with boats coming from Ao Nang beach.

ROCK CLIMBING

Krabi is now one of the most famous rock climbing centers in the world. There are over 100 protected routes accessible from Railey Beach. Most have been bolted by internationally renowned climbers and are looked after by Krabi's new generation of home grown climbers who are rapidly becoming as famous as the limestone walls they scale. Although Krabi did have a less than perfect safety reputation a few years ago, it has now matured into as safe a place to climb as anywhere in Europe or the States. But it is the views across the Andaman coast, great weather and an incredibly varied range of routes that make it one of the top two or three climbing destinations in the world. Class climbing rarely remains a secret for long and the walls do get crowded during the peak winter season when European and American climbers flock to Thailand's warm climes.

A thriving industry has sprung up to cater for the visitors and there are presently a number of climbing schools in Railey providing experienced instructors, gear rental and surprisingly well stocked shops selling everything from caribenas to shoes to specialised abseiling ropes. The most popular climbing areas are at 1-2-3; the huge wall at the end of Railey East and Thaiwand Wall; the magnificent cliff that overlooks Railey West.

For experienced climbers route maps are available detailing all the climbs in the area and partners are easy to find – just wander down to the 1-2-3 Wall and see what's going on.

Climbing Courses range from half-day introductory courses to the full three-day-course, which will take you through all the basic climbing techniques to a level where you will hopefully be able to lead a climb. The fee for a half-day course is **B**500, a full-day **B**1,000 and three days **B**3,000.

King Climbers

One of the original climbing schools and pioneers of rock climbing in Krabi. A well deserved reputation for reliability and employing good instructors. Located at Ya Ya bungalows on the path to Railey West.
☎ (01) 477 6624, (075) 63715,
📠 (075) 612 914,
email:
kingclimbers@iname.com
www.railey.com/kingclimbers.htm

Hot Rock

Located at Co Co Bungalows

PHRA NANG AREA

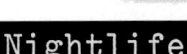

and run by another of Krabi's best climbers and his wife.
☎ (01) 677 3727.

Krabi Climbers
Located at Viewpoint bungalows.
☎ (01) 722 0115.

Tex Rock Climbing
Another member of Krabi's original climbers has a well-stocked shop offering equipment and courses.

SEA KAYAKING

Paddling tours and kayaks for rent are available from Railey Bay Resort.

PLACES TO SEE

DIAMOND CAVE

A two-kilometer hike up the hill along a path from Diamond Cave Bungalows is the Diamond Cave. The cavern stretches for 500-meters inside the rock and is quite spectacular with millions of crystalline formations that sparkle like diamonds under the light.

Be sure to take a torch and wear shoes.

PRINCESS LAGOON

About half way along the path between Railey East and Phra Nang Beach you will see a rope dangling down a steep dirt path. If you scramble up to the top you can follow a track to Phra Nang lagoon.

A large tidal body of water trapped inside the headland. Well worth the effort, but make sure you have decent footwear especially if it has been raining. Try to go at high tide.

Nightlife

As Railey is so small and easily navigable it is easy to keep up with any parties and special nights that are being put on – just keep an eye open for the advertisements.

Ya Ya's Bar
The stage for most of Railey's wild excesses. An open-air pub under large trees that is busy every night. Located at Ya Ya Resort on Railey East.

Sunset Bar
In front of Railey Bay Resort on Railey West and a Railey institution. The place to drink beer and sip cocktails as the sun goes down and sometimes for a good few hours after that.

Restaurants

Railey Bay Resort . . . .
. . . . **B100–200**
Even though they are trying to attract a better class of tourist the

Rock climbing...

'Inter-beaches' boats.

PHRA NANG AREA

Railey East shows its sporty side.

service here is as surly as ever and sometimes infuriatingly slow. Be sure to get your order in well before 22.00 as the kitchen closes when the chef has had enough. Having said that, the Thai food and seafood is very good, but the western food is best left alone.

Bo Bo's B30–100
The best Thai food on the beach – good noodles and one-plate meals. They also do a pretty good breakfast and have real coffee. The friendly bar is the best spot for daytime drinking and people watching.

Co Co's B100–200
Great for good value Thai food – the barbeque fish in three sauces is the best on the beach.

Accommodation

RAILEY WEST
Railey Bay B450–1,800
Large resort at the north of the beach just before the Rayawadee Hotel, with around 100 rooms sprawling all the way back to Railey East. Rooms range from fairly basic fan cooled huts to large air-con bungalows.
Rates are negotiable in low season and you can usually get better value elsewhere, but prices can be unreasonably increased during the peak period.
☎ (075) 611 944-5, ☎/📠 (01) 228 4516, (01)722 0112.

Railey Village Resort B800–2,500
Well run resort with a range of good fan and air-con rooms. Expensive for what you get, but then so is everywhere else on Railey. ☎/📠 (075) 612 415, ☎ (01) 464 6484.

Sand Sea Bungalows B900–2,750
Has been continually renovated over the last few years and is now probably the best on the beach. Fan and air-con rooms available. Also about the most reliable when it comes to holding a booking. ☎ (01) 722 0114, (01) 228 4426, 📠 (01) 722 0114.

Sunrise Resort . . . B300–800
In the middle of Railey East with small and basic bungalows. Not a very nice resort and the bungalows are well overpriced, but as they are one of the few budget options they are always full.
☎ (01) 228 4235.

Ya Ya Resort B450–700
Located on Railey East, but can be reached by walking through Railey Village Resort.
Three storey wooden buildings that fit nicely amongst the coconut palms and casuarina trees are the best value on the beach. Spacious, fan cooled and

PHRA NANG AREA

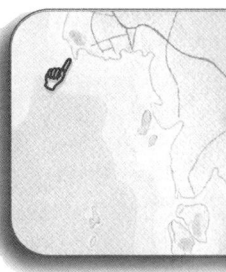

the trendiest place to hang out. Recommended.
☎/📠 (01) 464 4300.

Co Co Bungalows ... B200+
Very laid back old style bungalow resort with wooden huts scattered around the beach forest. Good budget option and popular with backpackers.
☎/📠 (075) 612 730.

**Diamond Cave Bungalows ...
.... B300–600**
Simple thatch roofed bungalows and nice cottages set back from the mangroves on Railey East. One of the best deals on the beach and a pretty setting. Recommended.
☎ (01) 477 0933.

Viewpoint B400–800
On the hill at the far north end of Railey East. Good quality fan cooled two story cottages in a garden stretching up the hill. A bit of a walk to the beach but nice and quiet. Shame the management can't be friendlier.
☎ (01) 722 0115.

Private Homes
*The northern section of Railey West is taken up by private homes. Mostly owned by farangs who built their own houses as part of a development project 20 years ago. The houses are all low rise and fit snugly into their surroundings. Many are available for rent and can accommodate from two to eight persons – a great way to stay in Railey if you are a group of friends.
For more details contact Dick Balsamo PO Box 8, Krabi 81000 or ☎ (01) 464 4338.*

Practical info

SHOPS
There are minimarts at Railey Village and Railey Bay resorts, but don't expect much more than film, sarongs, hammocks and other beach paraphernalia to be on sale. Climbing equipment and diving equipment is available from the climb and dive shops. There are no beach vendors on Railey beach, however on Phra Nang long tail boats pull up close to shore and sell all kinds of food and drinks - much cheaper than the hotel.

HEALTH
There is a first aid center (open 10.00-18.00) at Railey Bay Resort.

COMMUNICATIONS
The Internet has made it to Railey and you can go on line at Internet 55 behind Bo Bo restaurant. Phone calls can be made from any of the resorts; they will also handle stamps and postal services.

Lodging ...

PHRA NANG BEACH

This beautiful stretch of white sand is the domain of The Rayawadee Hotel. The beach is overlooked by another proud limestone cliff face dramatised by dangling stalactites and caves. Phra Nang Cave at the and of the beach is said to be one of the homes of the mythical princess Phra Nang and provides an awesome entrance to the beach if you arrive via the pathway from Railey East. The beach is only accessible by foot from Railey or by boat and it is now very popular with day-trippers from Ao Nang and can be crowded during high season.

The Rayawadee Hotel ......
.... B12,000–25,000

Formerly managed by the Dusit Group, this exclusive five-star hotel is the only resort on the beach. Designed to blend in with the environment it manages to remain unobtrusive without loosing anything in luxury and comfort. There are 179 rooms and cottages built out of wood and cement and painted in neutral colors. There are no fancy gardens but the rooms have beautiful interiors and the facilities are first class. The restaurants are very good but everything on sale in the hotel is very expensive.
☎ (075) 620 740,
📠 (075) 620 630.

At the far end of Phra Nang Beach you can follow a path through the beach forest up into a large cavern. Inside the cave there is a tunnel that is marked by ropes and ladders. If you follow the labyrinth, using the ropes and bamboo poles to help you scramble through, you will eventually find daylight and emerge from an opening in Thaiwand Wall. From this vantage point there are incredible views across Railey West and the whole peninsular. Climbers can abseil down to the land below and walk back to Railey Beach. This cave walk is not for the faint hearted, there is a lot of climbing and scrambling involved and it is best to go with someone who knows the way. Make sure you take a torch.

1-2-3 Wall at Railey East.

Koh Lanta

INTRODUCTION

Koh Lanta Yai is the latest hot destination for budget travelers to Thailand and it looks like it may well follow in Koh Samui's footsteps and become a fully-fledged international tourist destination. At the moment it is in the early stages of development, but the signs are there for rapid expansion into the mainstream market - which will include the dreaded package tourists. For now it is still a relatively unspoilt tropical island, with some beautiful beaches and quiet bays. There are no high-rise developments, no discos, no shopping malls and no beach vendors - just beaches, beach bungalows and restaurants. It is a destination for those looking for a quiet holiday. The main town, Saladan, is little more than two roads lined with new businesses catering for the growing tourist trade. The main beach, Klong Dao, has a few bars and hosts the occasional party, but it is still much, much more laid back than Phi Phi, Ao Nang or even Railey.

The beaches in the north and far south are the best, with most of the available accommodation in Klong Dao and scattered down the west coast. The east coast has no beaches and therefore no resorts and Lanta's traditional way of life is preserved there - 95% of the island's population are Muslim and you will see mosques as well as mangrove forests if you take the time to venture over to old Koh Lanta. The island has become far more accessible now that there is an airport in Krabi and there are daily ferries from Krabi and Phi Phi. The island can also be reached by bus from Trang, which is also served by an airport, as well as being on the main train line between Bangkok and Butterworth (Malaysia).

As with other islands off Thailand's west coast Lanta is only really visited between September and June due to the monsoon, which brings rain and rough seas. If you come out of season you may find it difficult to get there by boat and that most of the bungalows are closed, however you will be rewarded by bargain rates and plenty of empty beaches to wander along.

GETTING TO AND FROM LANTA

Express Boats to Krabi town; 08.00, 13.00. 1 hour 30 minute journey, cost B150.
From Krabi town: 08.00, 13.00, B150.
Express boats to Phi Phi: 08.00, 13.00 1 hour 15 minute journey, costs B170.
From Phi Phi: 08.00, 13.00, B170.
Express boats to minibuses to Trang depart from Saladan every hour from 09.00 until 14.00, 2 hours 30-minute journey, cost: B150.
From Trang, minibuses tickets can be purchased from any of the travel offices directly opposite Trang railway station and cost B150 each way. Minibuses depart on the hour from 11.00 until 14.00.

ORIENTATION

Lanta is 25 kilometers long and five kilometers wide at its broadest point. All the development and available accommodation is along the west coast. A paved road runs from the port town of Saladan along the west coast as far as Ban Klong Nin, where it turns inland to continue to Lanta town. A dirt road continues south to access the southern beaches. The busiest beach is Klong Dao just a few kilometers south of Saladan, Phra-Ae or Longbeach is the next beach south and is probably the best on the island. The beaches around the middle are generally not quite as good; they are a bit rockier and have coarser sand.

KOH LANTA

THE CHAO LEH
SEA GYPSIES OF THE ANDAMAN

The sea gypsies – chao leh in Thai – are unique to the Andaman coast and are scattered in small settlements from south Burma to northern Malaysia. Numbering around 4,000 people, they live on the ocean in boats, or simple shacks by the shore and seek their living from fishing. Ethnically and linguistically they are different from the Thais and they are thought to be descendents of the original Sakai negroid tribes of South Thailand. Physically they are shorter and stockier than the land dwellers and have thick curly hair.

Little is known about their history, they have no written language and very little in the way of cultural ideology or significant traditions. They believe in spirits rather than any formal religion and although many sea gypsies are nominally Muslim, their traditions owe more to Malay folklore than Islam. There are also Christian motifs amongst their mythology and they plant wooden crosses on the beach after their *loi rua* ceremony. *Loi Rua* is when elaborately decorated ceremonial boats are set adrift to cast away the accumulated sins and suffering of each community. The event lasts three days and takes place in the middle of June and November.

The sea gypsies form three distinct groups: the Moken, Moklen and Urak Lawoi. All three groups see themselves as one people and often intermarry, but their languages are only partially intelligible. Moken and Moklen are quite similar, but Urak Lawoi is closer to Malay than the other dialects. All three languages originally come from Malay, however Moken and Moklen have assimilated many aspects of Mon-Khmer, Thai and Burmese vocabularies.

The Mokken are the most primitive sea gypsy clan and number as few as 400. These are the original sea faring gypsies and the subject of many a seaman's tale. They bath at sea and move constantly, living in family groups on board small dugout boats. They can be found as far north as Burma's Tavoy Archipelago and in small communities off the north coast of Phang Nga province, including Koh Surin National Marine Park. The Moklen tend to live in shacks by the sea and are only found between Koh Phra Thong - off northern Phang Nga - and the northern tip of Phuket. The Urak Lawoi are the largest group, numbering around 2,500 people. They live in simple, but permanent huts on beaches from Phuket south to Phi Phi, Lanta and all the way south to the Tarutao archipelago.

On Phuket, the Urak Lawoi have formed large settlements on Sirey island and at Rawai, where although they live apart from the Thais, they have largely assimilated into Thai society. Tourist buses still deposit camera-toting foreigners into their villages, where they search amongst the poverty for brown haired children to photograph.

Most sea gypsy communities have been exploited mercilessly by land developers seeking title deeds to their coastal homelands and by tour operators searching for attractions for their clients. They have been forced onto the fringes of islands that they once roamed as they pleased and live in poverty and disarray. Limitations on fishing in some places have deprived them of their natural way of life and forced some of them to turn to the mainland for a living. Some communities have prospered from tourism and although the village at Koh Panyi has more Thai sellers than chao leh, at least some of the money spent there finds its way back to the poor sea gypsies. The chao leh are a people without ambition or material desires, seeking merely to subsist in their time-honored way. How they will fit into the harsh realities of modern Thailand is still unclear.

KOH LANTA

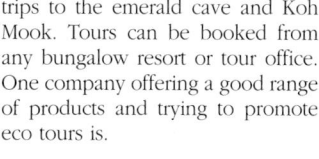

Waterfall beach in the far south is a beautiful bay with white sand and the prettiest place on the island.

GETTING AROUND

When you arrive in Saladan there will be a number of touts offering you free transport to their bungalows. If you have already decided where to stay this is the easiest and most economical way to get there. Otherwise you must take a taxi. Taxis on Lanta come in various forms: motorbike taxis are convenient for lone travelers going to Klong Dao or Longbeach; motorcycle sidecar taxis are good for couples or small groups going as far as Klong Nin. There are also *songtaews* on standby for longer trips. Saladan is very small and all the local transport is very easy to find. Fares are negotiable and range from **B**20 to Klong Dao up to **B**100 for a *songtaew* to Klong Jaak.

SIGHTS OF LANTA AND ISLAND TOURS

One of the main attractions for visitors to Lanta are the many small and beautiful islands that lie off its coastline. The most popular trips are to Koh Rok Nok, Koh Ngai and Koh Mook (see page 144 for details on these islands). Tours are by speedboat or longtail and include snorkeling and lunch. Speedboat trips get you there much quicker and cost around **B**900 - recommended for trips to the further island Koh Rok Nok. Longtail trips cost in the region of **B**500 and are recommended for trips to the emerald cave and Koh Mook. Tours can be booked from any bungalow resort or tour office. One company offering a good range of products and trying to promote eco tours is.

South Nature Tour
111 Moo 2, Saladan.
☎ (01) 228 4213.

Canoe Tours
Lanta Canoeing offers very interesting self-paddle tours through the mangroves off the east coast. Costs **B**800 for a one-day trip and pick up times depend on the tide. ☎ 01-228 4213.

Lanta Orchid Nursery
An orchid garden located at Long Beach.

ELEPHANT TREKKING

There are now a number of elephants on the island and they offer short treks into the interior or to viewpoints. Costs are around **B**500 for a 30-minute trek.

Around Lanta...

This is probably a temporary sight.

KOH LANTA

DIVING

Many of the best dive sights in the southern Andaman Sea are reachable from Lanta and there is now a thriving dive industry offering all the standard courses and dive tours. The closest sites are Koh Ha and Hin Bida but the best sites are Hin Daeng and Hin Muang. These are a long three and a half hour boat ride away, however some companies now run speed boats and some run overnight tours (staying on Koh Ngai) to make them easier to visit - however you get there it is unlikely you will be disappointed. There are also regular trips to the King Cruiser Wreck which is also around three hours away. A PADI Open Water Dive course costs around US$295 everywhere and daytrips run at US55 for the nearer sites and US$65 for the further ones. All tours include two dives, equipment and lunch and pricing seems to be fairly even. The main consideration when choosing a dive tour from Lanta is the quality of the boat and how fast it will get you there. All the dive operators have offices in Saladan and many now have offices on Klong Dao or the other beaches.

Atlantis Diving
Located near the pier at Saladan. PADI dive courses and day tours. Big dive boat takes 25 persons. ☎ (075) 612 914.

Dive Zone
Offices in Saladan and at Golden Bay cottages, Klong Dao. Offers all the same courses and tours. ☎ (01) 211 6938, www.thedivezone.com

Koh Lanta Diving Center
The first dive center on Lanta and probably the biggest operation as they have three boats, the bigger one being a very comfortable dive boat and the best choice for trips to Hin Daeng and Hin Muang. They also offer overnight tours sleeping on Koh Hai for US$150, including accommodation and four dives. Offices are at Saladan, Lanta bungalows (Klong Dao) and Tropicana Resort (Relax Bay). ☎ (01) 229 2103, email: christianmetz@t-online.de

Laguna Fun Dive
Located at Laguna beach Club, Klong Dao. All PADI courses and dive tours, but they use a speed boat, which makes the longer trips much more attractive. Two dive trips to Hin Daeng/Hin Muang cost US$69 and it takes one-and-a-half hours to get there - a considerable time saving. email: mail@lagunafundivers.de, www.lagunafundivers.de

Lanta Diver
Offers all the same tours and courses from offices in Saladan and Noble House Resort on Klong Dao. ☎ (01) 679 4940.

White and Blue Dive Club
Located at Saladan. ☎ (01) 478 9493, email: lanta@white-bluedive.com

The Raggae Pub is the best meeting place on Lanta.

KOH LANTA

SALADAN

The port of Saladan is barely more than a T-junction at the far north of the island. It is a small town bustling with tour agents, dive shops, minimarts and restaurants. There is a small clinic, lots of motorcycles for rent - if you can stand the daily fee of ฿250. There is a police box, a number of supermarkets, a few Internet cafes, a Kodak shop and a bank where you can change travelers cheques, cash and get credit card advances.

It is also the arrival and departure point for ferries to and from Phi Phi and Krabi. The pier is now about 200 meters east of the town.

KLONG DAO BEACH

The closest bay to Baan Saladan is also one of the loveliest on the island. It is a 3 kilometer long sweep of sand in a protected bay, perfect for swimming and sunbathing. Although this is the island's busiest beach it is still very quiet and peaceful. There are bungalow resorts all along the beach and anywhere you choose will not be more than a hundred meters from the sea. Prime beachfront bungalows are only a few short meters from the lapping waves at high tide.

The northern end is the quietest with the two resorts at the Deer's Neck headland being particularly peaceful. The southern end has the finest sand and heavier, although far from too much, development. There is a little strip of beach bars that provide what passes for nightlife and every now and again they can get quite lively as the young backpacker crowd comes to let their hair down.

Most of the available accommodation consists of standard Thai beach resorts. Which means that there is very little in the way of imaginative architecture or creative landscaping. The choice of bungalows range from basic ฿100 huts to large air-conditioned bungalows. At the time of writing there were no upscale resorts or hotels, but there was plenty of talk about the big boys looking for suitable land.

Bars, Restaurants

Swiss Bakery ..... ฿50–200
Located at Noble House Bungalows. A good alternative to Thai food with pastries, sandwiches and western food heavily featured on the menu.

VR Minimart ...... ฿25–100
Best value on the beach for cheap eats. The menu is scrawled on the wall in front of the shop and includes many travelers' favorites like muesli, banana pancakes, cheap breakfast sets and excellent noodle soup.

The Culture Restaurant .....
.... ฿100-200
Good Thai food and seafood right on the beach with a rustic Thai and pseudo western interior. Wicked seafood barbeques.

Nok Bar
Located in front of Golden Bay Cottages and has the best and most up to date music selections, an opinion that is supported by the fact that it is consistently the busiest bar on the beach.

Hunter Bar
A beer bar tacked onto Lanta Garden Home with a small pool table.

Beach Bars
There are a series of small box bars along from Chaba Lanta resort - no bar girls.

Otto Party Pub
An open air beach pub playing lots of reggae and other Thai beach classics (Eagles and Dire Straits live forever) as well taking occasional musical direction from visiting ravers. Still pretty low key but potentially the Reggae Pub of Koh Lanta.

KOH LANTA

Lone kayak on the high seas, an adventure off limits during the monsoon.

Flower Power Pub
Home of the Sunday beach party. Set beyond the bungalows to the far south of the beach this is where the late night stuff happens, when it happens.

Accommodation

Kaw Kwang Beach Resort B100–1,500
Located on the peninsular at the north of the beach with a wide range of bungalows, and still the best value on the beach. Well-run, friendly and helpful - although the staff are all tough salesmen, with everything done efficiently but for a price. Bungalows run from basic bamboo huts to air-con rooms, not luxury, but clean and comfortable. ☎ (01) 228 4106, (075) 621 373. Recommended.

Noble House . . . B600–1,000
Newcomer with six bungalows at the moment, but more on the drawing board. Well-designed, comfortable rooms.
☎ (01) 676 4940.

Diamond Sand Palace B600–1,500
One of the older resorts but still pretty good. The bungalows are a decent size and the staff is friendly. Good restaurant too.
☎/🖷 621 135,
email: diamondsand2000@hotmail.com

Laguna Beach Club B500–1,000
A new resort with lots of traditional coconut palm thatched roofs and nice big bungalows. One of the prettiest resorts on the beach.

Lanta Sea House B400–1,200
Pretty much in the center of the beach. Good size fan and air-con bungalows at reasonable prices. ☎ 612 713.

Lanta Villa B250–1,000
In a nice garden setting with plenty of tall casuarina trees for shade and lots of open space. This is one of the better deals on the beach. Fan and air-con rooms available. ☎ 620 629.

Southern Lanta Resort B1,000–3,000
Can claim to be the top resort on the beach as it is the only one with a swimming pool and other "resort facilities" such as a seminar room and Internet bookings. However the rooms are not very impressive and definitely over-

KOH LANTA

Lodging at Klong Dao...

priced. ☎ 218 947, 🖷 218 241, email: *southernlanta@kohlanta.com*

Sun and Sea Bungalows B600–800
New clean and functional rooms with fans and hot water. Part of Hans Bungalows growing concerns, but overpriced and void of any character.

Hans Bungalows B500–800
Friendly resort with lots of convenient services close by - bikes for rent, tours and even a massage school. Largish wood and bamboo rooms with fans.

VR Minimart B500–800
With a big open space right on the beach the temptation to build was obviously too much. They now have small old bungalow huts small new bungalow huts with fans and cold water. Both types are overpriced.

Chaba Lanta B400–700
Right in the thick of the beach bars - ideal for those who don't like to walk too far at night. Small wooden huts with fans.

Lanta Sand B400-800
Nice friendly little resort with all the huts cleverly built to face the sea. Fan and cold water. Located at the south end of the beach.

Sayang Beach Bungalows B200–300
Located on the quiet cove just south of Klong Dao, with new bungalows - a very peaceful retreat.

LONG BEACH (PRAE-AE)

The next beach after Klong Dao going south is also the best stretch of sand on the island. In fact it has to be one of the best beaches in Thailand, with fine white sand and clear waters, it could only be improved by adding the limestone cliffs of Phi Phi, but is far better as there is still very little development and hardly any people. However it is unlikely that the large tracts of vacant land will escape the developer's notice for long.

Already a Samui resort operator is building a three to four star resortel towards the north of the beach and Lanta Long Beach is renovating.

Blue Marlin Bar
Located near the end of the beach, just beyond the Reggae House and a better beach bar to hang out in. Friendly staff and a very laid back atmosphere.

Lanta Sandy Beach Bungalows B200–300
Clean and friendly resort at the north end of the beach. Nice and quiet and shaded by coconut palms.

Lanta Palm beach B200–300
The same family as Lanta Sandy Beach and really an extension of that resort. The two are pleasantly isolated and make a great place for a getaway beach holiday without being far from Klong Dao and Saladan.

The Sanctuary . . . B200–800
Laid back and friendly resort located towards the south end of the beach. This is the place to go for a chilled atmosphere, with friendly service and good value rooms. Good restaurant too – some tasty Indian offerings. Recommended.

Rapala Longbeach Resort B200–600
Wonderful location at the southern end of the beach, with fine sand and good swimming. Strange hexagonal bungalows but quite comfortable.
☎ (01) 228 4562.

Reggae House
A Rasta style open-air pub provides some laid back nightlife at the southern end of the beach. There are some bungalows but they are small and shabby.

141

KOH LANTA

RELAX BAY

A pretty cove south of Long beach with just one resort

Relax Bay Tropicana . . . .
. . . . B400–600
Comfortable, large and interesting bamboo and thatched bungalows with open roofed bathrooms providing a back to nature feel. Beautifully located.
☎ (01) 228 4213,
www.lanta.de/relaxbay

KLONG KHONG BEACH

The beach becomes a bit narrower and rockier as you get to the central section of the island; however there are some nice resorts and the swimming is still good.

Lanta Riviera B150–400
Fairly standard huts in a coconut garden. ☎ (01) 464 4354.
Lanta Coconut Green Field . . .
. . . . B250–300
Quite a pretty resort with 20 bamboo and thatch bungalows with fans. Also has a good bar and restaurant.
☎ (01) 415 0713.
Lanta Merry Hut Resort . . . . .
. . . . B250–300
A very pretty resort with 15 rooms in a beautifully landscaped garden. Lanta would be a much better place if everywhere used as much care and thought when building a resort. Highly recommended. ☎ (01) 210 3835.

KLONG NIN BEACH

Again the beach is not as good as elsewhere but there are some bargain bungalows to be found.

Lanta Nature Beach Resort . . .
. . . . B100–300
Standard bamboo and thatch bungalows, but clean and big enough to make them excellent value.

Lanta Miami B200–300
Basic huts and bungalows.
Nice Beach B150–200
Unexciting white wood huts. nothing special here.

HAAD NUI

Dreamteam B300–1,800
Medium to large resort that sprawls along a hill down onto the beach. Well run and popular bungalow resort with a wide range of rooms available from basic fan to air-con. The beach is OK but not as good as those further north, but the resort makes up for it in ambiance. Recommended.
☎ (01) 228 4184.

KANTIANG BAY

A small secluded bay with a lovely beach and clear water.

Sea Sun B200–400
Standard bungalows but nicely situated on the beach.
Kantiamu Seaview . B200–300
Unimaginative but clean and functional beach huts within sight of the sea.

KLONG JAK BAY

A beautiful bay right at the south of the island. If you are after a quiet, secluded piece of paradise this is it.

Waterfall Bay Resort . . . .
. . . . B600–900
Very well run and pretty resort with nice bungalows that appear to be well overpriced. However it remains popular due to a fantastic location and peaceful atmosphere. The staff is very helpful and speak excellent English.
☎ (01) 228 4014.
Sun moon Jungle Hut . . . . . .
. . . . B300–600
Reasonable bungalows, but lacking the service and ambiance of Waterfall Bay. However they are more realistically priced and share the same beach.

Trang & Tarutao

TRANG

The capital of Trang province is becoming a gateway to some of Thailand's most beautiful yet least known island getaways, including Koh Lanta.

The town itself is of little interest to travelers, but it is clean and well ordered and has been the beneficiary of some generous attention as the home town of Thailand's current prime minister. It has an airport that connects with Bangkok and it is on the main railway line between Bangkok and Butterworth in Malaysia. Foreign tourists are no longer a strange sight in Trang and there are now dozens of travel offices located opposite the train station all set up to provide onward tickets to Koh Lanta and the other islands.

There are a number of hotels, banks and a post office on the main - Rama 6 - road, which is directly opposite the railway station.

GETTING THERE

Trains from Bangkok departs at 13.55 (arrives at Trang Station at 07.15). From Trang trains leaves at 17.10 (arrives Bangkok at 09.05).
There are daily flights from (and to) Bangkok costing B2,305 each way on Thai Airways.

Accommodation

Thumrin Hotel B470–700
Air-con rooms with hot water fridge and TV. ☎ (075) 211 011, ☎ (075) 218 057.
Koteng Hotel B180–300
Basic fan rooms.
☎ (075) 218 622.
Trang Hotel
Air-con rooms with TV and fridge.
☎ 218 944.

KOH NGAI

Pronounced 'Hai', this is a beautiful unspoilt island south of Lanta with white sand beaches and very little else - superb for snorkeling with very clear waters. It has two resorts.

Koh Ngai Resort . . B700–900
Billed as a VIP resort and has reasonably comfortable air-con bungalows, a good restaurant and trips to the emerald cave and other islands. ☎ (075) 211 045 or Trang Office (075) 210 317.
Koh Ngai Villa B300
In another cove and good value, friendly resort with fan rooms right on the beach.

Both resorts are reached by boat from Trang via Pak Meng. Transfers leave from opposite Trang train station at 10.30 (cost B150).

Emerald Bay, secluded as can be.

TRANG AND TARUTAO

Koh Mook, has the charm of unsophisticated accommodation.

KOH MOOK

Also south of Lanta, but not as pretty as Koh Ngai. The main attraction is the Emerald Cave on its western side. The cave can be entered by longtail or canoe and inside opens up into a hong with a hidden lagoon and beach completely enclosed by the limestone walls of the island. Similar to the famous hongs of Phang Nga but far less known. It is well worth a visit.

Koh Mook Resort . . B150–300
The resort is on the east of the island and is run by a friendly and helpful family who cook superb seafood every night. The beach is mostly mud flats and mangroves and not ideal for swimming. Closed from July to September. Trang Office ☎ (075) 214 441, Resort ☎ (075) 212 613.

Koh Mook Resort is reached by boat from Trang via Pak Meng. Transfers leave from opposite Trang railway Station at 10.30 and cost B150.

TARUTAO

Koh Tarutao National Marine Park consists of 51 islands in the far south west of Thailand close to the Malaysian border. The archipelago is one of the most beautiful parts of the Andaman Cost and due to its location - and the impressive efforts of the parks authority - it experiences very little tourism. There are rooms available on the main island, Koh Tarutao and on Koh Adang. Accommodation is in park authority bungalows - camping is allowed on many of the islands. There are no resorts on any of the islands and private development is still prohibited, although there is increasing pressure to build here.

"Tarutao National Park - A Travelers Adventure Handbook" is available at the park's headquarters and it details all the park's facilities as well as giving trekking routes. It is essential reading for all visitors.

GETTING THERE
Boats to Tarutao Island leave from Pak Bara, 60 kilometers south west of Satun. They run daily between November and April leaving at 10.30 and 15.00 and cost B100 each way, the trip takes one-and-a-half hours.

Andaman coast

THE NORTHERN ANDAMAN COAST

North of Phuket the Andaman coast of Thailand stretches to the Isthmus of Kra where it meets the Burmese border. It is a tremendously varied coastline with sandy beaches and rocky headlands fringing tropical jungle. Route 4 winds its way along the length of Phang Nga province forming a barrier between the shore and the forest.

There are only a few sleepy towns on the road until it reaches Ranong and much of this part of Phang Nga province has been designated as national parks.

THAI MUANG

The first large settlement north of Phuket is Thai Muang, a typically dusty and non-descript Thai town. There is a public beach, but it is not particularly attractive. Just north of the town is Haad Thai Muang National Park where sea turtles come to lay eggs between November and February.

For golfers there is a nice 18-hole course at the southern end of the beach.

Thai Muang Beach Golf and Marina, Green Fees . . ฿2,000
An 18-hole championship course has been constructed by Dye designs close to the ocean. It is a flat course, but testing and has some wonderful views out to sea. There is a restaurant, conference center and accommodation in well-designed chalets. Room rates start at ฿2,200 per night and entitle you to half price golf. It offers reasonable value for money – especially when compared to Phuket – and the course is never that busy. A marina is still on the drawing board.
☎ (076) 571 533-4,
📠 (076) 571 214.

KHAO LAK

The prettiest section of coastline has become known as Khao Lak due to its proximity to the national park of that name. Khao Lak consists of a series of sandy beaches that stretch for five or six kilometers along the coast approximately 70 kilometers north of Phuket. A variety of resorts have opened along the coast, offering accommodation right on the beach. A village of sorts has invented itself, but the area is still very quiet and peaceful. Most of the resorts have sprung up over the last couple of years and evidence that more are planned can be seen all along the coast. The attraction of Khao Lak is peace and tranquillity and hopefully that will not be adversely affected by the arrival of more resorts. It is a very beautiful area, with the jungle overflowing onto the beach road and broad sandy beaches studded with granite boulders. Most visitors are European – Germans easily outnumber other tourists. The Similan islands are just 60 kilometers away. Khao Lak has a thriving dive industry offering great value courses and trips to Thailand's best dive sites. There is no nightlife to speak of, just a few beach bars and restaurants. This is a place to soak up the sun, relax and take things easy.

SEASONS

Like most of the Andaman coast, the tourist season is dependent on the monsoon. The season is October to May, with December and New Year being peak times. From June to September the area is practically deserted and many resorts and businesses close down. Swimming is dangerous at this time and it is often too rough for boats to go out. There is a lot of flotsam on the beach and it looks very different to the photogenic sands of high season. However the plus side is half price accommodation and empty beaches

ANDAMAN COAST

and the parks are at their best during this time, so it is a good time for nature lovers.

ORIENTATION

Khao Lak is the collective name for a series of beaches. Khao Lak beach is actually at the far south and borders Khao Lak National Park. The middle section is Nong Thong Beach – but more commonly referred to as Khao Lak. There is a denser concentration of resorts, restaurants and dive shops here and a strip of sorts along the beach. At the northern end is Bang Niang Beach, the quietest and most scenic area. Route 4 runs right through Khao Lak so it is very simple to navigate your way around.

GETTING THERE

BY BUS

Any bus running along Route 4 will stop at Khao Lak. Just tell the driver where you are staying and they will stop as close as possible. If you still haven't made your mind up, the easiest place to get out is at Sea Dragon Dive Center and then walk down the road to the beach. From Phuket you can take an air-con bus to Ranong, or a local bus to Takua Pa and jump out. From Surat Thani take the bus to Takua Pa and then a local bus to Tap Lamu, or an air-con bus to Phuket.

AIR AND TAXI

From Phuket Airport it costs ฿1,200 for a taxi to any resort on Khao Lak.

FROM BANGKOK

Take a bus from the Southern bus terminal to Ranong and then a bus to Tap Lamu, Thai Muang, or Phuket.

Beachlife

DIVING

There is now a flourishing dive industry in Khao Lak and it is gaining a reputation as a cheap place to learn to dive. PADI Open Water Courses can cost as little as ฿7,800.– the lowest price in Thailand bar Koh Tao. There is a nice reef close to the shore, which is ideal for training dives and not far away is some of the best diving in Asia. It is the nearest accommodation center to the Similan Islands - home to Thailand's most highly rated dive sites. Most operators in Khao Lak offer liveaboard dive tours to the Similans and some also offer trips to Surin and Burma.

Sea Dragon

Located in the center of Khao Lak – with a very visible office on Route 4. The oldest and probably still the main operator in Khao Lak. They have all PADI courses with dives on the local reefs as well as regular liveaboard trips to the Similans. They have a reputation as a very reliable, but no-frills operator, offering some of the cheapest dive tours to the Similans. A 3 day/2 night tour costs ฿11,400 and includes 7

The road from Ranong to Takua Pa.

ANDAMAN COAST

dives. ☎/📠 (01) 229 2418.

Kon Tiki
A branch of the reputable Phuket based school. A Scandinavian/German operation, they mainly book liveaboard trips on a number of different boats and aim exclusively at the German speaking market. Openwater courses cost B11,000.
☎/📠 (076) 443 339.

High Class Adventure Diving
Offers all PADI courses as well as liveaboard diving from two different boats. Located at Sabai Bungalows on Bang Niang beach. ☎/📠 (01) 958 8040.

Bars, Restaurants

There is a strip of bars and restaurants on the seafront north of Nang Thong Bay Resort. Tarzan bar is a bit of a hang out. Otherwise there are some small tour agents and shops, as well as places offering to rent snorkeling gear.

Green House Café
Just south of the center. Brand new bar/café yet to establish itself but may provide the nightlife for the area.

Khao Lak View Restaurant B60–160
Beautifully situated on the headland overlooking the whole of Khao Lak. If you are driving from Phuket this is the first place you see after passing the national park offices. The food is nothing special, but is a "must visit" for the view.

Taco House B50-150
A Mexican restaurant on the beach. It looks very out of place, but serves up a reasonable impression of Mexican food and does offer something different.

Joe's Steakhouse B100-200
On Ban Niang beach. Farang owned restaurant near the Sabai bungalows offering a western menu, including steaks. Pretty good too.

Beach restaurants
Beyond Bang Niang Resort are a clutch of thatched-roofed beach restaurants with big wooden benches right on the beach. Quiet, peaceful, a great place to eat good Thai food and look out over the ocean.

Accommodation

KHAO LAK BEACH

Baan Khao Lak B1,200–4,000
Brand new hotel on Khao Lak beach. Fan and air-con bungalows available, good facilities and nice jungle landscaping.

Khao Lak Laguna B1,800–4,600
Very pretty luxury resort with all facilities and a super location on the hill between route 4 and Khao Lak beach.
☎ 01-229 2247.

Khao Lak Sunset B850–2,500
Very new resort on the headland at the south of the beach. A range of bungalows and cottages from large Thai style bungalows to smaller fan rooms.
☎ (076) 421 807.

Khao Lak Nature Resort
Not finished at the time of going to print, but looks like another luxury "nature resort". Great location adjacent to the national park, looks like it may be a more interesting place to stay than the other upmarket resorts.

Poseidon Bungalows B150-500
Located south of Khao Lak, in a secluded bay. Basic thatched roofed bungalows with shared facilities and large huts with private bathrooms are available. Well run and friendly.
☎ (076) 443 258.

Food & lodging...

ANDAMAN COAST

The central part of Kao Lak beach (looking towards the north).

CENTRAL KHAO LAK (NONG THONG BEACH)

Khao Lak Tropicana Resort B880–1,650
An example of a developer spending lots of money on land and materials, but being too mean to employ a decent architect. An ugly resort north of the center of Khao Lak with fan and air-con bungalows.
☎/🖷 (076) 420 231-40.

Garden Beach Resort B500–600
One of the older resorts with a little more character than the rest. 62 large brick bungalows (shame about the green roofs). Friendly service and relaxed atmosphere.
☎ (076) 420 121-28, 🖷 (076) 420 121-28, 🖷 (076) 420 129-30. Recommended

Khao Lak Bungalows (Gerd and Noi)
A wide variety of bungalows in a pleasant garden just back from the beach. Some are very thoughtfully designed with big decks and French windows. Located north of the center.
☎ (01) 229 2197,
🖷 (01) 270 1804.

Khao Lak Green Beach B700–1,100
A new resort near the center of the beach. Very attractive resort, pleasantly landscaped with fan and air-con bungalows in the garden or right on the beach. Service is friendly although not particularly efficient.
☎ (076) 420 043-7, 🖷 (076) 420 047. Recommended.

Nang Thong Bay Resort B400–850
Another of the older resorts. About 35 bungalows ranging from fan rooms to air-con. The beach front rooms are the most expensive and the air-con rooms at the back are probably the best value. ☎ (076) 420 088,
🖷 (076) 420 090.

Nang Thong Bay Resort II B500-1000
South of Nang Thong resort with 30 or so cottages. Plenty of space with nice new air-con and fan bungalows. Newer and better than its sister, but with less character. ☎ (076) 420 078,
🖷 (076) 420 080.

Wang Torn Bungalows B300-700
Big new wooden bungalows running up a hill next to a stream. Great value, but on the wrong side of the road. Located on the road next to the Green House Café.

Tukta B300–400
A scruffy little resort with poorly kept rooms. Only really an option if you are on a tight budget. However the restaurant on the beach is really good.

ANDAMAN COAST

BANG NIANG BEACH

Bang Niang Beach Resort B600–1,800
A very new resort behind Chong Fa Resort. Tastefully built rooms and bungalows around a small pool and garden. Helpful and friendly staff, good facilities and pretty good value. ☎ (076) 422 140, 📠 (076) 431 345.

Chong Fa Beach Resort B180–1,000
Older resort right on the beach offering fan and air-con bungalows or rooms are in a two storey building. Laid back and peaceful. Pretty good value. Good restaurant.
☎/📠 (01) 229 1253.

Baan Soraya B500
6 nicely constructed and designed brand new rooms behind Chong Fa resort. No facilities, but friendly family/owners live in the big house behind.
☎ (076) 420 194.

Mai's Quiet Zone . . B300-600
At the northern extremes of Bang Niang is this traditional Thai beach resort. Wooden huts of various sizes and a super-laid-back atmosphere. To get there; follow the dirt track past Bang Niang Beach Resort and continue past the beach restaurants.

Sabai Bungalows . . B400-800
Set back from the beach near Bang Niang Beach Resort. Traditional wooden and bamboo bungalows with nice big decks – nice and quiet.
☎ (01) 229 2197.

Similana Resort B1,800–2,800
Located a couple of kilometers north of Bang Niang is the beautifully landscaped Similana Resort. Sitting on top of a headland with superb views, this is a 3-star resort with a difference. All the rooms have been crafted from local materials and particular attention has been paid to make sure that if fits in with the natural surroundings. Facilities include a swimming pool and a good restaurant, the beach is super-clean and the staff are helpful and friendly. Rooms are a little expensive for what you get, but you are paying for the atmosphere and isolation.
☎ (01) 211 2564, (02) 379 4586,
📠 (02) 731 6844, email: similana@asiaaccess.net.th.

Practical info

Next to Khao Lak Green Beach there is a small village (collection of huts) that runs down to the sea. This

Lodging at Khao Lak...

Beach side restaurant at Khao Lak - always laid back.

ANDAMAN COAST

is where taxis congregate; there are cars for rent and some small restaurants offering good cheap Thai food.

Nee and Lido Restaurant
On route 4 just south of town. Restaurant, Internet and cars for rent all in one place. Good value breakfasts for **B**69.
☎ (076) 330 789.

BANKS
Siam City Bank has an exchange booth on the main road opposite Sea Dragon's office. Otherwise most of the bigger resorts will change travelers cheques for a price. The nearest ATMs are in Thai Muang or Takua Pa.

HEALTH
There is a clinic on the main road near the bank; otherwise the nearest hospital is at Takua Pa. For anything serious it is best to go straight to Phuket.

SAWASDEE PLAZA
A big ugly plaza, full of shophouses for rent, is being built just south of town. Although development is an inevitable part of the area's evolution, this is a criminally ugly building. Shame, shame, shame.

THE SIMILAN ISLANDS

Koh Mu Similan Park consists of the famous granite islands that are so highly regarded - and visited - by divers. Designated as a national park, there are no resorts or developments on any of the islands, making them beautifully preserved examples of Thailand's islands and beaches. The National Parks Division of the Royal Forestry Office has a headquarters on Koh Miang – island #4 – and has accommodation available in the form of purpose-built dormitory bungalows, each capable of housing 20 people. It is also permitted to camp on almost all of the islands for a small fee. There is a restaurant at the parks office and there are longtail boats available to take you to the other beaches. There is also a pleasant nature trail across Koh Miang.

BOATS TO THE SIMILANS
Depart from Tap Lamu pier at 07.30 every day, takes 4 hours and costs **B**850 each way. Tickets are available from Met Sine Tours right by the pier.
☎ (076) 443 276.
Get to Tap Lamu by bus from Phuket, Ranong, Khao Lak or Takua Pa.

Alternatively, trips to the Similans can be arranged in Phuket. A boat trip from Patong Beach takes 4 hours by Songserm Travel Center ☎ (076) 222 570-4.

PERMITS
Permission for staying on the Similans must be obtained in advance from the Royal Forestry Department in Tap Lamu.
☎ *(076) 411 914,*
or the Marine National Parks Division: ☎ *(02) 579 7048.*

ANDAMAN COAST

THE SURIN ISLANDS

Koh Surin National Marine Park lies about 70 kilometers from Khuraburi in Northern Phang Nga province. The islands are excellent for exploring, there are several trekking trails and many of the reefs are accessible for snorkelers. The islands are very popular with Thai eco-tourists and can be busy at weekends and on public holidays. Accommodation is in dormitory style long houses run by the National Parks Office or in tents, which can be rented for **B**100. The parks office is on Koh Surin Neua and has a decent restaurant.

BOATS TO SURIN

Leave from the Parks Office about 6 kilometers north of Khuraburi town. The parks office can help you charter a boat or you can join a charter boat for **B**1,000 per person each way, otherwise it costs **B**8,000 to **B**15,000 to charter a whole boat. It is advisable to call first and see when – and if – boats are departing.
☎ (076) 491378.
Khuraburi is on the bus route between Takua Pa and Ranong.

Ask to be let off at Nong Yang – or mention Surin – and then take a motor-cycle taxi to the pier.

RANONG

The small capital of Ranong province is another gateway to the Andaman Coast. It is also just across the Chan river from Burma --and the border is open to foreigners.for visa runs There are several hotels in all categories and many places to eat. Across the border in Victoria Point there is an interesting market and some old colonial buildings.

Ranong has an airport and Bangkok Airways operates a daily service from Bangkok for **B**1,980 each way. There are also direct buses from Bangkok's southern bus terminal, Phuket and all the other centers in the south. Local buses to Takua Pa – stopping at Khuraburi – Khao Lak and Tap Lamu also run from the bus station.

The border is the most convenient place in the region for visa runs. It takes about 2 hours.

Similans & Surin islands...

Arrival quay at Kawtung, a typical Burmese trading post.

Khao Sok

KHAO SOK NATIONAL PARK

Just two hours drive from Surat Thani, heading west along highway 401 towards Phuket, is Khao Sok National Park. A 646-square-kilometer expanse of land blanketed with tropical and evergreen rainforest and dominated by towering limestone mountains and spectacular karsts.

Few tourists make the effort to get to the park, most preferring to lie on the beaches of Samui or Phuket, however those who do are rarely disappointed and find it quite incredible that one of Thailand's last remaining rainforests and a true wilderness is so close to these major tourist centers yet relatively unknown.

GETTING TO THE PARK

The park entrance is just west of the 109-kilometer marker, roughly two thirds of the way to Takua Pa from Surat Thani, and is on the north side of the road. Buses to Takua Pa leave Surat Thani bus station every 90 minutes, but make sure you ask to be let off at the park - it is three kilometers from the entrance to the park headquarters, but less to the nearest bungalow resort, and the chances are that someone from one (or more) resorts will be waiting to pick people up (in the high season at least).

Buses from Surat Thani to Phuket now DO NOT go past the park entrance, so make sure the bus is going to Takua Pa. Otherwise rent a car from Samui and drive yourself. Budget supply a very useful book with detailed maps and advice for getting to and staying in the park, when you rent one of their cars. Many local renters will not allow you to leave the island, so check first as it may invalidate any insurance they have.

If you don't have the time or inclination to do it yourself, book one of Siam Safari's award winning eco-tour adventures.

SIGHTS OF KHAO SOK

Within the far-flung boundaries are numerous waterfalls, enormous bat caves, the immense Chieo Lan Reservoir, and the Sok River, which

KHAO SOK

winds through thick jungle and past huge limestone cliffs that resemble a misty vision of another world. In dense regions of the park a few tigers and leopards still prowl, although they are hardly ever seen. Elephant, gaur, serow, banteng, Malay sun-bear, tapir, and wild pig also roam the forest and can be seen if you have the time and patience to go on a real safari. Wild gibbons, langur monkey and macaque are more likely to be spotted and are often heard, especially the distinctive whooping of the gibbon.

There are over 180 species of birds living in the park, including 5 species of hornbills. Birdwatchers from all over the world come to catalogue rare species, especially Guerney's Pita, which is one of the rarest species on the planet and lives only in Khao Sok.

Another species endemic to the park is a flower; Bua Phut, or "wild lotus", which is the largest flower in the world, reaching a diameter of 80-centimeters, and once a year it produces huge buds that emit a foul stench attracting the insects it uses for pollination.

TREKKING

From the visitor's center there are a number of trails leading into the jungle. They are all mapped in the official guide book or in Tom Henley's book and marked by signposts. However it is best to check with the rangers before going trekking, as some trails are poorly marked or inaccessible at certain times of the year. Many of the most interesting trails lead to waterfalls and can be done in a day; guides can be hired for around **B**300 to accompany you on these trails.

Bang Laep Nam Waterfalls
Trail #4 is a rather easy 5-kilometer walk.

Sip Et Chan Waterfalls
This 11-tiered waterfall is quite a sight and worth the tough 4-kilometer walk. It is at the end of the only trail going north and follows the Bang Laen river, which you will have to cross a number of times.

Tan Gloy Waterfalls
Trail #1 leads 9-kilometers to these impressive falls which have a good pool for swimming - allow for three hours hike each way.

Tan Sawn Falls
Follow trail #3 for 9-kilometers, but be sure to check first as this trail includes a wade along the river bed, which may not be possible in the wet season.

CHEOW LAN LAKE

The most interesting sights in the park can only be reached by going on overnight tours. These can be part of a package prearranged in Samui (or Bangkok or Phuket) or you can join a local tour organized by one of the resorts in Khao Sok. The Jungle House, and Khao Sok Rainforest Resort offer good trips and Nature Restaurant Bamboo House and Nung's do similar budget packages, which can be arranged at short notice, but you will need a minimum of four persons. Most tours take you to Cheow Lan lake, which is a beautiful expanse of water studded by islands and surrounded by spectacular limestone karsts and misty rainforest. There are three interesting caves to explore by boat or by canoe.

Accommodation is in raft huts that float on the lake and can only be used as part of a tour.

Some tours include a night safari, where you have a real chance of spotting some wildlife, and some include elephant trekking.

Another tour that is now popular is a canoe trip down the Sok river which cuts through the jungle amidst some beautiful scenery.

The best wildlife in the Kingdom...

KHAO SOK

PRICES

Prices for tours to Khao Sok departing from Samui or Surat Thani start at around B4,000. Siam Safari Nature Tours run tours out of Koh Samui.
☎ 415 123-4, 🖷 415 124,
email: info@siamsafari.com,
www.siamsafari.com

ACCOMMODATION

There is quite a good choice of accommodation available inside the park, mostly rustic wood cabins and simple bamboo huts or tree houses, which provide an alternative way to get back to nature.

The National Park division rents rather unimaginative bungalows for B600 to 900 and has camping facilities for B40 to 60, but few people stay there as the private guest houses have superior facilities and a much more congenial atmosphere.

Art's Jungle House .B300-800
Located down the trail that runs from Bamboo House, Art's also has a couple of tree houses as well as some well situated wooden cabins in a tropical garden. It is close to the river and has a good swimming area. Well run and very friendly - popular with backpackers and tour groups.
☎ /🖷 (076) 421 613.

Bamboo House . . . B150-450
Run by the park warden and also nicely situated with simple bamboo huts, with bathrooms and a few treehouses. Located on the road to the park headquarters, almost two kilometers from the entrance - good place to get trekking information.

Khao Sok Rainforest Resort B300-800
Probably the most comfortable accommodation in the park, with large cottages on stilts, with spacious balconies overlooking the forest and attached showers and toilets. ☎ 01-464 4361,
🖷 612 914.

Nung House B100-450
Slightly further down the track from Bamboo House and run by the warden's son. He has set up his own place with cheap bamboo huts with shared facilities, as well as a few better cabins.

Our Jungle Lodge . .B300-450
Beautifully located on a secluded riverbank beneath limestone cliffs, this is the prettiest resort in the park and is run by a friendly Irishman and his wife. They have treehouses, wooden cabins and cabins right on the river, all quite spacious and very private. Can be found by walking for about 15-minutes past Nung's. Recommended.
☎ 01-229 2337.

Monkeys are omnipresent throughout the park.

KHAO SOK

Tree Tops River Huts . . . .
. . . . B200-600
The original tree tops guest house and still the best, consists of five elevated tree houses, two cave lodges and five bamboo raft houses, with attached bathrooms, on Rajaphrabha Lake. Located close to the visitors center. Recommended.
☎ (076) 299 150.

BARS & RESTAURANTS

Nature Restaurant
Close to Our Jungle House and offers a pleasant change to the resorts. Good shakes and a nice atmosphere.

Nirvana Bar and Yogurt House
Small bar just past Nung's, the kind of place to get a healthy break.

PRACTICAL INFO

There is a **B**3 entrance fee which is payable at the checkpoint close to the visitors center. There are rough but useful maps available for **B**5, which include sketches of many of the trails, and it is recommended that you buy Tom Henley's excellent book "Waterfalls and Gibbon Calls".

There is also a display inside the center that shows details of the park. The visitors center is open from 08:00 to 16:00.

Khao Sok is a rain-forest so it has its own eco-system and climate. It is usually wet and humid and there are lots of leeches, so if you are going trekking make sure you have good shoes and always take lots of water with you.

The best time to visit is in January or February. From March to May it is hot and the rest of the year it can be wet, but don't let that put you off as in the wet season the flora is at its best.

Lodging at Khao Sok...

North of the park towards Ranong.

Back of the Book

	PAGE Nº
FESTIVALS & NATIONAL HOLIDAYS	158
PHOTO CREDITS	159
MEDICAL ADVISORY	160
- HOSPITALS	162
SELECTION OF: BOOKS, MAPS & WEBSITES	163
CONTACTS FOR ALL AIRLINES	164
EMERGENCY & IMPORTANT PHONE NUMBERS	
- IN BANGKOK	166
- ON THE ISLANDS	167
INDEX	168
INDEX OF OUR FAVORITE PLACES	170
MAP LEGEND	171
INDEX OF ADVERTISEMENTS	172
MAP OF PHRA NAMG AREA	173
MAP OF PATONG	174
MAP OF KARON & KATA	175
MAP OF PHUKET TOWN	176
MAP OF PHI PHI ISLANDS	178
MAP OF PHANG NGA BAY	179
MAP OF KOH LANTA	180

Festivals & Holidays

1st January: New Year's Day
  Celebrations for the start of the new year.
10th January: Children's Day
  On the second Saturday in January every year, there is a special celebration for children. Many places let children go in free or half price on this day.
16th January: Teacher's Day
  On this day every year, all of the schools in Thailand are closed as a special tribute to the teachers.
11th February: Makha Buchaa Day
  The full moon of the third lunar month marks the occasion when 1,250 of the Buddha's disciples came to hear him preach. Public holiday.
Early February: Chinese New Year
2nd April: HRH Princess Sirindhorn's Birthday.
6th April: Chakri Day
  Public holiday commemorating King Rama I who was the first of the Chakri kings.
13th, 14th, 15th April: Songkran Festival
  During April 13-15, everyone celebrates the traditional Thai new year. In every home, Buddha images are washed with rose scented water. People also pay respects to their elders by pouring a little water over their hands. Outside, people go a little wilder and buckets of water are thrown over anything that moves.
1st May: National Labor Day
  A holiday for some factory and office workers.
5th May: Coronation Day
  Public holiday. Commemorates the coronation of the king and queen in 1946.

Festivals and Events on PHUKET

April
  Turtle releasing festival at Nai Yang national park is incorporated into part of Songkran Festival. ☎ 327 407
June
  Loi Rua Festival – Sea gypsy boat ceremony celebrated by sea gypsies all along the coast. Contact TAT ☎ 212 213
July
  Phuket International Rugby Sevens. Contact Patrick ☎ 341 927
  Asian X Games on Patong beach with more than 250 competitors.
September
  Phuket International Fishing Tournament. ☎
October
  Vegetarian Festival. Contact: TAT ☎ 212 213
  Quiksilver Phuket Surfing Contest (over 50 surfers)
  Patong Carnival. Beauty pagents and fun fairs on Patong Beach.
Phuket International Football Cup at Dulwich College ☎ 238 711-20
November
  The Laguna Phuket Triathlon, organised by Phuket Laguna.
  Loi Rua Festival – Sea gypsy boat ceremony celebrated by sea gypsies all along the coast. Contact TAT ☎ 212213
December
  King's Cup Regatta. ☎

BACK OF THE BOOK

Festivals & public holidays...

10th May: Visakha Bucha Day
The full moon of the sixth lunar month is the most important date on the Buddhist religious calendar. It celebrates the Buddha's birth, enlightenment and death. Every year on this day, teachers at local schools take part in a candle-lit procession around the main chapel of village temples. They carry with them flowers, three incense sticks and a lighted candle. They walk around the chapel three times in a clock-wise direction. Afterwards they listen to a sermon from a monk. Public holiday.

11th May: Ploughing Day
Important ceremony to mark the official start of the rice-planting season.

19th July: Khao Phansa Day
Buddhist holiday

28th July: HRH The Crown Prince's Birthday

12th August: HM The Queen's Birthday
Celebrations for the Queen's birthday. This day is also Mother's Day and a public holiday.

23rd October: Chulalongkorn Day
A public holiday to commemorate King Rama V who did a lot of important things for Thailand. His many accomplishments include the abolition of slavery, the construction of the railways, the establishment of the post and telegraph services and the creation of the ministerial system.

3rd November: Loy Krathong
The most picturesque of the Thai festivals is held on the full-moon of the 12th lunar month. Little candle-lit *krathongs* are launched onto the water as an offering to Mother Water. People apologize for polluting the water and promise to do better in the future.

5th December: HM The King's Birthday
Celebrations for the King's birthday. This day is also Father's Day and a public holiday.

10th December: Constitution Day
Public holiday. Commemorates the proclamation of the constitutional monarchy in 1932.

31st December: New Year's Eve
Public holiday.

Photo Credits

Hamish Keith
Pages: 7, 27, 30, 31, 35, 56, 57, 58, 61, 62, 63, 64, 77, 79, 82, 83, 88, 101, 102, 105, 106, 108, 109, 110, 113, 116, 119, 121, 122, 125, 126, 127, 128, 130, 131, 132, 133, 134, 137, 138, 140, 143, 144, 148, 156, 173.

Dede Lurde
Pages: 10, 44, 68, 71, 73, 75, 76, 80, 85, 86, 89, 90b, 91, 92, 93, 94, 95, 97, 99, 100(2), 152, 155, 162, 168,

Roland Neveu
Pages: 5, 8, 17, 18, 22, 29, 38, 41, 42, 81, 90a, 111(2), 112, 124, 146, 151.

DR
Pages: 23, 34, 40, 46, 49, 50, 53, 54, 55, 150, 153, 154, 157.

Medical advisory

HEALTH GUIDE

Although it has joined the ranks of newly industrializing countries, Thailand is in the tropics and as such still has its share of health problems that you should be aware of before you travel.

Although medical facilities are now catching up with those in Western countries, the better hospitals are all privately owned and not cheap. It is therefore recommended that you purchase a travel health insurance, which includes a provision to have you air-lifted to safety if necessary. When purchasing your ticket with certain credit cards (Gold Cards in particular) you qualify for automatic accident coverage for the duration of the trip (check carefully as particular conditions usually apply).

Following is a list of primary threats to your health on the islands.

TOO MUCH SUN

The most common and easily prevented ailment for travelers to the island beaches. Make sure you keep plenty of good sunscreen with you at all times and drink lots and lots of water. Keep your head covered as much as possible and don't forget the water.

MOTORCYCLE AND CAR ACCIDENTS

Accidents on Phuket are frighteningly common. The only advice we can give is to be very careful and read our "getting around the island" section. If you do have an accident the few new hospitals are well equipped to deal with emergencies, but are also the most expensive.

DENGUE FEVER

A rather unpleasant mosquito-borne illness, carried by mosquitos active during daylight – for which there is no preventative treatment. If you are infected the fever can keep you bed ridden for a week or more accompanied by dizziness, loss of appetite and cold sweats. Since there is no treatment you just have to let the illness take its course.

HEPATITIS

The five types of viral hepatitis -- A, B, C, D and E -- are transmitted by a variety of means, mostly because of unsanitary conditions and through contact with bodily fluids (blood, saliva, urine, etc). In some cases it can be fatal. The main symptoms are stomach pains, lack of appetite, nausea, lassitude and yellowing of the eyes and skin.

Hepatitis A (HAV) can be transmitted through contaminated food and water, unpeeled fruit, salad, ice and seafood. There is a vaccine, consisting of two injections plus a booster shot given over six months, that will protect you for up to 10 years.

Hepatitis B (HBV) is transmitted sexually or by hypodermic injection and is carried by a high percentage of prostitutes. This potentially deadly virus is commonly transmitted from mother to infant and 300 million people are thought to be infected in Asia.

Hepatitis C (HCV) was only identified about five years ago and is found primarily among hypodermic needle users. Of the five, this strain of hepatitis has the highest rate of fatalities.

Hepatitis D (HDV) is associated with Hepatitis B.

Hepatitis E (HEV) is prevalent in North Africa, the Indian subcontinent and Mexico and is transmitted through contaminated food and water. It has no vaccine.

AIDS

Thailand has been lauded internationally for its efforts to halt the spread of the HIV virus and, in fact, recent reports suggest that the rate of new infections is actually dropping, a phenomenon unique to Thailand among Asian and other underdeveloped countries. But that doesn't mean you should let your guard down, since a huge number of people were already infected before the government began its now famous campaign to promote the use of condoms, and people still continue to become infected despite all efforts to the contrary. This can be blamed in large part on the country's thriving prostitution industry (the extent of which the government refuses to acknowledge), which accounts for the fact that the majority of the people infected are heterosexual, unlike countries in the more industrialized West. If you plan on engaging in any casual sex or visiting any of the country's ubiquitous brothels while in Thailand, be sure to use condoms that meet international standards -- not always although increasingly available here. It's better to be safe than sorry.

OTHER RISKS

Most other health risks are directly connected to unsanitary conditions or habits of personal hygiene. Among the most common are intestinal infections, so common in fact that you might as well resign yourself to suffering one or more while in the country. Most of the time they are due to the improper preparation of food or contaminated water, but don't let that stop you from enjoying the wide variety of food available. Avoid drinking tap water in any amount for any reason -- bottled water is readily available and generally germ-free. Just be sure the bottle is properly sealed when you purchase it. Ice served with drinks at restaurants is also something to be wary of but not nearly as much of a problem as it once was.

Diarrhoea

Diarrhoea is also a common affliction, and you should be aware that not all forms can be treated the same way since there are a variety of causes – viruses, bacteria, protozoa (like amoeba), salmonella and cholera organisms. Diarrhoea can contribute to dehydration, so be sure to drink plenty of water, get plenty of rest and consult a doctor promptly if symptoms persist for more than three days.

Intestinal worms

Intestinal worms are also common, and other more serious worms like hookworm can be contracted by walking on infected earth or beaches.

Other ailments

Ailments related to hygiene include prickly heat, a common itchy rash that can be avoided by taking frequent showers, drying the skin thoroughly afterwards and applying talcum powder. You should also be on the watch for athlete's foot and other fungal infections.

Snakebites

If you go camping, trekking or walking in the wild, be aware that Thailand is home to many venomous snakes (like several varieties of cobra, for instance). At night always carry a flashlight or torch. If you are bitten, stay calm and do not panic as this increases the rate at which your blood circulates and will only cause the poison to spread faster. Immobilize the bitten limb as much as possible, clean the wound and get to a doctor (or clinic) ASAP. Keep in mind that snake venom, if of the potentially lethal variety, usually takes hours rather than minutes to kill. In most situations, you probably will have enough time to seek effective treatment.

Other animal bites and stings

Scorpions (which are often encountered in national parks) don't usually pose a threat, but certain species can be dangerous (although rarely deadly). As with snakebites, stay calm if stung and get to the nearest hospital.

Geckos are usually harmless, but if cornered they can bite. If bitten, have a medical professional check for tetanus and diphtheria.

Bees and wasps. One person in 200 is severely allergic to bee or

HEALTH GUIDE

wasp venom. In such cases, a bee sting can be fatal. Those at risk should carry the necessary supplies for self-administration of epinephrine.

Coral and coral fish. Some fish, like the stonefish, can be dangerous although they're usually not aggressive. If you scratch yourself on coral, do not scrub or rub. We recommend you see a doctor as the wound is almost always more serious than it appears because some coral can be poisonous.

PHARMACIES AND CLINICS

There are many pharmacies and clinics all over the islands and are easily identified by green crosses. In addition to common over-the-counter remedies, some medications, that might require a doctors prescription in the west, can also be purchased. One thing you should bear in mind when visiting pharmacies is that the owner may try to get you to buy several different tablets to cure your ailment, although it will probably do you no harm to take them, it is likely that he is just maximizing his profits.

Hospitals

INSURANCE

Most hospitals accept patients who are covered by international insurance policies but you may want to verify this before (or as soon as) you check in. In any case, you may be asked for a credit card reference (just as when you check in at any hotel).

Modern hospitals in Phuket have English speaking staff and many of the doctors have some form of western training.

One of Phuket's favorite pastimes!

Books & Internet

Useful Books

GUIDES

Dive Sites of Thailand
Asiabooks, 1998, by Paul Lees. The most up-to-date guide on diving in Thai waters; beautiful illustrations.

Diving in Thailand
Written by Collin Piprell and photographed by Ashley J. Boyd. Published by Times Editions, Singapore,1995. Complete reference but outdated.

Thai Hawker Food
Published in Bangkok in 1993, but still a good reference (with drawings) to eat street side. **B**250.

Your Favorite Thai dishes
Published by AVA House, Bangkok, 1996. A reference guide with pictures, **B**250.

Waterfalls and Gibbon Calls
By Thomas Henley. Published in Phuket, 1996, (**B**250). The book to have if you plan to go to the Khao Sok National Park.

FICTION

Island
By Aldus Huxley. The classic story of paradise found on a tropical island. A great book.

The Beach
By Alex Garland. Incontestably the book for the season. The inspiration is directly out of Haad Rin Beach on Koh Phangan and a few reclusive spots of Angthong archipelago. But the movie was shot at Maya Bay on Phi Phi Leh island.

Maps

Krabi Province & around
1:300,000, by Prannok Witthaya in Bangkok.The best map for the area. Ref S002. **B**55

Nelles Maps-Thailand
1:1,500,000. A good and easy to read overall map. **B**175.

Periplus Travel Maps
A good series on Thailand (Thailand, Koh Samui, Phuket, etc…) at 1:1,000,000 and 1:100,000 -- city maps as well. **B**125 each.

Guide Map of Krabi/Koh Lanta
Another local map in English and Thai with illustrations. Very detailed and available locally only. **B**50.

You can find, in abundance, free maps of Phuket, but they are very partial to the advertising they contain and not so good in general, but if you need them to find restaurants and shops, that they will do.

Websites

Any good search-engine will land you several sites on Phuket, but the level and quality of information is not up to this guidebook standards. Most sites feature mostly their advertisers. Several personal sites give a different idea on the islands. A few sites offer booking directly (which bring them a commision).

A few to start with:
   www.sawadee.com
   www.phuket.com
   www.thaifocus.com
   www.amazing-thailand.com
   www.thaibiz.com
   www.phuketgazette.net
   www.tavel-phuket.com
   www.phuketxyber.com (flash site)
   www.thaiwave.com

Contacts–Airlines

IN BANGKOK

Local Airlines

Thai Airways International (TG)
- ☎ 628-2000 (24-hour booking number).
- ☎ 234 3100 (Silom office).
- ☎ 513 0121 (Vipavadee-HQ).
- ☎ 535 2846-7 (Airport).
- ☎ 535 2084-5 (Domestic).

Bangkok Airways (PG)
Queen Sirikit Center (HQ).
- ☎ 229 3456-63 (Reservations).
- ☎ 229 3434 (Ticketing).
- ☎ 535 2497-8 (Airport).

Angel Air (8G)
- ☎ 953 2260.
- ☎ 535 6287-8 (Airport).

Orient Thai Airlines (OX)
- ☎ 267 3210-2.
- ☎ 535 2021-2 (Airport).

PB Air . . . . ☎ 261 0220-5

Airlines-online

Aeroflot Soviet Airlines (SU)
- ☎ 251 1223-6.
- ☎ 523 4661-2 (Airport).

Air China (CA)
- ☎ 631 0728-34.
- ☎ 535 4661-2 (Airport).

Air France (AF)
- ☎ 635 1199, 635 1186-7
- ☎ 535 2112 (Airport).

Air India (AI)
- ☎ 235 0557-8.
- ☎ 535 2121-2 (Airport).

Air Lanka (UL)
- ☎ 236 9292-3.
- ☎ 535 2331-2 (Airport).

Air New Zealand (NZ)
- ☎ 254 8440-9.
- ☎ 535 3981-2 (Airport).

Alitalia (AZ)
- ☎ 634 1800-9.
- ☎ 535 2602-4 (Airport).

All Nippon Airways (NH)
- ☎ 238 5121, 238 5141.
- ☎ 535 2602-4 (Airport).

Asiana Airlines (OZ)
- ☎ 656 8610-7.
- ☎ 535 3450-3 (Airport).

Austrian Airlines (OS)
- ☎ 267 0873-9.
- ☎ 535 3936-7 (Airport).

Biman Bangladesh Airlines (BG)
- ☎ 235 7643-4, 233 3896-8
- ☎ 535 2151 (Airport).

British Airways (BA)
- ☎ 636 1747.
- ☎ 535 2220 (Airport).

Canadian Airlines (CP)
- ☎ 255 5862-5.
- ☎ 535 2229 (Airport).

Cathay Pacific Airways (CX)
- ☎ 263 0606, 263 0616.
- ☎ 535 2155-6 (Airport).

China Airlines (CI)
- ☎ 253 4242-3, 253 5733.
- ☎ 535 2160 (Airport).

China Eastern Airlines (MU)
- ☎ 636 6978.
- ☎ 535 4709 (Airport).

China Southern Airlines (CZ)
- ☎ 266 5688/5699.
- ☎ 535 2354-5/57 (Airport).

China Southwest Airlines (SZ)
- ☎ 662 1940-5.

China Yunnan Airlines (3Q)
- ☎ 216 3067-8.
- ☎ 535 4731-2 (Airport).

Czech Airlines (OK)
- ☎ 718 1839-40.
- ☎ 535 1866 (Airport).

Druk Air (KB)
- ☎ 235 6326-7.
- ☎ 535 1960 (Airport).

Egypt Air (MS)
- ☎ 231 0504-8.
- ☎ 523 7334 (Airport).

El Al Israel Airlines (LY)
- ☎ 671 6145-7.
- ☎ 535 3566-7 (Airport).

Emirates Airlines (EK)
- ☎ 260 7400-4.
- ☎ 535 1946-7 (Airport).

Ethiopian Airlines (ET)
- ☎ 237 9201-9.
- ☎ 535 3298 (Airport).

Eva Air (BR)
- ☎ 240 0890.
- ☎ 535 3531-5 (Airport).

Finnair (AY)
- ☎ 635 1234 (#101, 102).
- ☎ 535 2104-5 (Airport).

Garuda Indonesia (GA)
- ☎ 285 6470-3.
- ☎ 535 2171 (Airport).

Gulf Air (GF)
- ☎ 254 7931-4.
- ☎ 535 2313-4 (Airport).

Indian Airlines Limited (IC)
- ☎ 235 5534-5.

BACK OF THE BOOK

☎ 535 2420 (Airport).
Japan Airlines (JL)
☎ 692 5151-65.
☎ 535 2135-6 (Airport).
KLM Royal Dutch Airlines (KL)
☎ 679 1100 #1.
☎ 535 2191-2265 (Airport).
Kampuchea Airlines (KT)
☎ 267 3210-2.
☎ 535 3645 (Airport).
Korea Air (KE)
☎ 635 0465-72.
☎ 535 2335-6 (Airport).
Kuwait Airways (KU)
☎ 641 2864-7.
☎ 535 2338-9 (Airport).
Lao Aviation (QV)
☎ 236 9822-3.
☎ 535 3786-6 (Airport).
Lauda Air (NG)
☎ 267 0873-9.
☎ 535 2635-6 (Airport).
LOT Polish Airlines (LO)
☎ 233 0347-8.
☎ 535 2399 (Airport).
LTU Airways (LT)
☎ 267 1235-7.
☎ 535 1930 (Airport).
Lufthansa German Airlines (LH)
☎ 264 2400.
☎ 535 2211 (Airport).
Malaysia Airlines (MH)
☎ 263 0565-71.
☎ 535 2288 (Airport).
Malev Hungarian (MA)
☎ 535 5538-9.
Myanmar Airways (UB)
☎ 630 0334-8.
☎ 535 7420 (Airtport).
Northwest Airlines (NW)
☎ 652 1010.
☎ 535 6200 (Airport).
Olympic Airways (OA)
☎ 237 6164-7.
☎ 535 2058-9 (Airport).
Pakistan Airlines (PK)
☎ 233 5215-6.
☎ 535 2127-8 (Airport).
Philippine Airlines PR)
☎ 233 2350-2.
☎ 535 2312 (Airport).
Qantas Airways (QF)
☎ 636 1747.
☎ 535 2220 (Airport).
Quatar Airways (QR)
☎ 237 9201-3.
Royal Air Cambodge (VJ)
☎ 635 2261-6.
☎ 535 3679 (Airport).
Royal Brunei Airlines (BI)

☎ 233 0056.
☎ 535 2626-7 (Airport).
Royal Jordanian (RJ)
☎ 236 8609-17.
☎ 535 2152-3 (Airport).
Royal Nepal Airlines (RA)
☎ 216 5691-5.
☎ 535 2150 (Airport).
Saudi Arabian Airlines (SV)
☎ 266 7393-7.
☎ 535 2340 (Airport).
SAS Airlines (SK)
☎ 260 0444.
☎ 535 2716 (Airport).
Silk Air (MI)
☎ 236 0303.
Singapore Airlines (SQ)
☎ 236 0440, 236 0222.
☎ 535 2260 (Airport).
South African Airways (SA)
☎ 635 1410-14.
☎ 535 4702-3 (Airport).
Swissair (SR)
☎ 636 2160-6.
☎ 535 2371-2 (Airport).
TAP Air Portugal (TP)
☎ 638 2981.
☎ 535 5409-10 (Airport).
Turkish Airlines (TK)
☎ 231 0300-7.
☎ 535 2621-2 (Airport).
Turkmenistan Airlines (T5)
☎ 224 4410.
☎ 535 2680 (Airport).
United Airlines (UA)
☎ 253 0558.
☎ 535 2232 (Airport).
Uzbekistan Airways (HY)
☎ 261 5084-6.
Vietnam Airlines (VN)
☎ 656 9056-58.
☎ 535 2671 (Airport).

On Phuket

Bangkok Airways (PG)
☎ 212 341.
China Airlines (CI)
☎ 327 099-100 (Airport).
Dragon Air (KA)
☎ (076) 215 734.
Malaysian Airlines (MH)
☎ 216 675.
SilkAir (MI)
☎ 213 891.
Thai Airways (TG)
☎ 211 195, 212 946 (for domestic flights).
☎ 212 499 (international flights).

Staying in touch...

INDEX

Main Index

1-2-3 Wall 130

A–B

Ahaan jay 31
Airlines 164
Andaman Coast 145
Ao Chalong 91
Ao Nam Mao 128
Ao Nang 121
Ao Po 114
Ao Sane Beach 89
Asian X Games 158
Baan Talaad Kao 116
Bang Niang Beach 149
Bang Tao Beach 98
Bangla Road 63
Bareboating 43
Bargain 18
Beer Bars 69
Big waves 96
Bird nests 104
Boat Tours 40
Bua Phut 152
Bungy 36
Burma Banks 55
Bus 20

C–D

Canal Village 101
Cape Panwa 93
Cape Promthep 33
Car and Bike Hire 22
Chao Fah pier 116
Chao Leh 27
Cheow Lan Lake 153
Chicken Island 123
Coral island 93
Curries 30
Dawn of Happiness 128
Dengue Fever 160
Diamond Cave 131
Diarrhoea 161
Dive Sites 47
Diving tips 51
Dos and Don'ts 17
Driving 20

E–F–G

Elephant Trekking 36
Emerald Cave 144
Flights 20
Gaeng mussaman 31
Gai yang 29
Game fishing 41, 105
Gastronomy 28
Geckos 161
Gibbon Rehab 34
Go-Karts 36
Go-go bars 67
Golf courses 43
Guerney's Pita 152

H–I–J

Haad Khlong Muang 127
Haad Nopparatthara 127
Haad Nui 142
Haad Thai Muang Nat. Park 145
Haad Yao 110
Hawkers Food 71
Health Guide 160
Hepatitis 160
Hin Daeng 53
History 23
Hokkien mee 31
Hornbills 153
Horse riding 38
Hospitals 162
hoy tawd 30
Immigration offices 93
James Bond Island 113

K

Kamala Beach 95
Kantiang Bay 142
Kata Noi Beach 84
Kayaking 106
khanom jiin naam ya 30
Khao Lak 145
khao naa ped 31
khao pat 31
Khao Phra Taew 34
Khao Sok National Park 152
khao yam 30
Khuraburi 151
King Cruiser Wreck 50
King prawns 32
King's Cup Regatta 40
Klong Dao Beach 139
Klong Jak Bay 142
Klong Kong Beach 142
Klong Nin Beach 142
Koh Hae 41
Koh Hong 113
Koh Lanta 135
Koh Lone 34
Koh Miang 150

BACK OF THE BOOK

Index...

Koh Mook 144	Phi Phi Leh 103
Koh Ngai 143	Phra Nang 128
Koh Sirey 35	Phra Nang Beach 134
KohTapu 113	Phra Nang Cave 134
Koh Yao 114	Phuket Boat Lagoon 42
Krabi Canyon 122	Phuket Diving 50
Krabi Diving 52	*por pia thod* 29
Krabi town 115	Princess Lagoon 131
kuay tiaw nam 30	Public transport 21

L–M

Laem Sing Beach 33, 96	Racha Yai Island 94
Laem Trong 110	Railey Beach 129
Laguna Complex 98	Rainforest 153
Leopards 152	Ranong 151
Lighthouse 92	Rawai 89
Limestone islands 113	Rawai Beach 90
Liveaboards 46	Rawai fishing village 90
Lobsters 32	Relax Bay 142
Loh Bakao 110	Relax Beach 83
Loh Dalam Beach 104	Rock Climbing 130
Loi Rua Festival 158	*roti* 30
Long Beach 141	Rubber plantations 26
Low season 28	

S

ma la gaw 30	Safety 19, 22
mai pet 29	Sailing 42
Maiton Island 94	Saladan 139
Markets 30	*sap pa rot* 30
Massage 70	Scuba diving 45
Maya Bay 103, 111	Sea canoeing 39
Mergui Archipelago 55	Sea Gypsy 103
Mokken Sea gypsies 23	Sea turtles 145
moo yang 29	Seafood restaurants 90
Motorcycle taxis 22	Siam Safari Nature 37
Mu Surin Marine Park 49	Siamese Junk 40
Muslims 27	Silan 23

N–O

Nai Hharn Beach 88	Similan diving 47
Nai Thon Beach 101	Similan Islands 150
Nai Yang Beach 33,102	Sir Francis Light 24
Nhong Thong Beach 146	Smiling 18
Nui Beach 88	Social behavior 18

P–R

pad si yiw 31	Soi Eric 69
pad thai 31	Soi Katoey 69
Pak Bara 144	Standard Chartered Bank . . . 25
Pansea Beach 97	Stonefish 162
papaya pok-pok 29	Street food 30
Patak Road 85	Surfing 77
Peak season 28	Surin Beach 96
Penang 24	Surin Islands 151
pet pet 29	

T–U

Phang Nga Bay 113	Ta Khai 114
Phi Phi Diving 51	*taeng mo* 30
Phi Phi Don 103	Takua pa 151
	Tam Lod 122
	Tap Lamu pier 150
	Tarutao 144
	Temples & shrines 35

167

BACK OF THE BOOK

Tha Dan	113
Thai cuisine	29
Thai massage	98
Thai Muang	145
Thai style country pubs	118
Thai Village	35
Thaiwand Wall	130
Thalang	36
Tin	23
Ton Sai Bay	103
Traffic accidents	160
Trang	143
Trekking	157
Tuk Tuks	21
Two Heroines	24
Useful books	163

V-W-Y

Vegetarian Festival	158
Victoria Point	151
Viking Cave	111
VIP Buses	20
Wai	19
Websites	163
Whale sharks	49
Wild Lotus	152
Yawi	27
Wild Lotus	152

****

HOTELS, BARS RESTAURANTS INDEX

(THIS IS THE LIST OF THE PLACE WE RECOMMEND IN THE GUIDE)

Amari Coral Beach Resort	73
Argentina Grill & Steakhouse	71
Azzura Italian Restaurant	124
Azzurro Village	74
Ban Rim Pa	71
Boonsiam Hotel	118
Café Europa	117
Cha Guesthouse	118
Chao Fa Valley	118
Charlie Beach Resort	108
Chong Khao Bungalows	108
Club Andaman Resort	73
Da Maurizio	71
Dawn of Happiness Beach Resort	128
Diamond Cave Bungalows	133
Don's Barbecue	91
Dreamteam	142
Emerald Resort	128
Garden Beach Resort	148
Garden Cottage	102
Jimmy Lighthouse	92
Kan Eng Seafood	92
Kaw Kwang Beach Resort	140
Khao Lak Green Beach	148
Krabi Seaview Resort	126
Lanta Merry Hut Resort	142
Marina Cottage	80
Nai Harn Resort	89
Nikita Bar	91
On On Hotel	60
Our Jungle Lodge	154
Pardise Bar	68
Patong Penthouse	74
Pee Pee Viewpoint Resort	109
Phi Phi Pavillon Resort	109
Potpourrri Patong	72
Rimley Seafood	91
Ruen Thai Restuarant	117
Sam's Steakhouse	72
Thavorn Hotel	60
The Last Cafe	125
The Sanctuary	141
Toto Italian Restaurant	97
Tree Tops River Huts	155
Wasana GH	60
Yanui Beach Bungalows	89
Ya Ya Beach Seafood	124
Ya Ya Resort	132

BACK OF THE BOOK

DIVE SHOPS INDEX

Recommended Shops 47
....Andy Herrich Expeditions
............Asian Divers
..........Fantasea Divers
..........Phra Nang Divers
..........Siam Dive'n Sail
............Scuba Quest
..South East Asia Liveaboard

MAIN DIVE SHOPS (LISTED IN THE GUIDE)
Ao Nang Dive Shops 122
Karon DIve Shops 78
Kata Dive Shops 84
Khao Lak Dive Shops 146
Koh Lanta Dive Shops ...138
Patong Dive Shops 65
Phi Phi Dive Shops 105
Railey Dive Shops 129

Map Legend

 City, village
 Airport
 Ferry, Boat service
 Main Road
 Border post
 Historic site
 Mountain, Vista
 A/C Bus service
 Train service
 Hospital
 Golf, Sport fishing
 Beach, Resort
 Main diving site
 Water Sports
 NATIONAL PARK WILD LIFE RESERVE
 Main TAT office
 Internet Shop
 Restaurant
Hotels

Index...

Important Numbers

IN BANGKOK

Emergency No

Police Hotline **191**
also 246 1338-42 in Bangkok.
Crime. **195**
also 513 3844 in Bangkok.
Fire **199**
also 246 0199 in Bangkok.
Highway Police **193**
Traffic Control Center **197**
Tourist Police
Nationwide **1699**
Bangkok 255 2964/8
Pattaya 429 371
Phuket 219 878
Samui 421 281
Tourist Assistance Center
Nationwide (24h) 1155
Bangkok 281 5015
Phuket 212 213
Missing Persons Bureau
in Bangkok 282 1815
Ambulance-Police Hospital
in Bangkok 255 1133/6
in Phuket 212 297
Emergency Medical Services
Nationwide 1669
Bangkok 248 2222

Lost Credit Cards

Lost or stolen credit cards can be reported to the following:
American Express:
IBM Building, Phahonyothin Road, ☎ 273 0022.
Diner's Club:
Dusit Thani Building, Rama IV Road, ☎ 233 2645, 233 5775, 238 3660.
JCB:
☎ 256 1361, 256 1351, 256 2857.
Visa and MasterCard:
Thai Farmers Bank Building, Phahonyothin Road,
☎ 270 1801/10, 256 7326/7.
Lost or stolen traveler's checks can be reported to the following:
American Express (Thai) Co., Ltd.
S.P. Building, 388 Phahonyothin Rd, ☎ 273 5296.
The Thomas Cook Group Ltd.
12th Floor, Sathorn City Tower, 175 South Sathorn Rd.
☎ 679 5521/3.

Immigration

Bangkok Immigration Division
Soi Suan Phlu, Sathorn Tai Road,
☎ 287 3101/10.

Anti-Poison Center

Chulalongkorn Hospital
Chulaporn Bldg, Rama IV Road, Bangkok. ☎ 256 4214.
☎ 256 4328 (snake, dog bites).

Courier Services

AIRBORNE	☎ **712 4300**
DHL	☎ **207 0600**
DPE	☎ **237 4751-6**
FEDEX	☎ **367 3222**
TNT	☎ **249 5702-6**
UPS	☎ **712 3300-5**
WORLDPAK	☎ **258 3896**

Airport

Don Muang . . . . . . ☎ **535 1111**
Thai Airways 24 H information
Departures . . . . ☎ **535 1254**
Arrivals . . . . ☎ **535 1301**
Domestic . . . . . ☎ **535 1253**
☎ 1566, (02) 1566 outside Bangkok. With fax back service.
☎ 280 0060 (24 H Booking).

Miscellaneous

Hualampong Train Station
☎ 223 0341/8
Southern Bus Terminal
☎ 434 5558, 435 1200 (A/C)
TAT
(Tourism Authority of Thailand)
202 Le Concorde Bldg, Rachadapisek Rd Huaykwang, Bangkok 10310. ☎ 662-694 1222.
All airlines .see pages 164-165

BACK OF THE BOOK

Useful Numbers

IN PHUKET

☎ area code ....(076)

Emergency .....☎ 1699, 191
Ambulance .....☎ 212 297
Fire Brigade ....☎ 199
Phuket International Hospital .
............☎ 249 400
............☎ 210 935
Bangkok Phuket Hospital ....
............☎ 254 421-9
Phuket Ruampaet Hospital ...
............☎ 212 578
Mission Hospital .☎ 212 386 .
Siriroj Hospital ...☎ 215 666
Wachira Hospital .☎ 211 114
Phuket Immigration ....
............☎ 212 108
Airport ....☎ 327 230-4
  Airport office ...☎ 422 513

POLICE STATIONS
  Tourist Police ....☎ 211 036
  ....☎ 212 468
  Emergency .....☎ 191
  Provincial Police .☎ 212 115

MISCELLANEOUS
  Telecom Center ..☎ 216 861
  Post & Telegraph .☎ 211 020
  ATT Direct ..☎ 001-999-111-1
  Phone Directory ..☎ 13
  Overseas Phone .☎ 100
  Bus Station .....☎ 211 480
  Bangkok Airways .☎ 225 033
  Thai Airways ....☎ 212 946
  TAT ....☎ 212 213
  City Hall ......☎ 211 366
  Dulwich College .☎ 238 711
  Patong Arin Clinic ☎ 341 159
  Wattana Clinic ..☎ 340 690

CAR RENTALS
  Avis ....☎ 327 358
  Avis Patong ....☎ 340 608
  Budget ....☎ 427 188
  Hertz ....☎ 340 037
  Via Rent-A-Car ..☎ 341 660

IN KRABI

☎ area code ....(075)

Hospital ......☎ 611 203
Emergency ....☎ 1699
Police ....☎ 611 222
Immigration ....☎ 611 097
Tourist Info ....☎ 611 381

MISCELLANEOUS
  Thai Airways ...☎ 612 888
  Bangkok Bank ..☎ 611 186
  Phone Center ..☎ 611 123
  City Hall ......☎ 611 120

BOAT SERVICES

SONGSERM/FERRYLINES OFFICES
  Bangkok (HQ).☎ 984 5600/49
  Kaosan (BKK) ..☎ 281 1463/5
  Phuket ....☎ 222 570/4
  Krabi ....☎ 611 288
  Surat Thani City .☎ 286 340
  Surat Thani Port ..☎ 285 125/6

Important phone numbers...

BACK OF THE BOOK

Advertising Index

	page...
Asian Trails	2
Siam Dive n' Sail	6
Asian Adventures	9
Phuket Country Club	11
Siam Safari	11
SeaCanoe	15

Special Thanks

The author and the publisher would like to extend his gratitude to the following people and organizations, all of which generously gave their time, knowledge and opinions to help this book come into being:

Asia Voyages and their sailing crews in the Phang Nga Bay.

Dede for his last run for pictures during Easter holidays.

The boat 'Tantawan', based at the Phuket Marina and his owner.

A unique photographic book available at bookstores and online at www.asiahorizons.com

GLOSSARY

Amphur (or amphoe)	district
Ao	small bay (usually with a beach)
Ban (or baan)	village (or house)
Changwat	province
Doi	mount (hill)
Haad (or Hat)	beach
Hin	stone
Khao	mountain
Klong	canal (or small river)
Koh	island
Laem	cape, headland
Loh	bay
Mae (like in Mae Haad)	literally means 'mother'
Maenam	river
Muang	city
Namtok	waterfall
Samlor	pedicab (can be motorized)
Songthaew	modified passenger pick-up truck
Talaad (or Talat)	market
Thale	the sea
Tham	cave
Wat	pagoda

BACK OF THE BOOK

Maps....

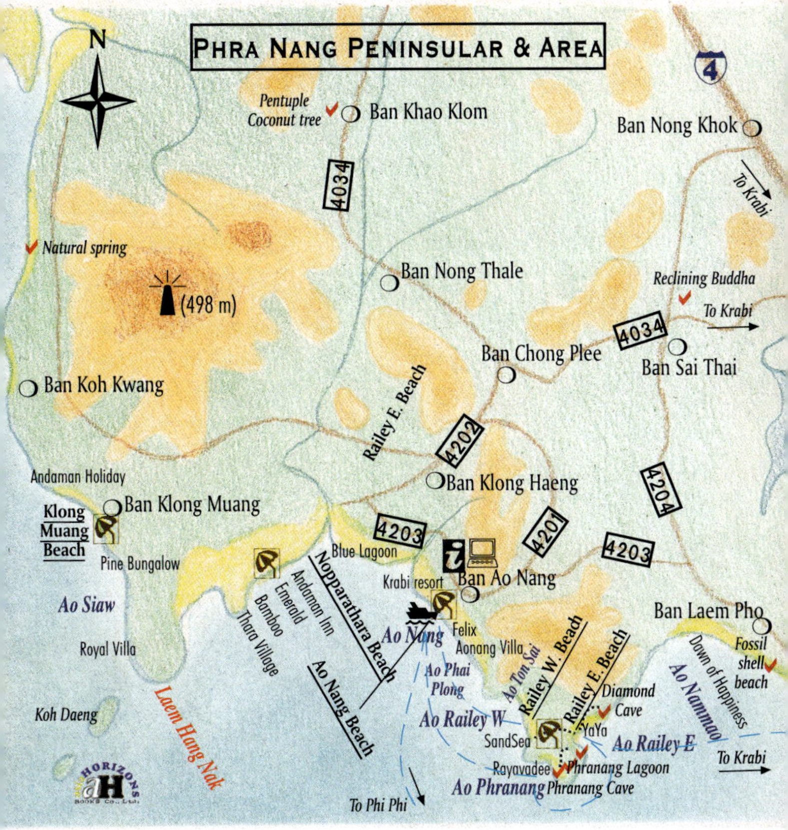

PHRA NANG PENINSULAR & AREA

- Ban Khao Klom
- Pentuple Coconut tree
- Ban Nong Khok
- 4034
- To Krabi
- Natural spring
- (498 m)
- Ban Nong Thale
- Reclining Buddha
- To Krabi
- Ban Chong Plee
- 4034
- Ban Sai Thai
- Ban Koh Kwang
- Railey E. Beach
- 4202
- Andaman Holiday
- Ban Klong Haeng
- 4204
- Klong Muang Beach
- Ban Klong Muang
- 4203
- 4201
- 4203
- Pine Bungalow
- Blue Lagoon
- Ban Ao Nang
- Ban Laem Pho
- Ao Siaw
- Andaman Inn
- Emerald
- Bamboo
- Thara Village
- Krabi resort
- Nopparathara Beach
- Felix Aonang Villa
- Dawn of Happiness
- Fossil shell beach
- Royal Villa
- Ao Nang Beach
- Ao Nang
- Ao Phai Plong
- Ao Ton Sai
- Railey W. Beach
- Railey E. Beach
- Ao Nammao
- Koh Daeng
- Laem Hang Nak
- Ao Railey W
- Diamond Cave
- SandSea
- YaYa
- Ao Railey E
- To Krabi
- Rayavadee
- Phranang Lagoon
- Ao Phranang
- Phranang Cave
- To Phi Phi

HORIZONS

173

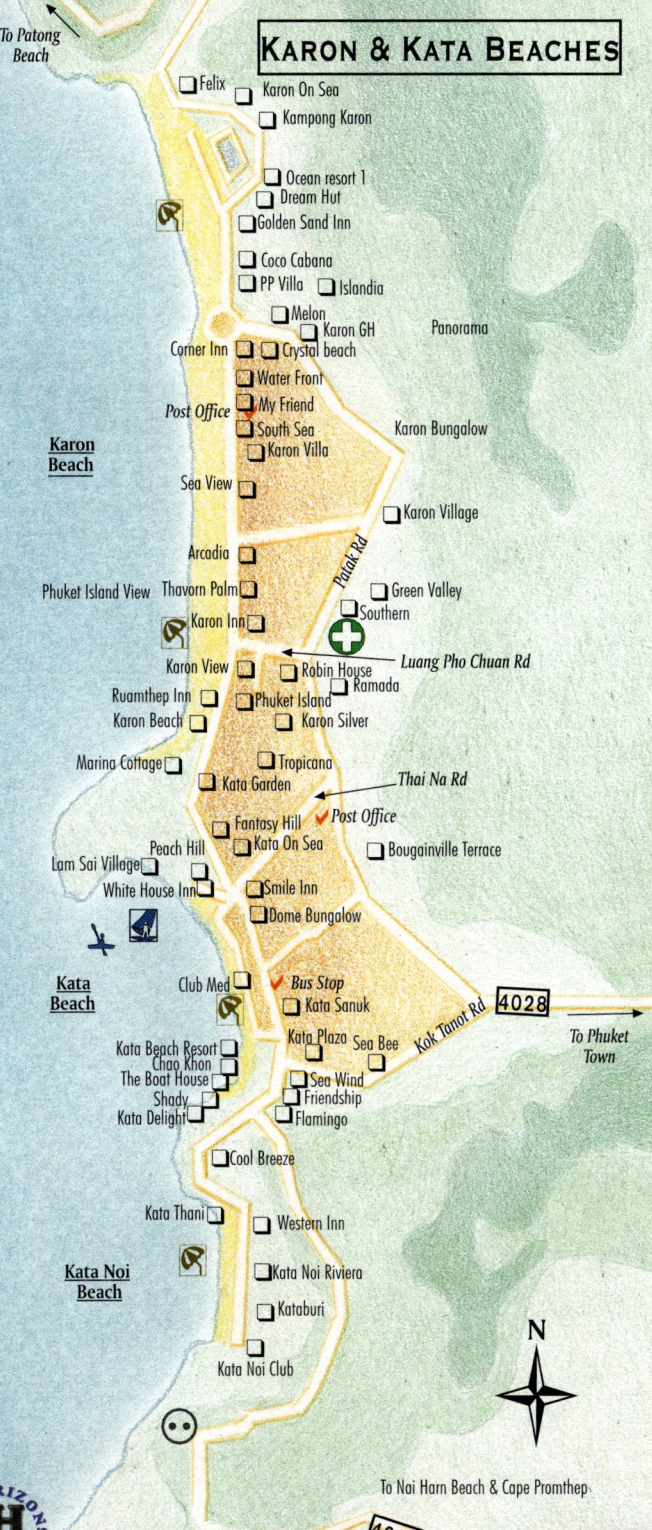